Diet cure
For Common Ailments

Other Books By The Same Author

— A Complete Handbook Of Nature Cure

— A Handbook Of Natural Beauty

— Nature Cure For Children

— Naturopathy For Longevity

— Healing Through Natural Foods

— Indian Spices And Condiments As Natural Healers

— Foods That Heal

— Herbs That Heal

— Natural Home Remedies For Common Ailments

— Vitamins That Heal

— Conquering Diabetes Naturally

— Conquering Cancer Naturally

Diet cure

For Common Ailments

Dr. H.K. Bakhru

JAICO PUBLISHING HOUSE
Mumbai Delhi Bangalore Kolkata
Hyderabad Chennai Ahmedabad Bhopal

Published by Jaico Publishing House
121 Mahatma Gandhi Road
Mumbai - 400 001
jaicopub@vsnl.com
www.jaicobooks.com

© Dr. H.K. Bakhru

DIET CURE FOR COMMON AILMENTS
ISBN 81-7224-072-4

First Jaico Impression: 1988
Second Revised Edition: 1998
Eleventh Jaico Impression: 2008

No part of this book may be reproduced or utilized in
any form or by any means, electronic or
mechanical including photocopying, recording or
by any information storage and retrieval system,
without permission in writing from the publishers.

Printed by
Snehesh Printers
320-A, Shah & Nahar Ind. Est. A-1
Lower Parel, Mumbai - 400 013.

About the Author

Dr. H.K. Bakhru enjoys a countrywide reputation as an expert naturopath and a prolific writer. His well-researched articles on nature cure, health, nutrition and herbs appear regularly in various newspapers and magazines andthey bear the stamp of authority.

A diploma holder in naturopathy, all his current 13 books on nature cure, nutrition and herbs titled, 'A Complete Handbook of Nature Cure', 'Diet Cure for Common Ailments', 'A Handbook of Natural Beauty', 'Nature Cure for Children,' 'Naturopathy for Longevity', 'Healing Through Natural Foods', 'Indian Spices and Condiments as Natural Healers', 'Foods That Heal', 'Herbs That Heal', 'Natural Home Remedies for Common Ailments', 'Vitamins that Heal', 'Conquering Diabetes Naturally' and 'Conquering Cancer Naturally' have been highly appreciated by the public and repeatedly reprinted. His first-named book has been awarded first prize in the category 'Primer on Naturopathy for Healthy Living' by the jury of judges at the 'Book Prize Award' scheme, organized by 'National Institute of Naturopathy', an autonomous body under Govt. of India, Ministry of Health.

Dr. Bakhru began his career on the Indian Railways, with a first class first postgraduate degree in History from Lucknow University in 1949. He retired in October 1984 as the Chief Public Relations Officer of the Central Railway in Mumbai, having to his credit 35 years of distinguished service in the Public Relations organisations of the Indian Railways and the Railway Board.

An associate member of the All India Alternative Medical Practitioner's Association and a member of the Nature Cure Practitioners' Guild in Mumbai, Dr. Bakhru has extensively studied herbs and natural methods of treating diseases. He has been honoured with 'Lifetime Achievement Award', 'Gem of Alternative Medicines' award and a gold medal in Diet Therapy by the Indian Board of Alternative Medicines, Kolkata, in recognition of his dedication and outstanding contributions in the field of Alternative Medicines. The Board, which is affiliated with the Open International University for Complementary Medicines, established under World Health Organisation and recognised by the United Nations Peace University, has also appointed him as its Honorary Advisor. Dr. Bakhru has also been honoured by Nature Cure Practitioners' Guild, Mumbai with Nature Cure Appreciation Award for his services to Naturopathy.

Dr. Bakhru has founded a registered Public Charitable Trust, known as D.H. Bakhru Foundation, for help to the poor and needy. He has been donating Rs. 25,000 every year to this trust from his income as writer and author.

Foreword

Man, the highest creation of God, is, by divine plan, born healthy and strong. It is when nature's rhythm and cycle are upset that the human system loses its natural capacity to renew and rejuvenate itself. Disorders and ailments set in when the body's natural processes are strained and impaired through physical and moral excesses. Prevention of disease is indeed better than cure. Even if born with some inherited affliction, the individual can eliminate it or at least control it by putting to the best use all the elements available freely in Nature.

Health is ensured by observing the laws of nature. Their transgression inflicts the justifiable penalty of suffering and disease. In nature, the beneficial germs which preserve health and make for mental and emotional well being are far higher in number than those of destruction which inflict disease. Hence, given the opportunity and encouragement to flourish and exert their influence, these germs can combat the unhealthy ones and bestow glowing health.

Reasonable care of oneself, is worship. Essential health care ensures an independent, active, fruitful and fulfilled life while chronic illnesses render man a troublesome invalid dependent on others' compassion.

Shri H.K. Bakhru has been contributing numerous articles on various diseases and their cures through dietetics and nature cure treatments, which when put into practice can be of immense benefit to the connoisseur as well as the layman. The book, appropriately titled 'Diet Cure for Common Ailments', covers the whole gamut of ailments which can be cured merely by proper food habits and regulation of one's life, without recourse to medicinal treatment. The book is based on the theories and fundamentals of Nature Cure that go to preserve health and vitality and regain these when lost. It will undoubtedly be a boon not only to laymen but also to nature cure practitioners as a reference guide because of its practical utility.

Nature Cure has carved a niche in the realm of Curative Sciences in our country and abroad, though the protogonists of the drugless healing system have included a lot of other unorthodox treatments in their curative disciplines. Nature Cure, through its correct application brings about amazing changes that baffle the practitioners of modern medicine, devoid as it is of the crippling side-effects of drug treatments. The all-pervading truth is "Nature alone possesses the power of healing." There are not many institutions which cater to this system. Hence, many a patient cannot take advantage of it. Shri Bakhru's book will serve as a useful guide to those who wish to treat themselves through this system at home.

I highly appreciate the commendable efforts and labour put in by Shri H.K. Bakhru in compiling this monumental treatise of immense value to posterity.

Dr. R.G. Krishnatray,
Director, Nature Cure Hospital,
Juhu Scheme, Bombay.

Preface

I was afflicted with several serious diseases from an early age. At the age of 16, I contracted pleurisy and typhoid fever of long duration, simultaneously. Both these illnesses left me extremely weak. In subsequent years I suffered from numerous critical ailments, including hyperacidity with severe heartburn, breathing trouble, stroke, suspected brain tumour, chronic duodenal ulcer, spondylosis, mylagia, hiatus hernia with peptic oesophageal ulcers, suspected heart disease, insomnia, backache and prostate enlargement.

The modern medical system failed to provide me any relief from these diseases and I underwent a great deal of physical suffering and mental anguish for almost 40 long years. Eventually, at the advanced age of 55, I made a determined bid to give up all drugs and take resort to the natural methods of treatment.

I obtained substantial relief by taking recourse to the time-tested methods of nature cure, in which diet plays a major role. It was mainly through diet control that I succeeded in controlling several serious disabilities. This convinced me that a properly and carefully planned diet programme can go a long way in rooting out disease and restoring health and youthfulness.

This conviction, based on personal experience, prompted me to write a series of articles on Diet Cure for Common Ailments, which were published in many leading newspapers Encouraged by the reader's response, I have compiled them in a book form for the benefit of a wider readership.

— H.K. BAKHRU

Preface to Second Revised Edition

There is a growing awareness today about the importance of diet in the maintenance of good health and in the prevention and treatment of diseases. More and more people are now adopting dietary treatment for overcoming their health problems. This trend, coupled with success attained in treating diseases through appropriate diet, has promoted me to revise my book, Diet Cure For Common Ailment.

This book has proved quite popular since its first publication in 1988 and it has already gone into six Jaico Impressions. It has now been revised and enlarged to include more diseases, which respond favourably to dietary treatment, as well as illustrations, and treatment charts. Illustrations would give better understanding of the diseases. Treatment charts provide not only the diet chart, but also other time-tested natural methods of treatment, making the book truly a book for self-treatment of common ailments. It would, however, be advisable to consult a nature cure practitioner in case of serious illnesses.

— Dr. H.K. BAKHRU

CONTENTS

Chapter 1:	Introduction: Diet in Health and Disease	1
Chapter 2:	Acidosis	9
Chapter 3:	Acne	14
Chapter 4:	Alcoholism	19
Chapter 5:	Allergies	25
Chapter 6:	Anaemia	31
Chapter 7:	Appendicitis	36
Chapter 8:	Arteriosclerosis	41
Chapter 9:	Arthritis	46
Chapter 10:	Asthma	53
Chapter 11:	Backache	58
Chapter 12:	Bronchitis	64
Chapter 13:	Cancer	69
Chapter 14:	Cataract	76
Chapter 15:	Cholera	81
Chapter 16:	Cirrhosis of the Liver	86
Chapter 17:	Colitis	91
Chapter 18:	Common Cold	96
Chapter 19:	Conjunctivitis	101
Chapter 20:	Constipation	105
Chapter 21:	Cough	111
Chapter 22:	Depression	116
Chapter 23:	Diabetes	121
Chapter 24:	Diarrhoea	127
Chapter 25:	Dysentery	132
Chapter 26:	Dyspepsia	137
Chapter 27:	Eczema	142
Chapter 28:	Epilepsy	148
Chapter 29:	Fatigue	154
Chapter 30:	Fever	160
Chapter 31:	Gall Bladder Disorders	165
Chapter 32:	Gastritis	170
Chapter 33:	Goitre	174
Chapter 34:	Glaucoma	179
Chapter 35:	Gout	184
Chapter 36:	Heart Disease	189
Chapter 37:	Hialus Hernia	196
Chapter 38:	High Blood Cholesterol	201

CONTENTS

Chapter 39:	Hypertension	207
Chapter 40:	Infuenza	212
Chapter 41:	Insomnia	217
Chapter 42:	Jaundice	222
Chapter 43:	Kidney Stones	227
Chapter 44:	Low Blood Pressure	233
Chapter 45:	Lower Blood Sugar	238
Chapter 46:	Malaria	243
Chapter 47:	Migraine	248
Chapter 48:	Nephritis	254
Chapter 49:	Neuritis	259
Chapter 50:	Obesity	264
Chapter 51:	Peptic Ulcer	271
Chapter 52:	Piles	277
Chapter 53:	Prostate Disorders	282
Chapter 54:	Psoriasis	288
Chapter 55:	Rheumatism	293
Chapter 56:	Sexual Disorders	298
Chapter 57:	Sinusitis	306
Chapter 58:	Stomatitis	311
Chapter 59:	Stress	315
Chapter 60:	Thinness	320
Chapter 61:	Tonsillitis	326
Chapter 62:	Tooth Decay	332
Chapter 63:	Tuberculosis	337
Chapter 64:	Varicose Veins	342
Chapter 65:	Women's Ailments	347

CHAPTER 1

Introduction : Diet in Health and Disease

Your food shall be your medicine — Hippocrates.

Diet plays a vital role in the maintenance of good health and in the prevention and cure of disease. In the words of Sir Robert McCarrison, one of the best known nutritionists, "The right kind of food is the most important single factor in the promotion of health; and the wrong kind of food is the most important single factor in the promotion of disease." The human body builds up and maintains healthy cells, tissues, glands and organs only with the help of various nutrients. The body cannot perform any of its functions, be they metabolic, hormonal, mental, physical or chemical, without specific nutrients. The food which provides these nutrients is, thus, one of the most essential factors in building and maintaining health. The other essential factor is that, these nutrients must also be appropriately utilised by the body.

Nutrition, which depends on food, is also of utmost importance in the cure of disease. The primary cause of disease is a weakened organism or lowered resistance in the body, arising from the adoption of a faulty nutritional pattern. There is an elaborate healing mechanism within the body but it can perform its function only if it is abundantly supplied with all the essential nutritional factors. It is believed that at least 45 chemical components and elements are needed by human cells. An adequate diet must contain each of these 45 substances, called essential nutrients. Two of these nutrients are oxygen and water. The other 43 are classified into five main groups, namely, carbohydrates, fats, proteins, minerals, and vitamins. All 45 of these nutrients are vitally important and they work together. Therefore, the absence of any of them will result in disease and eventually in death.

Research has shown that almost all diseases can be attributed, directly or indirectly, to an undersupply of various nutrients. These deficiencies occur due to various factors, such as, the intense processing and refining of foods, the time lag between the harvesting and consumption of vegetables and fruits, the chemicals used in bleaching, flavouring, colouring and preserving foods and the chemical fertilisers, fungicides, insecticides and sprays used for treating the soil. Vitamin losses also occur due to the storage, paring and grating of vegetables, from soaking in water and from the heat of cooking.

One of the fundamental principles of nature cure is that most diseases have the same basic underlying cause, namely, the steady accumulation in the system of waste materials through years of wrong food habits. Apart from nutritional deficiencies, other factors contributing to this are a faulty nutritional pattern, constant overeating, excessive consumption of proteins and the body's inability to properly digest them and sluggish metabolism. As wrong food habits is the most potent cause of disease, a healthy and balanced diet alone can prevent further accumulation of toxic waste matter in the system, purify the blood and allow all bodily structures to work at a high level of efficiency.

Research shows that diseases produced by combinations of deficiencies can be corrected when all the nutrients are supplied, provided irreparable damage has not been done. A well-balanced and correct diet is thus of utmost importance for the maintenance of good health and the healing of diseases. Such a diet, obviously should be made up of foods which, in combination, would supply all the essential nutrients. It has been found that a diet which contains liberal quantities of seeds, nuts and grains, vegetables and fruits would provide adequate amounts of all the essential nutrients. These foods have, therefore, been aptly called basic food groups and a diet containing these food groups as an optimum diet for vigour and vitality. This diet has been named the Airole Diet after its exponent, Dr Paavo O. Airole, the internationally famous nutritionist and naturopathic physician. It is briefly described in the following lines:

Seeds, nuts and grains:

These are the most important and the most potent of all foods and contain all the important nutrients needed for human growth. They contain the germ, the reproductive power which is of vital importance for the lives of human beings and their health. Millet, wheat, oats, barley, brown rice, beans and peas are all highly valuable in building health. Wheat, mung beans, alfalfa seeds and soya beans make excellent sprouts. Sunflower seeds, pumpkin seeds, almonds, peanuts and soya beans contain proteins of high biological value. Seeds, nuts and grains are also excellent natural sources of essential unsaturated fatty acids necessary for health. They are also good sources of lecithin and most of the B vitamins. They are the best natural sources of vitamin C, which is perhaps the most important vitamin for the preservation of health and prevention of premature ageing. Besides, they are rich sources of minerals and supply the necessary bulk in the diet. They also contain auxones, the natural substances that play an important role in the rejuvenation of cells and prevention of premature ageing. Sprouted seeds are a good source of vitamin C and A. All seeds and nuts should ideally be eaten raw but those which can be sprouted, should be consumed in that form to derive maximum nutritional value. Some grains such as rice, wheat, millet, rye and barley can be cooked in the form of cereals and bread.

Vegetables:

They are an extremely rich source of minerals, enzymes and vitamins. However, faulty cooking and prolonged careless storage, destroy these valuable nutrients. Most of the vegetables are, therefore, best consumed in their natural raw state in the form of salads.

There are different kinds of vegetables. They may be edible roots, stems, leaves, fruits and seeds. Each group contributes to the diet in its own way. Fleshy roots have high energy value and are a good source of vitamin B. Seeds are relatively high in carbohydrates and proteins and the yellow ones are rich in Vitamin A. Leaves, stems and fruits are excellent sources of minerals, vitamins, water and roughage.

To prevent loss of nutrients in vegetables, it would be advisable to steam or boil vegetables in their juices on a slow fire and the water or cooking liquid should not be drained off. No vegetable should be peeled unless it is so old that the peel is tough and unpalatable. In most root vegetables, the largest amount of minerals is directly under the skin and these are lost if the vegetables are peeled. Soaking of vegetables should also be avoided if taste and nutritive value are to be preserved.

An intake of about 280 grams of vegetables per day per person is considered essential for the maintenance of good health. Of this, leafy vegetables should constitute 40 per cent, roots and tubers 30 per cent and the other vegetables like brinjals, ladies fingers and cauliflower 30 per cent.

Fruits:

Like vegetables, fruits are an excellent source of minerals, vitamins and enzymes. They are easily digested and exercise a cleansing effect on the blood and digestive tract. They are highly alkaline and contain a high percentage of water and a low percentage of proteins and fats. Their organic acid and high sugar contents have immediate refreshing effects. Apart from seasonal fresh fruits, dry fruits, such as raisins, prunes and figs are also beneficial.

Fruits are at their best when eaten in the raw and ripe state. Much of their nutritional value in terms of salts and carbohydrates is lost in cooking. They are most beneficial when taken as a separate meal by themselves, preferably for breakfast. If fruits are eaten with regular food, they should form a fairly large part of the meal. Fruits, however, make better combination with milk than with meals. It is also desirable to take one kind of fruit at a time. For the maintenance of good health, at least one pound of uncooked fruits should form part of the daily diet. In case of sickness, it will be advisable to take fruits in the form of juices. However, juices should be drunk immediately after their extraction as they begin to decompose quickly and turn into harmful substances.

Each food group should roughly form the bulk of one of the three principal meals. Fruits can be taken in the morning for breakfast; seeds, nuts and cereals for lunch and vegetables for dinner. This order can, however, be interchanged to suit one's requirements.

About 75 to 80 per cent of the diet should consist of foods in their natural uncooked state, because cooking destroys much of the nutritional value of most foods. Sprouting is an excellent way of consuming seeds, beans and grains in their raw form as in the process of sprouting the nutritional value is multiplied. New vitamins are created and the protein quality is improved. Foods should be eaten only in their natural form, that is whole, unprocessed, unrefined and preferably grown organically, without chemical fertilisers and sprays. Organically grown fruits and vegetables contain more enzymes and have greater health-building and disease-preventing potential.

The three basic health-building foods mentioned above should be supplemented with certain special foods such as milk, vegetable oils and honey. Milk is an excellent food. It is considered as 'Nature's most nearly perfect food.' According to Charak, the great author of the Indian system of medicines, milk increases strength, improves memory, revitalizes the body, maintains strength and promotes long life. The best way to take milk is in its soured form — that is, yogurt and cottage cheese. Soured milk is superior to sweet milk as it is in a predigested form and more easily assimilated. Milk helps to prevent intestinal putrefaction and constipation. High quality unrefined vegetable oils should be added to the diet. They are rich in unsaturated fatty acids, vitamin C and F and lecithin. The average daily amount should not exceed two tablespoons. Honey too, is an ideal food. It helps increase calcium retention in the system, prevents anaemia besides being beneficial in kidney and liver disorders, colds, poor circulation and complexion problems. It is one of Nature's finest energy-giving food. It is easily digested and assimilated.

A diet of the three basic food groups, supplemented with the special foods mentioned above, will ensure a complete and adequate supply of all the vital nutrients needed for health, vitality and prevention of diseases. It is not necessary to include animal protein like egg, fish or meat in this basic diet, as animal protein, especially meat, always has a detrimental effect on the healing processes. A high animal protein is harmful to health and may cause many of our most common ailments.

Daily menu:

Based on what has been stated above, the daily menu of a health-building and vitalising diet should be on the following lines:

Upon arising: A glass of lukewarm water with half a freshly squeezed lemon and a spoonful of honey, or a glass of freshly squeezed juice of any available seasonal fruit such as apple, pineapple, orange, mosambi or grapes.

Breakfast: Fresh fruits such as apple, orange, banana, grapes or any available seasonal fruits, a cup of unpasteurised milk and a handful of raw nuts such as almonds, cashewnuts and peanuts.

Lunch: A bowl of freshly prepared steamed vegetables such as carrot, cabbage, cauliflower, potatoes, squash or

beans, using sea salt, vegetable oil or butter for seasoning, one or two whole wheat chappatis and a glass of butter-milk.
Mid-afternoon: A glass of fresh fruit or vegetable juice or coconut water or sugar cane juice.
Dinner: A large bowl of fresh salad made up of vegetables like tomatoes, carrot, beet, onion, etc., with lemon juice dressing, any available sprouts such as alfalfa seed or mung beans along with one tablespoon of fresh butter, and cottage cheese or a glass of butter-milk.
Bed-time snacks: A glass of fresh milk or one apple.

The above menu is a general outline around which an individual diet can be built. It can be modified and changed to adapt to specific requirements and conditions. The menu for lunch and dinner is interchangeable. Water should not be taken with meals, but half an hour before or an hour after meals. Milk, butter-milk and vegetable soups can be taken with meals.

Diseases can be overcome by sensible natural dietetic treatment. Disease is actually a self-initiated effort of the body to throw off the accumlations of waste materials which are interfering with its functioning. Since most conditions of ill-health are systemic in their origin and have the same underlying causes, the basic treatment is likewise the same.

In the beginning of the dietetic treatment, the patient should undergo a short cleansing juice fast so that the body may throw off all the accumulated toxins and wastes. In this regimen, the person should take the juice of a fresh orange or any other juicy fruit diluted in the proportion of 50:50 with water. Alternatively, vegetable juices such as carrot, cucumber, beet and spinach may be taken. Each day, while fasting, the bowels should be cleansed with a warm water enema. In certain conditions, the patient may adopt an exclusive fruit diet for a few days in the beginning of the treatment instead of juice fasting. In this regimen, three meals a day of fresh juicy fruits such as oranges, grapes, grapefruits, apples, pineapples, peaches and pears may be taken at five-hourly intervals. After the short juice fast or the all-fruit diet as the case may be, the patient may gradually embark upon a well-balanced diet of three basic food groups, namely seeds, nuts and grains, vegetables and fruits as already outlined. Further, juice fasts or periods on the all-fruit diet may be undertaken at intervals of two or three months depending on the progress being made.

CHAPTER 2

Acidosis

Acidosis is a condition in which the acidity of body fluid is abnormally high. The normal body chemistry is approximately 20 per cent acid and 80 per cent alkaline. In normal health, the reaction of the blood is alkaline and that is essential for our physical and mental well-being.

The prepoderance of alkalis in the blood is due to the fact that the products of the vital combustions taking place in the body are mostly acid in character. Carbohydrates and fats form about nine-tenths of the normal fuel of the body. In normal health, this great mass of material is converted into carbondioxide gas and water. This huge amount of acid is transported by the blood to the various points of discharge, mainly lungs. By virtue of its alkalinity, the blood is able to transport the acid from the tissues to the discharge points. Whenever the alkalinity of the blood is reduced, even slightly, its ability to transport the carbon dioxide gets reduced. This results in the accumulation of acid in the tissues.

Symptoms

The symptoms of acidosis are hunger, indigestion, burning sensation and pain in the pharynx, nausea, vomiting, headache, various nervous disorders and drowsiness. It is the breeding ground for most diseases. Nephritis or Bright's disease, rheumatism, premature old age, arteriosclerosis, high blood pressure, skin disorders and various degenerative diseases are traceable to this condition. It lowers the vitality of the system, thereby increasing the danger of infectious diseases.

Causes

The main cause of acidosis or hypo-alkalinity of the blood is faulty diet, in which too many acid-forming foods have been consumed. In the normal process of metabolism, various acids are formed in the system and in addition, other acids are introduced in food. Whenever there is substantial increase in the formation of acids in the system and these acids are not properly eliminated through the lungs, the kidneys, and the bowels, the alkalinity of the blood is reduced, resulting in acidosis.

Other causes of acidosis are depletion of alkali reserve due to diarrhoea, dysentery and cholera, accumalation of carbon dioxide in asphyxia as in circulatory and pulmonary diseases and accumulation of acetone bodies resulting from starvation, vomiting and diabetes mellitus.

Dietary Treatment

Acidosis can be prevented by maintaining a proper ratio between acid and alkaline foods in the diet. Certain foods leave alkaline ash and help in maintaining the alkalinity of the blood, while others leave acid ash which reduce the blood alkalinity. All flesh foods leave highly acid ash and lower the alkali reserve of the blood and tissue fluids to a very large extent. Eggs do the same but less strongly than meats. Cereals of all kinds, including breads, are also acid forming foods, though much less than meats. All fruits, with exceptions like plums and prunes, and all green and root vegetables are highly alkaline foods and help to alkalinize the blood and other tissue fluids.

Thus, our daily diet should consist of four-fifths of alkaline forming foods such as fresh fruits, tubers, legumes, leafy and root vegetables, and one-fifth of acid forming foods such as meat, fish, bread and cereals. Eating sensibly in this manner will ensure the necessary alkalinity of the blood, which will keep the body in perfect health.

Whenever a person has acidosis, the higher the ratio of

alkaline-forming foods in his diet, the quicker will be the recovery. Acids are neutralised by alkalis. It is therefore imperative that persons suffering from this disorder are given adequate alkaline-forming foods to offset the effects of acid-forming foods and leave a safe margin of alkalinity.

The most agreeable and convenient means of alkalising the blood are citrus fuits and fruit juices. The alkalising value of citrus fruits are due to the large percentage of alkaline salts, mainly potash, which they contain. About half a litre of orange juice contains 0.8 gms. of potassium. Lemon juice contains 0.55 gms. and grape juice 0.5 gms. of this alkali in half a litre.

In the diet during acidosis, breakfast may consist of fresh fruits, lunch may comprise raw vegetables, with acid and sub-acid fruits and for dinner, raw and cooked green vegetables or light-starchy vegetables like beet, carrot, cauliflower, egg-plant and squashes may be taken,. Sweet fruits may be added to this after a week or so.

Certain home remedies have been found beneficial in the treatment of acidosis. The foremost among these remedies is the use of raisins (munaqqa). This dry fruit, with its excess of alkalinity, is helpful in maintaining the acid balance of the body. Studies conducted by Saywell in the University of California have shown that the free use of raisins, say about 100 gms. daily, will greatly reduce the acidity of the urine. The urinary ammonia is also reduced. The organic acid of the raisins is completely exidized.

The use of spinach (palak) is valuabe in combating acidosis. This leafy vegetable is a rich source of calcium and other alkaline elements, which are helpful in keeping the tissues clean and for preserving the alkalinity of the blood.

Tomato (tamatar) is another effective remedy for acidosis. It is essentially an alkaline vegetable. This vegetable increases the alkalinity of the blood and decreases that of the urine and neutralises the acid compounds of the body such as phosphates, urea and ammonia. Its regular use is therefore, highly beneficial in the treatment of acidosis.

TREATMENT CHART FOR ACIDOSIS

A - DIET

I. A fast on orange juice for three days. During this period, orange juice diluted with water should be taken every two hours from 8 a.m. to 8 p.m. and bowels cleansed with warm water enema.

II. An all-fruit diet for 3 to 5 days. In this regimen, take three meals a day of fresh juicy fruits such as apples, pears, peaches, papaya, grapes, oranges and pineapples.

In case of acidosis, the patient should take liberal quantities of alkaline-forming foods like fruits.

III. Thereafter, gradually adopt a well-balanced diet on the following lines :-
1. *Upon arising:* A glass of lukewarm water with half a freshly-squeezed lime and a teaspoon of honey.

2. *Breakfast:* Fresh fruit such as apple, grapes, pear, peach, pineapple, papaya and a glass of milk, sweetened with honey.
3. *Lunch:* A large bowl of salad of fresh green vegetable such as lettuce, carrot, cabbage, cucumber, tomatoes, radish, red beets and sprouts such as alfalfa and mung beans with lemon juice dressing, acid and su-acid fruits.
4. *Mid-afternoon:* A glass of citrus fruit juice.
5. *Dinner:* A bowl of freshly-prepared steamed or lightly-cooked vegetables like beet, carrot, cauliflower, egg-plant and squashes.

AVOID: Tea, coffee, sugar, white flour, all products made with sugar and white flour, all refined foods, fried foods, fresh foods condimentas and pickles.

B - OTHER MEASURES

1. Daily dry friction and sponge.
2. Breathing and other light exercises like walking, swimming and bicycling.

CHAPTER 3

Acne

Acne is perhaps the most common chronic skin disease. It is an inflammatory condition of the sebaceous (that is, fat) glands and hair follicles usually found on the face, the neck, chest and shoulders. Approximately, eight out of ten young people between the ages of 12 and 24 suffer from some degree of acne. It is closely related to the disturbance in the hormones experienced at puberty. The majority of patients recover between the ages 20 and 30 years. But it is still common in men over 30 years. In women, it rarely lasts beyond the early thirties and is normally worse before each menstrual period. The disease causes a great deal of embarassment at an age when people tend to be sensitive about personal appearance.

The skin, covering the entire body, is a marvellous and intricate mechanism. It serves three main purposes, namely protection of the inner organism, regulation of body temperature and elimination of cell waste and systemic refuse. The skin is directly connected to and intimately bound up with the working of the whole system. All skin diseases, including acne, are the outcome of malfunctioning of the body as a whole.

Symptoms

Acne is characterised by the presence of comedones or blackheads, pimples, small superficial sebaceous cysts and scars. There are over half a dozen forms of acne. All of them are concerned with the sebaceous glands or the glands connected with hair follicles. The most common form of acne is blackheads. The areas cheifly affected are the forehead, temples, cheeks, chin, the chest and back.

In rare cases, almost the entire body may be covered with blackheads with extensive scarring.

Causes

All forms of acne have their origin in wrong food habits, such as irregular hours of eating, improper food, excess of starch, sugar and fatty foods. Chronic constipation is another major cause of acne. If the bowels do not move properly, the waste matter is not eliminated as quickly as it should be and the blood stream becomes saturated with toxic matter. The extra efforts of the skin to eliminate this excess waste result in acne and other forms of skin disease. Yet another important cause of acne is a devitalised condition of the skin resulting from unhygienic living habits. Other contributing factors to the disorder are excessive use of tea, coffee, alcohol and tobacco, strenuous studies, and sedentary habits which lead to indigestion and general debility.

Dietary Cure

The treatment of acne by the administration of salves or ointment does not serve any purpose. They only suppress the action of the sebaceous glands temporarily. In nature cure, the main emphasis is on diet and certain water applications. To begin with, the patient should resort to an all-fruit diet for about a week. This regimen should consist of three meals a day, consisting of fresh juicy fruits, such as apples, pears, grapes, grapefruits, pineapples and peaches. Citrus fruits, bananas, dried, stewed or tinned fruits should not be taken. Unsweetened lemon or plain water, either hot or cold, should be drunk and nothing else. During this period, a warm water enema should be taken daily to cleanse the bowels and all other measures adopted to eradicate constipation.

After a week of the all-fruit diet, the patient can gradually adopt a well-balanced diet with a predominantly alkaline base. Emphasis should be on raw foods, especially fresh fruits and vegetables, sprouted seeds, raw nuts and whole grain cereals, particularly millet and brown rice.

Further, short periods on the all-fruit diet for three days or so may be necessary at monthly intervals till the skin's condition improves.

Strict attention to diet is essential for recovery. Starchy, protein and fatty foods should be restricted. Meat, sugar, strong tea or coffee, condiments, pickles, refined and processed foods should all be avoided, as also soft drinks, candies, ice cream and products made with sugar and white flour.

The following diet should serve as a guideline:
1. *Breakfast:* Fresh fruits, and milk. For a change, dried fruits may be added occasionally.
2. *Lunch:* Steamed vegetables, whole grain bread or chappatis with butter and curd or butter-milk.
3. *Dinner:* A large bowl of raw vegetable salad and sprouts, such as alfalfa seeds or mung beans, with prunes or other dried fruit as dessert.

Two vitamins, namely, niacin and vitamin A, have been used successfully to treat acne. The vitamin therapy, comprising of niacin 100 mg. three times daily and vitamin A in large doses upto 50,000 units per day, should not exceed one month. Vitamin E is also vitally important for preventing scarring from acne and in removing old scars.

For local treatment, hot fomentation should be applied to open up the pores and squeeze out the waste matter. Then rinse with cold water. Sun and air baths, by exposing the whole body to sun and air, are highly beneficial. Washing the affected area with lemon juice has also proved helpful. Healing packs made of grated cucumbers, oatmeal cooked in milk and cooked, creamed carrots, used externally, have been found effective. Packs should be applied and kept on for half an hour and then washed off with cold water. A hot Epsom salt bath twice a week will be highly beneficial in all cases of acne. This bath is prepared by adding three lbs. of Epsom salt to 60 litres of water having a temperature of about 100°F. The patient should remain in the bath from 25 to 35 minutes till he perspires freely. After the bath, the patient should cool off gradually.

TREATMENT CHART FOR ACNE

A - DIET

I. An exclusive diet of fresh juicy fruits for five days. Take three meals a day at five-hourly intervals and use warm water enema daily during this period.

II. Therefore, adopt the following diet:-
1. *Upon arising:* A glass of lukewarm water with half a freshly-squeezed lime and a teaspoon of honey.

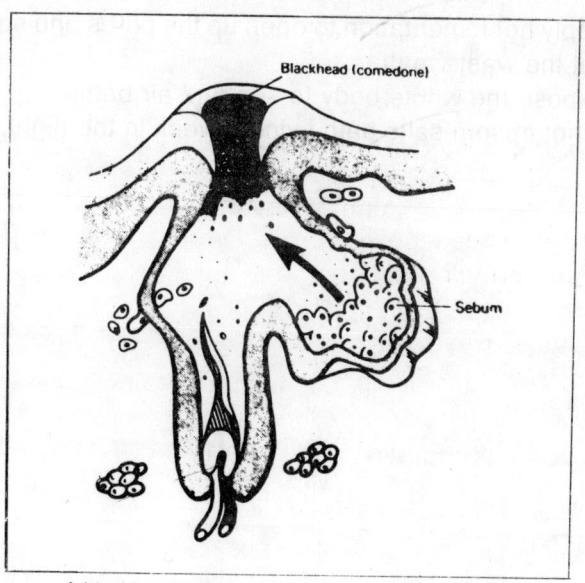

A blackhead is formed by sebum blocking a pore.

2. *Breakfast:* Fresh fruits such as apple, orange, grapes, papaya, mangoes, a cup of fresh milk, sweetened with honey or buttermilk.
3. *Lunch:* A bowl of steamed vegetables, whole wheat

chappatis with butter and a glass of buttermilk.
4. *Mid-afternoon:* A glass of fresh fruit or vegetable juice or sugarcane juice.
5. *Dinner:* A bowl of fresh green vegetable salad, with lime juice dressing, sprouted seeds and fresh home-made cottage cheese or a glass of buttermilk.
Restrict: Starchy, protein and fatty foods, as well as salt intake.

Note:
1. Repeat the exclusive diet of fresh juicy fruits every month for three days till the skin condition improves.
2. Take liberallly Vitamin A-rich foods.

B - OTHER MEASURES

1. Apply hot fomentation to open up the pores and squeeze out the waste matter.
2. Expose the whole body to sun and air baths.
3. A hot epsom-salts bath twice a week in the night.

CHAPTER 4

Alcoholism

Alcoholism is a chronic disorder, in which a person is unable to refrain from frequent and excessive consumption of alcohol for physical or psychological reasons. The World Health Organisation has listed alcoholism as one of the three most deadly killer diseases of the 20th century. Alcoholism is also a very serious social problem. It often brings poverty and a certain amount of crime and frequently results in marital unhappiness and broken homes. It also leads to numerous traffic accidents.

Alcohol is not a product found in nature. It results from decomposition and as such belongs to a family of poisons. Ethyl alcohol, the main intoxicating ingredient in wine, beer and distilled liquor is a toxic drug which depresses the brain and nervous system. Alcohol cannot be called a food for it enters the alimentary canal and is not changed or digested in any way. It is quickly absorbed in the blood stream and then travels to every part of the body, adversely affecting vital organs like the brain and liver. About 90 per cent of the alcohol is slowly oxidised in the liver and the remaining 10 per cent is eliminated by breathing and through urination. An average peg of whisky, 12 ounces of beer or 5 ounces of wine take one full hour to be oxidised in the liver.

Symptoms

According to W.H.O., "Alcoholics are those excessive drinkers whose dependence on alcohol has attained such a degree that it shows a noticeable mental disturbance or interference with their bodily or mental health, their interpersonal relations and their smooth social and economic functions, or who show the pro-dromal signs of such development."

Alcoholics have a puffy face with bloodshot eyes, hoarse voice and rapid pulse. They are suspicious, irritable and over-emotional. Vomiting, delirium, impaired judgement and disturbed sleep are some of the common symptoms.

The chronic alcoholic, who would rather drink than eat, fails to get enough vitamins. The few vitamins acquired by him are drained out of his system in the process of burning the alcohol in his body. Vitamin deficiency can lead to delirium tremens, convulsions, neuritis, disorders of the eyes and impaired memory. Excessive drinking often causes premature graying of hair due to vitamin deficiency. Chronic alcoholism results in a depletion of minerals in the body, particularly magnesium, which produces symptoms like tremor of the hands, feet and tongue, convulsions, mental clouding and sweating.

Alcohol tends to be habit-forming. The more you have, the more you want. The more you drink, the less you eat. Soon the body is out of gear, because it has been getting an unsuitable and inadequate type of fuel. Excessive drinking imposes a strain on the liver. It gradually destroys its functions and often causes cirrhosis of the liver. It leads to disorders of the stomach and bowels. It can cause brain damage as brain cells are often affected by it. Alcohol also affects the heart which becomes weak and flabby.

Causes

Alcoholism results from excessive drinking. Sometimes a person sinks comparatively rapidly into alcoholism and at other times, years may pass before a person becomes a full-fledged alcoholic. A person generally takes to drinking as a means to enliven social life, to overcome anxiety or to induce sleep. He becomes an alcoholic if he gets dependent on alcohol physically and psychologically. He resorts to heavy drinking because of his inability to deal with the stress and strain of life.

Dietary Considerations

The chronic alcoholic must first of all make a firm resolve to stop drinking. He should abstain from alcohol all at once for the habit cannot be got rid of in gradual stages. The most effective way to treat alcoholism is to build the body's nutritional integrity so as to prevent the craving for stimulants like drinks. The patient should be put on a cleansing juice fast for at least 10 days in the beginning. During this period, he should have the juice of an orange every two hours from 8 a.m. to 8 p.m. The juice may be diluted with warm water, if desired. Nothing else should be taken as otherwise the value of the fast would be entirely lost. Alternatively, vegetable juices may be taken. Each day while fasting, bowels should be cleansed of poisonous matter thrown off by the self-cleansing process set up by the body. This can be achieved by a warm water enema.

During the juice fast, the patient will usually feel no craving for alcohol. This will give a good 10-day start towards breaking the drinking habit and will help remove not only the physical but also the psychological dependence. After the initial fast on juices, the optimum diet of vital nutrients is essential. Such a diet should consist of whole grain cereals, nuts, seeds and sprouts, fresh fruits and vegetables. The breakfast may consist of fresh fruits and milk. Steamed vegetables, whole wheat chappatis and butter-milk may be taken for lunch. The dinner may comprise a good sized raw salad and sprouts.

It is advisable that in the beginning of the treatment, the patient is given a suitable substitute to relieve the craving for alcohol if and when such a craving occurs. The best substitute drink is a glass of fresh fruit juice, sweetened with honey, if desired. In the alternative, wholesome candy may be taken. The patient should always have easily available juices, candy or other snacks to be taken between meals if he feels a craving for a stimulant. All refined foods such as sugar, white rice, macaroni products and white flour and meat should be avoided. The patient should eat several small meals a day in preference to two or three large ones and avoid strong condiments such as pepper, mustard and chilli. He should not smoke as this will only increase his desire for alcohol.

Dr. Roger J. Williams, a world renowned researcher on alcoholism from the nutritional point of view, states that if the alcoholic is supplied with certain nutrients missing from his body, the craving can be halted and even reversed. He has worked out a specific nutritional supplement containing the nutrients necessary for an alcoholic, which is as under:

Vitamins

Vitamin A : 20,000 I.U.
Vitamin C : 200 mg.
Vitamin D : 1,000 I.U.
B vitamins
Thiamine : 4 mg.
Riboflavin : 4 mg.
Pyridoxin : 6 mg.
Niacinamide : 40 mg.
Pantothenate : 40 mg.
B - 12 : 10 mg.
Choline : 200 mg.
Insitol : 200 mg.
Vitamin E : 200 mg.

Minerals

Calcium : 300 mg.
Phosphate : 250 mg.
Magnesium : 100 mg.
Copper : 1 mg.
Iodine : 0.1 mg.
Iron : 10 mg.
Manganese : 1 mg.
Zinc : 5 mg.

In addition to proper nutrition, plenty of rest and outdoor exercise are necessary. The healthy condition of the appetite centre, which controls the craving for alcohol is improved by excercise.

ALCOHOLISM

TREATMENT CHART FOR ALCOHOLISM

A - DIET

I. Take the juice of oranges or carrots diluted with water for five days every two hours during the day. Use warm water enema during this period.

Raw Juice therapy is most effective remedy for alcoholic

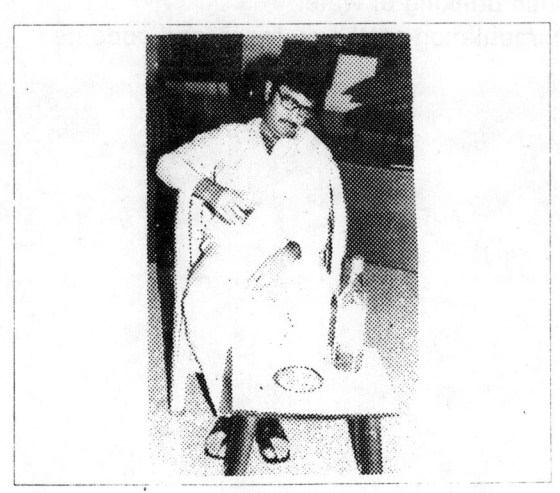

The chronic alcoholic, who would rather drink than eat, fails to get enough vitamins.

II. Therefore, adopt the following diet:-
1. *Upon arising:* A glass of lukewarm water with half a freshly-squeezed lime and a teaspoon of honey.
2. *Breakfast:* Fresh fruits and a cup of milk
3. *Mid-morning:* A glass of fresh fruit juice.
4. *Lunch:* Steamed vegetables, whole wheat chappatis and buttermilk.
5. *Mid-afternoon:* A glass of carrot juice or sugarcane juice.
6. *Dinner:* A good sized raw vegetable salad and sprouts

NOTE: (1) In case of craving for alcohol, take a glass of fresh fruit juice or a wholesome snack.
(2) Take frequent small meals rather than two or three large ones.

AVOID: Sugar, white rice, macroni and white flour products, meats, strong condiments and smoking.

B - OTHER MEASURES

1. Exercise and yogic asanas for general health.
2. Plenty of rest.
3. Copious drinking of water.
4. Hot fomentation on the stomach and abdomen.

CHAPTER 5

Allergies

The word 'allergy' means an altered or abnormal tissue reaction after exposure to a foreign antigen. An allergic reaction may occur when there is contact between a foreign protein — an allergen — and body tissues that are sensitive to it. The allergens may reach the tissues by direct contact with the skin or mucous membranes, or through the blood stream after absorption.

Allergic reactions may occur within a few minutes of the patient coming in contact with the allergen or they may be delayed for several hours or even several days. Almost any part of the body can be affected by allergies. The portion of the body which is affected is called a shock organ. Common sites are nose and eyes, the skin, chest, intestines and ears.

Allergic reactions are caused by a wide range of substances and conditions. These include pollen, dust, cosmetics, and animal hair; poisonous plants, serums, vaccines and drugs; physical agents such as heat, cold and sunlight; as well as a variety of foods.

Food and Allergy

The protein component of a food is considered to be the causative factor in food allergy, although foods which cause an allergic reaction may vary widely in protein content. Also, allergic response to a food may be either immediate or delayed.

Among the numerous allergens in the food department, the more common ones are oranges, milk, eggs, wheat, fish, chocolates, cabbage, potatoes, tomatoes and strawberries. Additives and refinements are also responsible for the rise in allergies. The trouble is not only in the foods themselves, but in what is done to them. They are sprayed, gassed, coloured, preserved for longer life and generally perverted.

Symptoms

The symptoms of allergy are as varied as the substances causing the reaction. These include recurring headache, migraine, dizziness, irritability, nervousness, depression, neuralgia, sneezing, conjunctivitis, eczema, heartburn, hay fever, indigestion, constipation, diarrhoea, gastric ulcer, asthma, overweight, high blood pressure, chest pain, heart attacks, a stuffy or runny nose, shortness of breath, swelling of the face and eyes, etc. The same food can cause different symptoms in different people. Many allergies are multiple and may be caused by multiple allergens.

Causes

Allergy is an indication of lowered resistance and internal disharmony caused by dietetic errors and faulty style of living. It is believed that the major cause of allergy is feeding babies such food as cereals, meat, corns, whole milk, etc., before they reach the age of 10 to 12 months. These foods cause allergic reactions as babies lack the proper enzymes needed for their digestion before that age. Babies should be breast-fed for at least eight months as this is nature's way of providing all the required nutrients during this period.

Another important cause of allergy is today's processed foods loaded with numerous chemical additives, many of which cause powerful reactions. An allergic condition can result from diet imbalance. There can be a breakdown in the body's ability to handle sugar due to excessive intake of refined sugar and consequent blood sugar irregularities, or mineral and vitamin imbalances due to defective dietary patterns.

Emotional and psychological stresses can also lead to allergies. According to Dr. Hans Salye, the world's premier researcher on stress, allergic symptoms are often nothing more than the body's reaction to stress. A person can, through chronic stress, become sensitive to common foods or commonplace substances like petrol fumes.

Dietary Treatment

There are various ways to tackle many of the allergic disturbances. First, the allergens must be identified. This is a difficult but not impossible task. Second, once they are identified, they should be avoided. Third, and most important, general health and resistance should be built up to establish immunity to them.

There are two methods of detecting disturbing foods. The first method is the trial-and-error elimination diet. This automatically eliminates many hazards and foods. Keep to organic, untreated, unprocessed foods as far as possible, and you will eliminate another set of hazards such as pesticides, various sprays and other poisons. After having eliminated as many disturbing factors as possible, a self-search should be carried out to ascertain any suspicious symptoms from foods. It is advisable to try an elimination diet, excluding suspected foods for two weeks until the cause is detected. Occasionally, by changing the brand or the type, you can find a food substitute that does not upset you. For example, chocolate upsets many, so try carob, which tastes the same but has not been found disturbing.

Another way to detect the cause of allergy is by Dr. Coca's "pulse test". The method is as follows: check your pulse before a meal. Then limiting that meal to one food only, wait for half an hour after eating and take your pulse again. A slight increae is considered normal, even up to 16 extra beats. If your pulse does not rise above 84, you may be allergy-free. But if your pulse rises beyond that point, and remains high an hour after the meal, you have found your food allergy. The best way, however, to prevent or overcome allergies is to strengthen the overall physical resistance so as not to fall an easy prey to every allergen that comes along. To start with, the patient should fast on fresh fruit juices for four or five days. Repeated short juice fasts are likely to result in better tolerance to previous allergies. After the fruit juice fast, the patient can take a mono diet of vegetables or fruits such as carrots, grapes or apples, for one week. After that one more food is added to the mono diet. A week later the third food is added and so on. After four weeks, the protein foods can be introduced, one at a time. In case an allergic reaction to a newly introduced food is noticed, it should be discontinued and a new food tried. In this way all real allergens can be eventually eliminated from the diet.

The body requires a large alkaline reserve for its daily activity. The problem of acid formation throughout the day from wrong foods, fatigue, mental stress and lack of sleep can be met by the competency of the alkaline reserves. Boosting the normal body reserve of alkalines by liberal use of alkaline forming foods is essential for those suffering from allergies.

The foods which should be excluded from the diet are tea, coffee, chocolate, cola drinks, alcohol, sugar, sweets and foods containing sugar, refined cereals, meats, fish, chicken, tobacco, milk, cheese, butter, smoked, salted and pickled foods and foods containing any chemical additives, preservatives and flavouring. These foods cause either toxic accumulations, overstimulation of the adrenal glands, strain on the pancreatic enzyme production or disturb the blood sugar balance.

For preventive purposes, the entire C complex vitamins — known as the bioflavonoids, are recommended. They gradually strengthen cell permeability to help immunise the body from various allergies, especially hay fever. Often the addition of B_5 or pantothenic acid brings great relief to allergy sufferers. Multiple allergies may result from poor adrenal gland functioning. In such cases liberal amounts of pantothenic acid helps cure them, although the recovery will take several weeks. An adequate intake of vitamin E is also beneficial as this vitamin possesses effective anti-allergic properties, as some studies have shown.

TREATMENT CHART FOR ALLERGIES

A - DIET

I. Fresh fruit juices for three to five days.

II. After the fruit juices, adopt a mono diet of vegetables or fruits like carrots, grapes or apples, for one week.

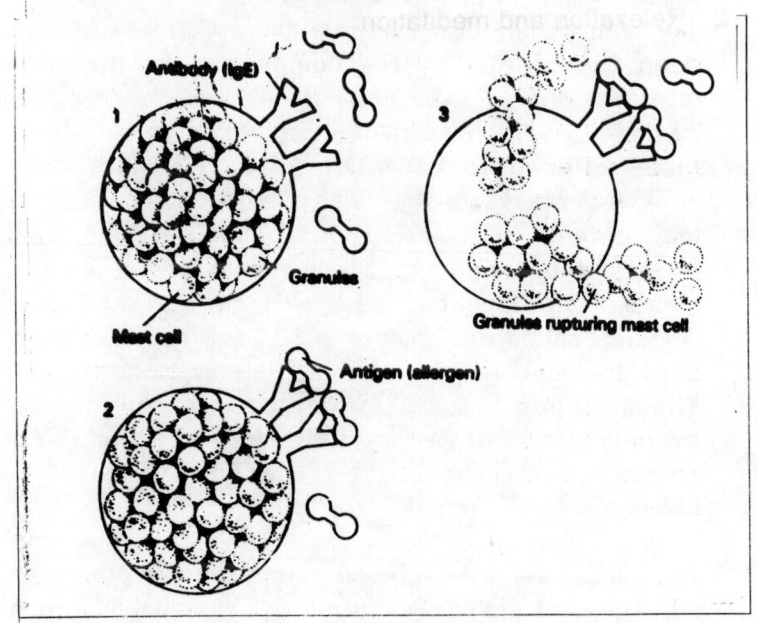

Allergy refers to abnormal tissue reaction after exposure to a foreign antigen.

III. Therefore, add one more food to mono diet. A week later, add the third food and so on.

IV. After four weeks, the protein foods can be introduced, one at a time.

NOTE:
(1) In case of an allergic reaction to a newly introduced food, it should be discontinued and a new food tried. So as to eventually eliminate all real allergens.
(2) Make liberal use of alkaline-forming foods such as fresh fruits, fruit juices and raw vegetables.

AVOID: Tea, coffee, alcohol, tobacco, chocolate, cola drinks, sugar, sweets and other sugary foods, refined and processed foods, flesh foods and pickles.

B - OTHER MEASURES

1. Regular exercise and yogic asanas.
2. Relexation and meditation.

CHAPTER 6

Anaemia

Anaemia may be defined as a condition in which there is a decrease in the quantity of haemoglobin, in the number of red blood cells, in the volume of packed cells, or in any combination of these. It usually results from consumption of refined foods and is among the most common diseases affecting human beings.

Nearly half of the blood flowing in our veins and arteries consists of red blood cells which carry oxygen to the tissues. Approximately, one trillion (100 million) new blood cells are formed daily in the bone marrow. The raw material required in the production of these cells are iron, proteins and vitamins, especially folic acid and vitamin B12. Of these, iron and proteins are essential in building up the red colouring matter, called haemoglobin.

Red cells live approximately 120 days and are being destroyed and replaced daily. Each person should have 100 per cent of haemoglobin or about 15 grams to 100 cc of blood, and a blood count of five million red cells per millimeter. A drop in the haemoglobin content results in anaemia.

Symptoms

The patient usually complains of weakness, fatigue, lack of energy and dizziness. Other symptoms include a haggard look, premature wrinkes, dull and tired looking eyes, poor memory, shortness of breath on slight exertion, headache, slow healing of wounds, palpitation of heart and mental depression. The skin and mucous membranes look pale, the nails appear brittle and there may be sores at the corners of the mouth.

Causes

Low formation of red blood cells in the bone marrow, either due to defects in the bone marrow itself or to an inadequate intake of iron, vitamins and protein, is one of the main causes of anaemia. Other important causes may be heavy loss of blood due to injury, bleeding piles and excessive menstruation in women. Besides, a lack of digestive acid or hydrochloric acid needed for digestion of iron and proteins or emotional strain, anxiety and worry which interferes with the manufacture of hydrochloric acid in the body could also lead to anaemia.

Intestinal parasites or worms are yet another cause of anaemia. Hookworms, pinworms, roundworms and tapeworms feed on the supply of blood as well as the vitamins. Symptoms of intestinal worms are itching at the rectum, restlessness during night with bad dreams, diarrhoea, foul breath, dark circles under the eyes and a constant desire for food. Garlic, fresh papaya and grated raw carrot can help vanquish some types of intestinal parasites.

Dietary Treatment

Diet is of the utmost importance in the treatment of anaemia. Refined foods like white bread, polished rice, sugar and desserts rob the body of the much-needed iron. Iron should always be taken in its natural organic form in food as the use of inorganic iron can prove hazardous. It may cause destruction of protective vitamins and unsaturated fatty acids, serious liver damage, miscarriage during pregnancy and delayed or premature births.

The diet should be predominantly alkaline. The emphasis should be on raw fruits and vegetables which are rich in iron. Iron rich vegetables are spinach, green onions, squash, carrots, radishes, beets, celery, yams, tomatoes and potatoes (with jackets). Fruits which are rich in iron are bananas, apples, dark grapes, apricots, plums, raisins and strawberries. Bananas are particularly beneficial as they also contain, besides easily assimilable iron, folic acid and B12, both of which are extremely useful in the treatment of anaemia.

Other iron-rich foods are whole wheat, brown rice, beans, soyabeans, sunflower seeds, crude blackstrap molasses, eggs and honey. Honey is also rich in copper which helps in iron absorption. The diet should also be adequate in proteins of high biological value such as milk, home-made cottage cheese and eggs.

Vitamin B-12 is a must for preventing or curing anaemia. This vitamin is usually found in animal protein and especially in organic meats like kidney and liver. A heavy meat diet is often associated with a high haemoglobin and high red cell count, but it has its disadvantages. One cause of anaemia is intestinal putrefaction, which is primarily brought on by a high meat diet. Moreover, all meats are becoming increasingly dangerous due to widespread diseases in the animals which are slaughtered. There are, however, other equally good sources of vitamin B12 such as dairy products, like milk, eggs, cheese and peanuts. Wheat germ and soyabean also contain some B12. Vegetarians should include adequate amount of milk, milk products and eggs in their diet. For prevention of anaemia, it is essential to take the entire B complex range which includes B-12, as well as the natural foods mentioned above. Eating lacto-ovo products, which are complete proteins containing vitamin B-12, is good insurance against the disease. A liberal intake of ascorbic acid is necessary to facilitate absorption of iron. At least two helpings of citrus fruits and other ascorbic acid rich foods should be taken daily.

Mention must be made of beets which are extremely important in curing anaemia. Beet juice contains potassium, phosphorus, calcium, sulphur, iodine, iron, copper, carbohydrates, protein, fat, vitamins B1, B2, niacin, B6, C and vitamin P. With its high iron content, beet juice regenerates and reactivates the red blood cells, and supplies the body with fresh oxygen. According to

Dr. Fritz Keitel of Germany, "The juice of red beet strengthens the body's powers of resistance and has proved to be an excellent remedy for anaemia, especially for children and teenagers, where other blood forming remedies have failed."

The anaemic person should commence the dietary treatment by an exclusive fresh fruit diet for about five days. During this period, he should take three meals of fresh juicy fruits at five-hourly interval. This may be followed by fruit and milk diet for about 15 days. In this regimen, the meals are exactly the same as for all-fruit diet, but with milk added to each fruit meal. The patient may begin with two pints the first day and increase by half a pint daily upto four or five pints a day. After the fruit and milk diet, the patient may gradually embark upon a well-balanced diet based on three basic food groups, namely seeds, nuts and grains vegetables and fruits.

TREATMENT CHART FOR ANAEMIA

A - DIET

I. An all-fruit diet for five days. Take three meals a day of fresh juicy fruits at five-hourly intervals and use warm water enema during this period.

II. Fruit and milk diet for further five days, adding milk to each fruit meal.

III. Thereafter, adopt the following diet:-
1. *Upon arising:* 25 black raisins soaked overnight in water alongwith water in which they are soaked and the water kept overnight in a copper vessel.
2. *Breakfast:* Fresh fruit, a glass of milk sweetened with honey and some nuts, especially almonds.
3. *Lunch:* A bowl of freshly-prepared steamed vegetables, two or three whole wheat chappatis, butter and a glass of buttermilk.
4. *Mid-afternoon:* A glass of carrot or apple juice

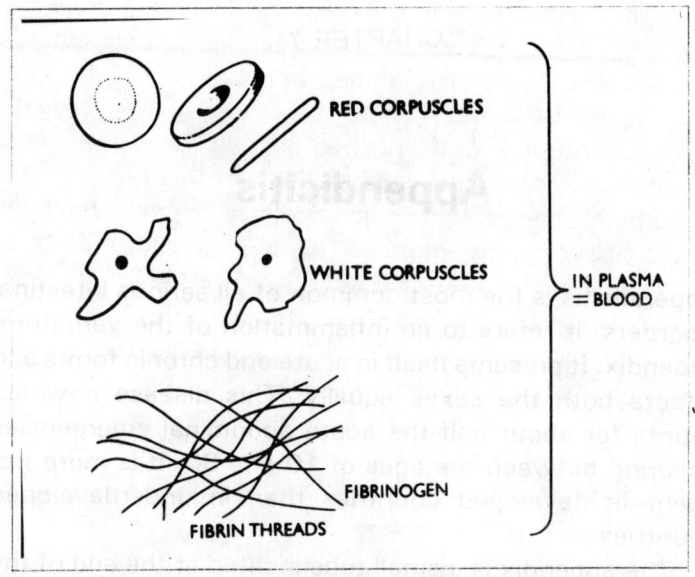

Composition of Blood

5. *Dinner:* A large bowl of fresh green vegetable salad and al-alfalfa or mung bean sprouts.

NOTE: An exclusive fruit diet for three days, followed by fruit and milk diet for further three days should be repeated at regular intervals.

AVOID: Meats, sugar, white flour, tea, coffee, refined and processed foods, soft drinks, fried foods, condiments and pickles.

B - OTHER MEASURES

1. Drink 8 to 10 glasses of water supply.
2. Cold water bath twice daily, cold friction and wet abdomen pack once daily.
3. Massage once a week.
4. Brisk walks, yogic asanas, breathing exercises, fresh air and sun bath.
5. Adequate rest and sleep.

CHAPTER 7

Appendicitis

Appendicitis is the most common of all serious intestinal disorders. It refers to an inflammation of the vermiform appendix. It presents itself in acute and chronic forms and affects both the sexes equally. This disease now accounts for about half the acute abdominal emergencies occuring between the ages of 10 and 30. It is more frequent in developed countries than in underdeveloped countries.

The appendix is a small tube located at the end of the caecum, the first part of the large intestine. It is usually three to four inches long. Its structure is made of the same tough fibrous outer covering as protects the entire alimentary canal. There is a layer of muscular tissue under the outer covering and then a layer of lymphoid tissue. The function of the appendix, which is performed by this lymphoid tissue, is to neutralise the irritating waste material generated in the body or the organic poisons introduced through the skin or membranes.

Symptoms

Appendicitis usually begins with a sudden pain in the centre of the abdomen, which gradually shifts to the lower right side. The pain may be preceded by general discomfort in the abdomen, indigestion, diarrhoea or constipation. The patient usually has a mild fever varying from 100° to 102°F. Nausea is common, and the patient may vomit once or twice. The muscles of the right side of the abdomen become tense and rigid. The patient gets some comfort by drawing up the right leg. The pain increases on the right side on pressing the left side of the abdomen. Coughing and sneezing makes the pain worse.

APPENDICITIS

If the inflammation continues to increase, the appendix may rupture and discharge its pus into the abdominal cavity. This may result in a serious state known as peritonitis. The temperature rises and the patient becomes pale and clammy. This condition may call for urgent operation. In the chronic state of appendicitis, the patient may suffer from recurrent pain in the right lower abdomen with constipation, loss of appetite and mild nausea.

Causes

Appendicitis is caused by a toxic bowel condition. When an excessive amount of poisonous waste material is accumulated in the caecum, the appendix is irritated and over-worked and becomes inflamed. It is an attempt on the part of nature to localise and 'burn up' the toxins. This condition is brought about by wrong food habits and enervation of the system. Inflammation of the bowel lining due to the habitual use of aperient drugs (laxatives), is a potent predisposing factor in the development of appendicitis. Further inflammation and infection comes from certain germs which are usually present in the intestinal tract.

Dietary Treatment

The patient should be put to bed immediately at the first signs of severe pain, vomiting and fever. Rest is of utmost importance in the treatment of this disease. The patient should resort to fasting which is the only real cure for appendicitis. Absolutely no food should be given. Nothing except water should enter the system. Low enemas, containing about one pint (½ litre) of warm water should be administered every day for the first three days to cleanse the lower bowel. Hot compresses may be placed over the painful area several times daily. Abdominal packs, made of a strip of wet sheet covered by a dry flannel cloth bound tightly around the abdomen, should be applied continuously until all acute symptoms subside.

When the acute symptoms subside by about the third day, the patient should be given a full enema, containing about three pints of warm water and this should be repeated daily until all inflammation and pain have subsided. The patient can be given fruit juices from the third day onwards. This simple treatment, sensibly applied, will overcome an appendicitis attack.

After spending three days on fruit juices, the patient may adopt an all-fruit diet for a further four or five days. During this period, he should have three meals a day of fresh, juicy fruits. Thereafter, he should adopt a well-balanced diet based on three basic food groups namely, seeds, nuts and grains, vegetables and fruits.

In case of chronic appendicitis, a short fast should be followed by a full milk diet for two to three weeks. In this regimen, a glass of milk should be taken every two hours from 8 a.m. to 8 p.m. on the first day, a glass every hour and a half the next day and a glass every hour the third day. Then the quantity of milk should be gradually increased so as to take a glass every half an hour, if such a quantity can be tolerated comfortably. After the full milk diet, the patient should gradually embark upon a well-balanced diet with emphasis on fresh fruits and green leafy vegetables.

Certain vegetable juices, especially carrot juice, in combination with the juices of beets and cucumbers, have been found valuable in the treatment of appendicitis. Regular use of tea made from fenugreek seeds has also proved helpful in preventing the appendix from becoming a dumping ground for excess mucous and intestinal waste.

The patient of appendicitis should adopt all measures to eradicate constipation, if it is habitual. Much relief can be obtained by the application of hot fomentation and abdominal packs every morning and night. Abdominal massage is also beneficial. Once the waste matter in the caecum has moved into the colon and thence eliminated, the irritation and inflammation in the appendix will subside and surgical removal of the appendix will not be necessary. The surgical operation should be resorted to only in rare cases, when the appendix has become septic.

TREATMENT CHART FOR CHRONIC APPENDICITIS

A - DIET

I. An all-fruit diet for 2 or 3 days, with three meals a day of fresh juicy fruits at five-hourly intervals.

II. Fruit and milk diet for further 3 days. In this regimen, milk may be added to each fruit meal.

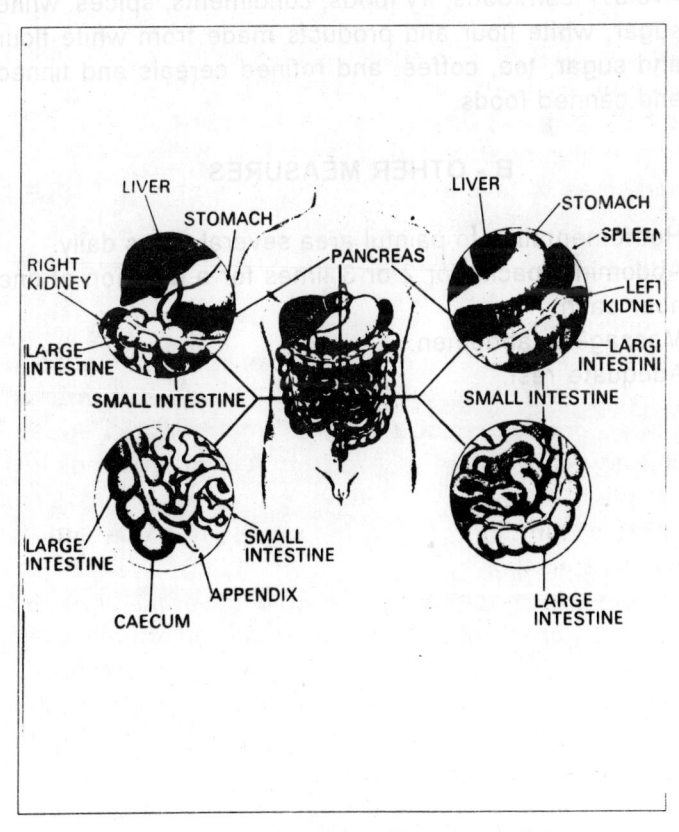

Diagram showing the position of appendix

III. Therefore, adopt a well-balanced diet on the following lines:
1. *Upon arising:* A glass of lukewarm water with half a freshly-squeezed lime and a teaspoon of honey.
2. *Breakfast:* Fruits and milk, followed by nuts, if desired.
3. *Lunch:* Steamed vegetables as obtainable, 2 or 3 whole wheat chappatis and a glass of buttermilk.
4. *Mid-afternoon:* A glass of fresh fruit or vegetable juice or sugarcane juice.
5. *Dinner:* A bowl of fresh green vegetable salad, with lime juice dressing, sprouted seeds and fresh home-made cottage cheese or a glass of buttermilk.
6. *Bedtime:* A glass of fresh milk or an apple.
   Avoid: Flesh foods, fry foods, condiments, spices, white sugar, white flour and products made from white flour and sugar, tea, coffee, and refined cereals and tinned and canned foods.

B - OTHER MEASURES

1. Hot fomentation to painful area several times daily.
2. Abdominal packs for 2 or 3 times for a duration of one hour each.
3. Massage to abdomen.
4. Adequate rest.

CHAPTER 8

Arteriosclerosis

Arteriosclerosis is one of the most common diseases of the blood vessels. It refers to a thickening of the walls of the arteries due to the presence of calcium or lime. It has become a common ailment in modern times, accounting for much of the disability and high death rate among older people.

Arteriosclerosis is usually preceded by atherosclerosis, a kind of degeneration or softening of the inner lining of the blood vessel walls. The most risky places for such degeneration are the coronary vessels of the heart and the arteries leading to the brain. Arteriosclerosis results in the loss of elasticity of the blood vessels, with a narrowing of the smaller arteries, which interferes with the free circulation of the blood. These changes may gradually extend to capillaries and veins.

Arteriosclerosis is more frequent in men than women, especially in the younger age group. It has been estimated that 40 per cent of all men over 40 years of age have a significant degree of obstruction of their coronary arteries and this can lead to a heart attack at any time.

Symptoms

The symptoms of arteriosclerosis vary with the arteries involved. Signs of inadequate blood supply generally appear first in the legs. There may be numbness and coldness in the feet and cramps and pains in the legs even after light exercise. If the coronary arteries are involved, the patient may have sharp pains, characteristic of angina pectoris. When arteries leading to the brain are involved, the vessel may burst, causing haemorrhage in the brain tissues. A cerebral vascular stroke, with partial or complete paralysis of one side of the body may result, if there is blockage with a blood clot. It may also lead to loss of memory and a confused state of mind in elderly people. If arteries leading to the kidneys are involved, the patient may suffer from high blood pressure and kidney disorders.

Causes

The most important cause of arteriosclerosis is excessive intake of white sugar, refined foods and a diet high in fat i.e., rich in cholesterol. A sedentary life and excesses of all kinds are the major contributing causes. Hardening of the arteries may also be caused by other diseases such as high blood pressure, obesity, diabetes, rheumatism, Bright's disease, malaria and syphilis. Emotional stress also plays an important part, and heart attacks are more common during periods of mental and emotional disturbances, particularly in those engaged in sedentary occupations. Heredity also plays its role and this disease runs in families.

Dietary Treatment

If the causes of arteriosclerosis are known, remedial action should be taken promptly to remove them. To begin with the patient should resort to a short juice fast for five to seven days. All available fresh, raw vegetable and fruit juices in season may be taken. Grapefruit juice, pineapple juice, lemon juice and juices of green vegetables are specially beneficial. A warm water enema should be used daily to cleanse the bowels during the period of fasting.

After the juice fast, the patient should follow a diet made up of the three basic food groups, namely, seeds, nuts and grains, vegetables and fruits, with emphasis on raw foods. Plenty of raw and sprouted seeds and nuts should be used. Cold pressed vegetable oils, particularly safflower oil, flax seed oil and olive oil should be used regularly. Further short fasts on juices may be undertaken

ARTERIOSCLEROSIS

at intervals of three months or so, depending on the progress being made.

The patient should take several small meals instead of a few large ones. He should avoid all hydrogenated fats and an excess of saturated fats, such as butter, cream, ghee and animal fat. He should also avoid meat, salt and all refined and processed foods, condiments, sauces, pickles, strong tea, coffee, white sugar, white flour and all products made with them. Foods cooked in aluminium and copper utensils should not be taken, as toxic metals entering the body are known to be deposited on the walls of the aorta and the arteries. Smoking, if habitual, should be given up as smoking consricts the arteries and aggravates the condition.

Recent investigations have shown that garlic and onions have a preventive effect on the development of arteriosclerosis. Vitamin C has also proved beneficial as it helps in the conversion of cholesterol into bite acids.

The patient should undertake plenty of outdoor exercise and eliminate all mental stress and worries. Warm baths or carefully graduated cold baths are helpful. Prolonged neutral immersion baths at bed time on alternate days are also beneficial.

TREATMENT CHART FOR ARTERIOSCLEROSIS

A - DIET

I. Raw juice diet for 5 days. Take a glass of fresh fruit or vegetable juice, diluted with water, every two hours during the day and use warm water enema daily.

II. Therefore, adopt the following diet:-
1. *Upon arising:* A glass of lukewarm water with half a freshly-squeezed lime and a teaspoon of honey.
2. *Breakfast:* Fresh fruits, a glass of milk, sweetened with honey and few nuts.
3. *Lunch:* A bowl of freshly-prepared steamed vegetables, two or three whole wheat chappatis and a glass of

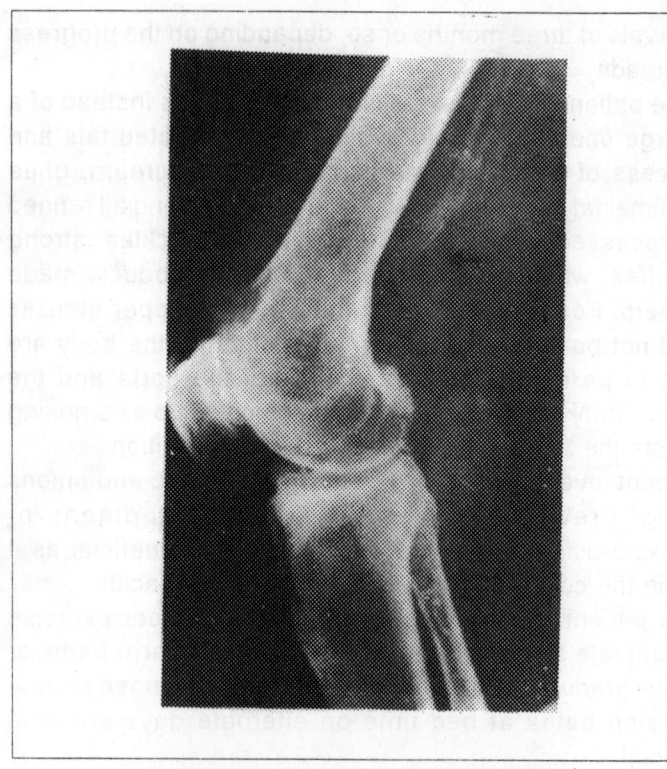

Advanced arteriosclerosis in lower extremity

    buttermilk.
4. *Mid-afternoon:* A glass of vegetable or fruit juice.
5. *Dinner:* A large bowl of fresh green vegetable salad, and sprout with olive oil and lemon juice dressing. This may be followed by a hot course, if desired.
6. *Bedtime Snack:* A glass of milk or one apple.

Note:
1. Short periods on raw juice diet may be spent at intervals of three months.
2. Take several small meals instead of few large ones.

AVOID: Hydrogenated fats and excess of saturated fats, excess of salt, tea, coffee, sugar, white flour, all products made with sugar and white flour, all refined foods, fried foods

ARTERIOSCLEROSIS

and flesh foods, condiments, pickles, foods cooked in aluminium vessels and smoking.

SPECIALLY BENEFICIAL: Grapefruit juice, pineapple juice, lemon juice and green vegetable juices, garlic and onion.

B - OTHER MEASURES

1. Brisk walks for 45 minutes morning and evening.
2. Avoid mental stress and worries.
3. Neutral immersion bath for one hour daily at bedtime.

CHAPTER 9

Arthritis

The word 'arthritis' means 'inflammation of joints.' It comes from two Greek words, *athron* meaning joints and *itis* meaning inflammation. It is a chronic disease process. In the early stages, the whole body is usually involved and one or two joints may become completely deformed, leaving the patient handicapped and somewhat weakened.

There are two categories of joints, namely, synarthrosis or those which do not move very much and do not have a cavity, and diarthrosis or those which move freely and have a joint cavity. The first type of joints are found in the head and spinal column. The second type, which is most frequently affected by arthritis, is more common and is found in the shoulders, elbows, wrists, fingers, knees, ankles and toes.

Arthritis assumes various forms, the most frequent being osteoarthritis and rheumatoid arthiritis. Inflammation is the main feature of arthritis, which is a reaction of the joint tissues to some form of damage or injury.

Osteoarthritis

Osteoarthritis is a degenerative joint disease which usually occurs in the older age-group. It is more frequent in women than in men. The disease results from structural changes in the articular cartilage in the joints, usually those which are weight-bearing such as the spine and knees.

The chief symptoms of osteoarthritis are pain and stiffness in the joints. The pain usually increases after exercise. Other symptoms include watery eyes, leg cramps, allergies, arteriosclerosis, impairment in the functioning of the gall-bladder and liver disturbances. The possible causes include malnutrition, continuous physical stress, obesity, glandular insufficiency, calcium deficiency and shortage of hydrochloric acid.

Rheumatoid Arthritis

Rheumatoid arthritis is a serious disease which affects not only the joints of the fingers, wrists, hips, knees and feet but also the muscles, tendons and other tissues of the body. The onset can be at any time from childhood to old age but usually appears between the ages 25 and 50. It is three times more common in women than in men. The disease is due to an inflammatory process of the synovium or lining of the joints accompanied by swelling and eventual deformity.

Rheumatoid arthritis is often called the "cooked food disease". It usually develops gradually over several months with persistent pain and stiffness in one or more joints. Ultimately the whole body is affected. Symptoms include anaemia, colitis, constipation, gall bladder disturbances, low blood pressure, deformed hands and feet. The condition may be caused by hormonal imbalance, physical and emotional stress, infection severe fright, shock and injury. Hereditary factors may also be responsible for the onset of this disease.

Dietary Cure

According to the modern medical profession, there is no cure for arthritis and the patient must learn to live with it. Naturopathy, however, believes in dietetic cure of the disease. Most chronic arthritis patients are heavy eaters and often take food furnishing 3,500 to 4,000 calories. As they cannot utilise all the starchy elements of this intake, toxins accumulate and an excessive acid waste results in the aggravation of prevalent joint condition. A low caloric diet consisting of about 2,000 calories minimum carbohydrate content is advisable. T should, however, include an adequate amount of calcium, phosphorus and iron.

ARTHRITIS

The diet of the arthritis patient should be alkaline in nature and include fruits and vegetables for protection and proteins and carbohydrates for energy. It may consist of a couple of fresh raw vegetables in the form of salads and at least two cooked vegetables. Cabbage, carrot, celery, cucumber, endive, lettuce, onion, radish, tomato and watercress may be used for raw salad. The cooked vegetables may include asparagus, beets, cauliflower, cabbage, carrots, celery, brinjal mushroom, onions, peas, beans, spinach, squash, tomatoes and turnips.

In severe cases, it will be advisable to put the patient on a vegetable juice therapy for about a week. Green juice extracted from any green leafy vegetable mixed with carrot, celery and red beet juice is specifically helpful for arthritis. The alkaline action of raw juices dissolves the accumulation of deposits around the joints and in other tissue. Fresh pineapple is also valuable as the enzyme in fresh pineapple juice, bromelain, reduces swelling and inflammation in osteoarthritis and rheumatoid arthritis. Repeated juice fasts are recommended at intervals of every two months.

The raw potato juice therapy is considered one of the most successful biological treatment for rheumatic and arthritic conditions. It has been used in folk medicine for centuries. The old method of preparing potato juice was to cut the potato into thin slices without peeling the skin and place overnight in a large glass filled with cold water. The water should be drunk in the morning on an empty stomach. Fresh juice can also be extracted from potatoes and drunk diluted with water 50:50, first thing in the morning.

Certain foods are harmful for arthritis patients and these must be excluded from the diet. These include aerated waters of any kind, all cheese except cottage cheese, bacon, ham, sausages and preserved meats, pastries, cakes, pies, sweet buns and white bread, all salad dressings, all soups made from meat stock, rice and white flour products. Candy, sweetmeats, sugar, ice

ARTHRITIS

cream, condiments, tea and coffee should also be avoided. Fruits permitted in arthritis are apples, lemons, oranges, bananas, pears, the various berries, apricots, pineapples, plums and melons.

Vitamin A and D play an important role in warding off infections, thereby preventing arthritis. Oranges, papayas, carrots, whole milk and butter, all green leafy vegetables, tomatoes and raw bananas are rich in Vitamin A. Vitamin D is chiefly obtained from exposing the skin to sunshine. Sunlight is an important factor in the prevention of arthritis.

Constipation should be avoided as it poisons the system and adds to the irritation and inflammation of the joints. Light exercises such as walking is beneficial. Maintaining a normal body weight is also an important factor in preventing arthritis. Obesity places excess stress on weight-bearing joints and interferes with the smooth functioning of tendons, ligaments and muscles.

The body should be kept warm at all times. Joints should not be bandaged tightly as this limits movement and interferes with the free circulation of blood. There should be plenty of ventilation in the bedroom. Rest is very important for those suffering from arthritis, who should not overdo their work, exercise or recreational activities.

TREATMENT CHART FOR ARTHRITIS

A - DIET

I. Raw juice therapy for five days. Take green juice extracted from any green leafy vegetable, mixed with carrot and red beet juice. Use warm water enema daily during this period.

II. After the raw juice therapy, the following restricted diets should be adopted for atleast three months.
1. *Upon arising:* 30 black rasins soaked overnight in water along with water in which they are soaked and water kept overnight in copper vessel.

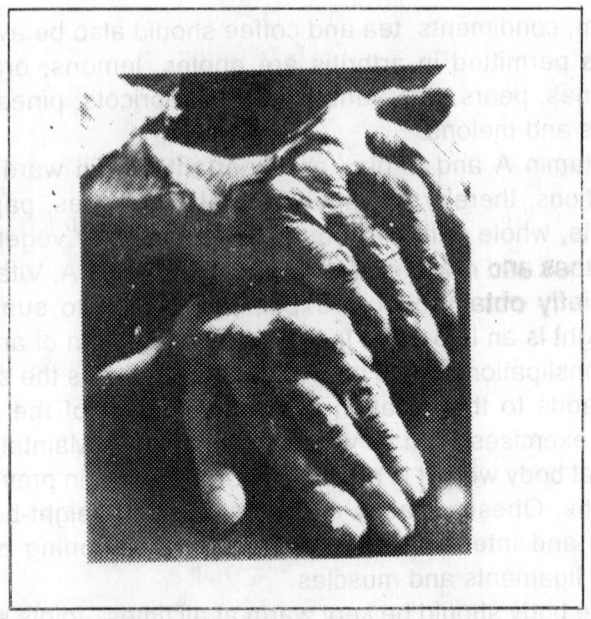

Arthritis showing swoolen wrists and fingures.

2. *Breakfast:* A glass of milk and carrot or orange juice.
3. *Lunch:* Salad of raw vegetables, steamed or boiled vegetables, one or two chappatis, butter and buttermilk.
4. *Evening:* Coconut water or sugarcane juice
5. *Dinner:* Fresh fruits and milk.

III. Thereafter, a well-balanced diet consisting of seeds, nuts and grains, vegetables and fruits may be taken. This diet should be supplemented with special foods like milk, milk products, vegetable oils and honey.

RESTRICT: Salt intake.

NOTE: No meal should be taken in the evening once a week

B - OTHER MEASURES

1. Neutral immersion bath for one hour daily before retiring

at night.
2. Steam bath once a week.
3. Avoid cold baths.
4. Yogic asanas like bhujangasana, shalabhasana and shavasana.
5. Ultrasonic diathermy and exposure of the affected parts to infrared rays.

CHAPTER 10

Asthma

Asthma is an allergic condition resulting from the reaction of the system to one or more allergens. It is the most troublesome of the respiratory diseases. The asthma patient gets frequent attacks of breathlessness, in between which he is completely normal.

Symptoms

Asthma is an ancient Greek word meaning "panting or short-drawn breath". Patients suffering from asthma appear to be gasping for breath. Actually, they have more difficulty in breathing out than breathing in and it is caused by a spasm of the smaller air passage in the lung. The effect is to blow the lungs up because the patient cannot drive the air properly out of the lungs before he has to take another breath. All asthmatics have more difficulty at night, especially during sleep.

The onset of asthma may be abrupt or gradual. Sudden onsets are often preceded by a spell of coughing. When the onset is gradual, the attack is usually brought on by respiratory infection. A severe attack causes an increase in heart-beat and respiratory rates and the patient feels restless and fatigued. There may be coughing, tightness in the chest, profuse sweating and vomiting. There may also be abdominal pain, especially if coughing is severe. The wheezing sound identified with asthma is produced by the air being pushed through the narrowed bronchi.

Causes

Asthma is caused by a variety of factors. For many it is due to an allergy which may be caused by weather conditions, food, drugs, perfumes and other irritants which vary with different individuals. Allergies to dust are the most common. Some persons are sensitive to the various forms of dust like cotton dust, wheat dust and paper dust, certain types of pollens, animal hair, fungi and insects. Foods which generally cause allergic reactions are wheat, eggs, milk, chocolates, beans, potato and beef.

For others, asthma may result from psychic factors. According to some studies about 25 per cent of the young asthmatics have in common a "deeper-seated emotional insecurity and an intense need for parental love and specific protection". Heredity also plays an important role, and it has been estimated that when both parents have asthma or hay fever, in more than 75 per cent cases, the offspring also have allergic reactions.

Asthma has also been attributed to malnutrition. According to the late Dr. Royal Lee, a nutrition expert, malnutrition in general, with adrenal insufficiency, hypoglycemia and intolerance for carbohydrates are the factors leading to asthma in adults. Dr. Carl J. Reich of Canada also considers asthma as a maladaptive state of the body due to deficiency of certain nutritional elements.

Dietary Treatment

The modern medical system has not been able to find a cure for asthma. Drugs and vaccines have only a limited value in alleviating symptoms. Most of these are habit forming and the dose has to be increased from time to time to give the same amount of relief. They also tend to make asthma chronic. Allergy — which is the immediate cause of asthma — itself is an indication of lowered resistance and internal disharmony caused by dietetic errors and a faulty style of living. The real cure, therefore, lies in the stimulation of the functioning of slack excretory organs and appropriate diet patterns to eliminate toxic and waste matter and reconstruct the body.

To begin with, the patient should fast for three to five days on lemon juice with honey. During this period the bowels should be cleansed daily with a warm water enema. After the fast, the patient may resort to an all-fruit diet for a further five to seven days to nourish the system and eliminate the toxins. Thereafter, other foods may be gradually added to the diet. Further short fasts and periods on all-fruit diet may be required in certain cases at intervals of two or three months depending upon the progress being made.

A vegetarian diet is best for asthma. Ideally, his diet should contain a limited quantity of carbohydrates, fats and proteins which are acid-forming foods, and a liberal quantity of alkaline foods consisting of fresh fruits, green vegetables and sprouted seeds and grains. The breakfast may consist of fresh fruits with prunes or other dried fruit. Steamed vegetables with whole wheat bread or chappatis may be taken for lunch and dinner may consist of a large salad of raw vegetables such as cucumber, lettuce, tomato, carrot and beets with cottage cheese, prunes or other dried fruit. The last meal should preferably be taken before sunset or at least two hours before going to bed.

The patient should avoid foods which tend to produce phlegm, such as rice, sugar, lentils and curds as also fried and other difficult-to-digest foods. he should also avoid strong tea, coffee, alcoholic beverages, condiments, pickles, sauces and all refined and processed foods. Initially, milk and milk products should be totally avoided. After noticeable recovery, a small quantity of milk may be added in the diet.

Asthmatics should always eat less than their capacity. They should eat slowly, chewing their food properly. They should drink eight to ten glasses of water every day, but should avoid taking water with meals.

Asthma, particularly when the attack is severe, tends to destroy the appetite. In such cases, do not force the patient to eat. He should be kept fasting till the attack is over. He should, however, take a cup of warm water every two hours. An enema taken at that time would be beneficial.

Honey is highly beneficial in the treatment of asthma. It is said that if a jug of honey is held under the nose of an asthma patient and he inhales the air that comes into contact with the honey, he starts breathing easier and deeper. The effect lasts for about an hour or so. This is because honey contains a mixture of 'higher' alcohols and ethereal oils and the vapours given off by them are soothing and beneficial to the asthma patients. Honey usually brings relief whether the air flowing over it is inhaled or whether it is eaten or taken either in milk or water. Some authorities recommend one year old honey for respiratory disease.

A recently completed study by Dr. Robert D. Reynolds Ph.D., a researcher with the U.S. Department of Agriculture, has shown that a vitamin B_6 deficiency congtributed to an asthmatic condition and the intake of even 50 milligrams of this vitamin twice a day can relieve the wheezing and other symptoms. Says Dr. Reynols, "The daily B_6 supplements stop the wheezing in about a week and the asthmatic attacks themselves occur less frequently and are of shorter duration".

The patient should also follow the other laws of nature. Air, sun and water are great healing agents, Regular fasting once a week, an occasional enema, breathing exercises, fresh air, dry climate, light exercises and a correct posture go a long way in treating the disease.

TREATMENT CHART FOR ASTHMA

A - DIET

I. All-fruit diet for three days. During this period, take three meals a day of fresh juicy fruits at five-hourly intervals.

II. Thereafter, adopt the followng diet:-

1. *Upon arising:* A glass of lukewarm water mixed with half a freshly-squeezed lime and a teaspoon of honey.
2. *Breakfast:* Fresh fruits, a cup of fresh milk sweetened

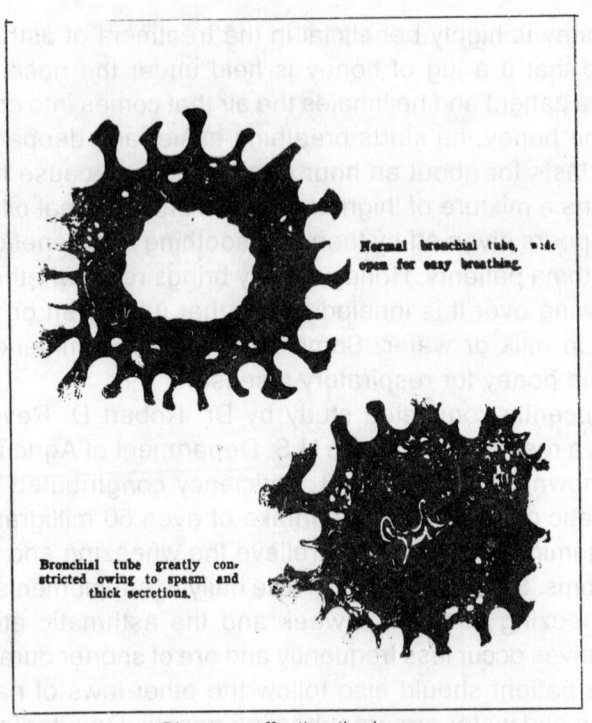

Normal bronchial tube, wide open for easy breathing.

Bronchial tube greatly constricted owing to spasm and thick secretions.

Diseases affecting the Lungs

with honey and nuts.
3. *Lunch:* A bowl of steamed vegetables, whole wheat chappatis with butter.
4. *Mid-afternoon:* A glass of fresh fruit or vegetable juice.
5. *Dinner:* A bowl of fresh green vegetable salad, with lime juice dressing, sprouted seeds and home-made cottage cheese.
6. *Before retiring:* Few dates and milk.

AVOID: Flesh foods, sugar, white flour, products made from sugar and white flour, tea, coffee, condiments, pickles, refined and processed foods and fried foods.

NOTES: If any of the common food allergens like orange, milk, eggs, wheat, chocolates, cabbage, potatoes and tomatoes aggravate the trouble, the same should not be consumed.

B - OTHER MEASURES

1. Wet chest packs for one hour daily.
2. Brisk walks, yogic asanas and deep breathing exercises.
3. A hot epsom-salts bath twice a week in the night.

CHAPTER 11

Backache

Backache is one of the most common ailments. It has assumed staggering dimensions these days. It generally results from sedentary living habits and hazardous work patterns. Emotional stress, which brings about spasm of the muscles, may also cause backache.

The back, known as the life bone of the body, is a complex structure of muscles, bone and elastic tissue. The spine is made of 24 blocks of bone, piled one on top of the other. Sandwiched between these bony blocks are cushions of cartilage and elastic tissues, called intervertebral discs. These discs act as shock absorbers for the back. Mobility would be impossible without these discs.

Symptoms

In most cases of backache, the pain is usually felt either in the middle of the back or lower down. It may spread to both sides of the waist and the hips. The patient is unable to move and is bedridden, in cases of acute pain.

Most backache patients suffer from cervical or lumbar spondylosis. It is a degenerative disorder in which the vertebral bone or the intervertebral disc becomes soft and loses shape. As a result of this, the spine loses its flexibility.

Causes

The main causes of backache are muscular tension, joint strain, poor posture, incorrect nutrition and lack of exercise. The condition may result from acute or chronic illnesses like kidney or prostate problems, female disorders, influenza and arthritis. Other causes include stress and strain, sitting for a long time, improper lifting of weights, high heels and emotional problems.

Another major cause of back problems is lack of exercise. Modern conveniences have made office work easier. This can lead to obesity which puts a great strain on the back. When muscles are not exercised and remain weak, the chances of injury to them is increased manifold.

Dietary Treatment

The diet of persons suffering from backache should consist of plenty of raw vegetables and fresh fruits. Raw vegetables for salad may include carrot, cabbage, cucumber, radish, onion and lettuce. The patient should also take at least two steamed or lightly-cooked vegetables such as cauliflower, cabbage, carrot, spinach and liberal quantities of fresh fruits.

The patients should have four meals daily. They may take fresh fruits and milk for breakfast, steamed vegetables and whole wheat chappatis for lunch, a fresh fruit or juice in the evening and a bowl of raw salad and sprouts for dinner.

The patient should avoid fatty, spicy and fried foods, curd sweetmeats, sugar condiments as well as tea and coffee. Those who smoke and take tobacco in any form should give up completely.

Proteins and vitamin C are necessary for the development of a healthy bone matrix. Vitamin D, calcium phosphorus and the essential trace minerals are essential for healthy bones. Foods that have been processed for storage to avoid spoiling have few nutrients and should be eliminated from the diet. Vitamin C has proved helpful in relieving low-back pain and averting spinal disc operations.

Certain food remedies have been found beneficial in the treatment of backache. The most important of these is the use of garlic (lahasoon). Two or three capsules of this vegetable should be taken daily in the morning. It will give good results. An oil prepared from garlic and rubbed on the back will give great relief. This oil is prepared by frying 10 cloves of garlic in 60 grams of oil in a frying pan. They should be fried slowly till they are brown. After it is cooled, it should be applied vigorously on the back and allowed to remain there for three hours. The patient may thereafter have a warm water bath. This treatment should be continued for atleast 15 days.

Lemon (Bara Niboo) is another useful remedy for backache. The juice of this fruit should be mixed with common salt and taken by the patient. It will give relief.

The use of chebulic myroblan (harad or haritaki) is also beneficial in the treatment of backache. A piece of this herb should be taken after meals. This will give quick relief.

Other Measures

Certain safety measures, especially for people in sedentary occupations, are necessary to relieve and prevent backache. The most important of these is exercise which improves the supply of nutrients to spinal discs, thereby delaying the process of deterioration that comes with age and eventually affects everybody. Safe exercises include walking, swimming and bicycling. Controlling one's weight is another important step towards relieving backache as excess weight greatly increases the stress on soft back tissues.

Persons with back problems should sleep on a firm matress on their sides with knees bent at right angles to the torso. They should take care never to bend from the waist down to lift any object, but instead should squat close to the object, bending the knees but keeping the back straight and then stand up slowly.

Neck tension arising from long hours at the desk or behind the wheel of the car can be relieved by certain neck exercises. These include rotating the head clockwise and anti-clockwise allowing the head to drop forward and backward as far as possible and turning the head to the right and left as far as possible several times. These exercises help to loosen up contracted neck muscles which may restrict blood supply to the head.

Hot fomentations, alternate sponging or application of radiant heat to the back will also give immediate relief. Yogic asanas which are beneficial in the treatment of backache are bhujangasana, shalabhasana, halasana, uttanpadasana and shavasana.

TREATMENT CHART FOR BACKACHE

A - DIET

I. An all-fruit diet for 3 to 5 days. In this regimen, take three meals a day of fresh juicy fruits such as apple, pear, peach, papaya, grapes, orange and pineapple.

II. Thereafter, gradually adopt a well-balanced diet on the following lines:-

1. *Upon arising:* A glass of lukewarm water with half a freshly-squeezed lime and a teaspoon of honey.

2. *Breakfast:* Fresh fruit such as apple, grapes, pear, peaches, pineapple, papaya and a glass of milk, sweetened with honey.

3. *Lunch:* A bowl of freshly-prepared steamed vegetables such as carrot, cabbage, cauliflower, squash and beans and two or three whole wheat chapatis.

4. *Mid-afternoon:* A glass of vegetable or fruit juice.

5. *Dinner:* A large bowl of fresh green vegetable salad. Use all available vegetables such as lettuce, carrot, cabbage, cucumber, tomatoes, radish, red beets and onion and sprouts such as alfalfa and mung beans with lemon juice dressing.

AVOID: Tea, coffee, sugar, white flour, all products made with sugar and white flour, all refined foods, fried foods, fatty substances, curd, flesh foods, condiments and pickles.

RUPTURED SPINAL DISC (BLACK) PRESSING ON SPINAL CORD AND NERVE ROOTS CAUSING SEVERE PAIN

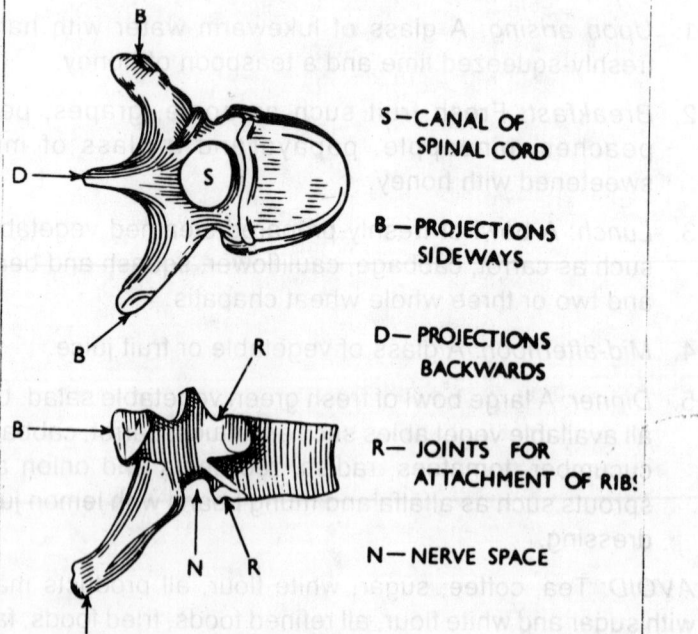

S — CANAL OF SPINAL CORD

B — PROJECTIONS SIDEWAYS

D — PROJECTIONS BACKWARDS

R — JOINTS FOR ATTACHMENT OF RIBS

N — NERVE SPACE

B - OTHER MEASURES

1. Safe exercises like walking, swimming and bicycling.
2. Weight control.
3. Sleep on firm mattress.
4. Never bend from the waist to lift any object, but squat close to the object.
5. Neck and shoulder exercises.
6. Apply hot fomentation and radiant heat to the back.
7. Yogic asanas like bhujangasana, shalabhasana, halasana, uttanpadasana and shavasana.

CHAPTER 12

Bronchitis

Bronchitis refers to an inflammation of the bronchi or air passage of the lung. It is a breathing disorder affecting the expiratory function. In most cases, some infection also occurs in the nose and throat.

Bronchitis may be acute or chronic. In chronic cases, the disease is of long duration. It is more serious than the acute type as permanent changes may have occurred in the lungs, thereby interfering with their normal movements. Chronic bronchitis is a condition of ageing and presumably degeneration of the respiratory tract that has been subjected to years of irritation by atmospheric pollutants, inhaled organism and, in smokers, to many years of self-inhaled irritants. It has been more frequent in males than in females and morality rate is also higher in males.

Symptoms

In most cases of bronchitis, the larynx, trachea and bronchial tubes are acutely inflamed. The tissues are swollen due to irritation. Large quantities of mucus are secreted and poured into the windpipe to protect the inflamed mucous membranes. There is usually some fever, and diffculty in breathing as well as a deep, chest cough. Other symptoms are hoarseness, pain in the chest, lack of energy and depression. The breathing trouble continues till the inflammation subsides and mucus is removed. In chronic cases, besides excessive production of bronchial mucus, there is infection and lung destruction.

Causes

Acute bronchitis may very often occur as a sequel to a common cold or as a result of an attack of influenza. The severity of the disease depends on the extent of the spread of infection which is aggravated by exposure to cold, damp and smoke.

The disease becomes chronic due to recurring attacks of acute bronchitis and wrong food habits. The habitual use of refined foods such as white sugar, refined cereals and white flour products result in the accumulation of toxic matter in the system and this toxic waste collects in the bronchial tube. Other causes of bronchitis are excessive smoking, living or working in a stuffy atmosphere and the use of drugs to suppress earlier diseases. Atmospheric pollution and climate are important causal factors for the onset of the disease. The greater the pollution, the higher will be the rate of chronic bronchitis.

Dietary Treatment

In acute cases of bronchitis, the patient should fast on orange juice and water till the symptoms subside. The procedure is to take the juice of an orange in a glass of warm water every two hours from 8 a.m. to 8 p.m. During this period, the bowels should be cleansed daily with a warm water enema. After the juice fast, the patient should adopt an all-fruit diet for two or three days.

In case of chronic bronchitis, the patient may adopt an all-fruit diet for five to seven days in the beginning of the treatment. In this regimen, he should have three meals a day of fresh juicy fruits such as apples, pears, grapes, grapefruits, oranges, pineapples, peaches and melons. Bananas, and dried or stewed or tinned fruits should not be taken. For drinks, unsweetened lemon water or cold or hot plain water may be taken.

After the all-fruit diet, the patient should follow a well-balanced diet based on the three basic food groups, namely, seeds, nuts and grains, vegetables and fruits, as outlined in Chapter 1 on Diet in Health and Disease. The patient should avoid meats, sugar, tea, coffee, condiments, pickles, refined and processed foods, soft drinks, candies, ice cream and products made from sugar and white flour.

Certain vegetables juices have been found valuable in the treatment of bronchitis. The combined juice of carrot and spinach is especially beneficial. Formula proportions considered helpful in this combination are carrot 10 ounces and spinach 6 ounces to prepare 16 ounces or 1 pint of juice.

A hot Epsom salt bath every night or every other night will be highly beneficial during the acute stages of the attack. The patient should remain immersed in the bath for about 20 minutes. In case of chronic bronchitis, this bath may be taken twice a week. Hot towels wrung out and applied over the upper chest are also helpful. Fresh air and outdoor exercises are also essential to the treatment of bronchitis and the patient should take a long walk every day.

TREATMENT CHART FOR BRONCHITIS

A - DIET

I. An exclusively diet of fresh juicy fruits, with three meals a day at five-hourly intervals.

II. Thereafter, adopt the following diet:-

1. *Upon arising:* A glass of lukewarm water mixed with half a freshly-squeezed lime and a teaspoon of honey.
2. *Breakfast:* Fresh fruits, a cup of fresh milk sweetened with honey and nuts.
3. *Lunch:* A bowl of steamed vegetables, whole wheat chappatis with butter.
4. *Mid-afternoon:* A glass of fresh fruit or gegetable juice.
5. *Dinner:* A bowl of fresh green vegetable salad, with lime juice dressing, sprouted seeds and home-made cottage cheese.
6. *Before retiring:* Few dates and milk.

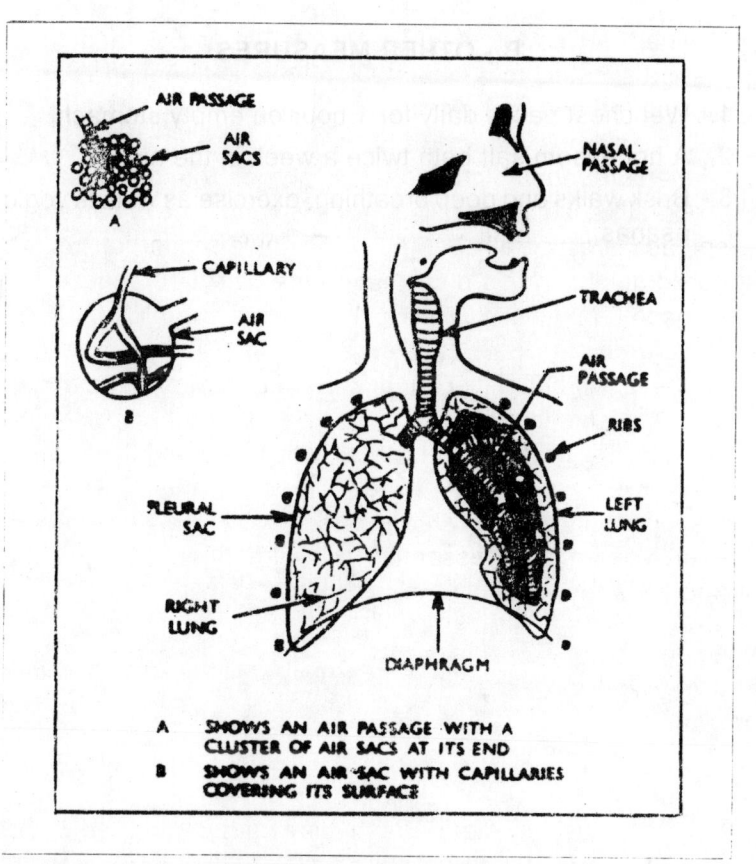

THE RESPIRATORY ORGANS
A   Shows an air passage with a cluster of air sacs at its end
B   Shows an air sac with capillaries covering its surface

Avoid: Flesh foods, sugar, white flour, products made from white sugar and white flour, tea, coffee, condiments, pickles, refined and processed foods and soft drinks.

Important: If any of the following common food allergens agravate the trouble, the same should be avoided, oranges, milk, eggs, wheat, chocolates, cabbage, potatoes, and tomatoes. Diet should include lots of garlic, green vegetables, manganese rich foods such as pear, beans and nuts.

B - OTHER MEASURES

1. Wet chest packs daily for 1 hour on empty stomach.
2. A hot epsom-salt bath twice a week in the night.
3. Brisk walks and deep breathing, exercise as well as yogic asanas.

CHAPTER 13

Cancer

Cancer, the most dreaded disease, refers to all malignant tumours caused by the abnormal growth of a body cell or a group of cells. It is today the second largest killer in the world, next only to heart ailments. The term covers more than 200 diseases.

There are billions of cells in the body which, under normal circumstances, develop in a well organised pattern for the growth of the body and the repair of damaged tissue. When cancer sets in, a group of cells start multiplying suddenly in a haphazard manner and form a lump or tumour. Cancer can spread very rapidly and eventually prove fatal, if not treated properly and in time.

The majority of cancers occur in the age group 50-60. Sex does not determine the incidence of the disease though it does affect the site of growth. In men, cancer is usually found in the intestines, the prostate and the lungs. In women, it occurs mostly in the breast tissues, uterus, gall-bladder and thyroid.

Symptoms

The symptoms of cancer vary according to the site of the growth. The American Cancer Society has prescribed seven signs or danger signals in general which may indicate the presence of cancer. These are: a sore that does not heal; change in bowel or bladder habits; unusual bleeding or discharge; thickening or lump in breast or elsewhere; indigestion or difficulty in swallowing; obvious change in wart or mole and persistent and nagging cough or hoarseness. Other symptoms may include unexplained loss of weight, particularly in older people, a change in skin colour and changes in the menstrual periods, especially bleeding between periods.

Cancers have a latency period varying from 5 to 40 years between the intial exposure to a carcinogen and the time the symptoms appear. In a large number of cases, either trivial symptoms are noted or there are none at all. One has, therefore, to be vigilant to recognise the first sign of the disease. The best way of diagnosing cancer is through a process called 'biopsy', in which a piece of suspect tissue is examined and tested under a microscope.

Causes

The prime cause of cancer is not known. Certain cancer-causing substances, known as carcinogens, however, increase the chances of getting the disease. About 80 per cent of cancers are caused by environmental factors. Forty per cent of male cancers in India are linked with tobacco, a known cancer-causing agent. The consumption of *pan,* betelnut, tobacco and slaked lime has been linked with cancer of the tongue, lips, mouth and throat. Cigarette and *bidi* smoking and *hukka* puffing are linked with lung and throat cancers. Heavy consumption of alcoholic drinks can cause oesophagal, stomach and liver cancers. Occupational exposure to industrial pollutants such as asbestos, nickel, tar, soot and high doses of X-Rays can lead to skin and lung cancers and leukaemia.

Other factors contributing to cancer are viral infections, trauma, hormone imbalance and malnutrition. Many well-known biologists and naturopaths believe that a faulty diet is the root cause of cancer. Investigations indicate that the cancer incidence is in direct proportion to the amount of animal protein, particularly meat, in the diet. Dr. Willard J. Visek, a renowned research scientist explained recently a link between excessive meat-eating and cancer. According to him, the villain is ammonia, the carcinogenic by-product of meat digestion.

Dietetic Treatment

The effective treatment of cancer consists of a complete change in diet, besides total elimination of all environmental sources of carcinogens, such as smoking and carcinogenic chemicals in air, water and food. As a first step, the patient should cleanse the system thoroughly, relieve himself of constipation and make all the organs of elimination — the skin, lungs, liver, kidneys and bowels — active. Enemas should be used to cleanse the colon. For the first four or five days, the patient should take only juicy fruits like oranges, grapefruits, lemons, apples, peaches, pears, pineapples and tomatoes. Vegetable juices are also useful, especially carrot juice.

After a few days of the exclusive fruit diet, the patient may be given a nourishing alkaline based diet. It should consist of 100 per cent natural foods, with emphasis on raw fruits and vegetables particularly carrots, green leafy vegetables, cabbage, onion, garlic, cucumber, asparagus, beets and tomatoes. A minimum requirement of high quality protein, mostly from vegetable sources such as almonds, millet, sesame seeds, sprouted seeds and grains, may be added to this diet.

Dr. Ann Wigmore of Boston, U.S.A., the well-known naturopath and pioneer in the field of living food nutrition, has been testing the effect of a drink made of fresh wheatgrass in the treatment of leukaemia. She claims to have cured several cases of this disease by this method. Dr. Wigmore points out that by furnishing the body with live minerals, vitamins, trace elements and chlorophyll through wheatgrass juice, it may be able to repair itself.

Johanna Brandt, the author of the book 'The Grape Cure', has advocated an exclusive grape diet for the treatment of cancer. She discovered this mode of cure in 1925, while experimenting on herself by fasting and dieting alternately in the course of her nine-years battle with cancer. She claims to have cured herself by this mode of treatment. She recommends fast for two or three days so as to prepare the system for the change of diet. The patient should drink plenty of pure cold water and take lukewarm water enema daily with the strained juice of lemon during this period. After the short fast, the patient should have a grape meal every two hours from 8 a.m. to 8 p.m. This should be followed for a week or two, even a month or two, in chronic cases of long standing. The patient should begin the grape cure with a small quantity of one, two or three ounces per meal, gradually increasing this to double the quantity. In course of time, about half a pound may safely be taken at a meal. The patient may lose strength under the grape diet and under the complete fast, but this is due to the presence of poisons in the system. The patient regains his strength and even puts on weight in some cases with the same diet after the poisons are expelled. Normally, the grape diet should be continued until weight loss stops.

Recent research has shown that certain vitamins can be successfully employed in the fight against cancer and that they can increase the life expectancy of some terminal cancer patients. According to recent Swedish studies, vitamin C in large doses can be an effective prophylactic agent against cancer. Noted Japanese scientist, Dr. Fukunir Mirishige and his colleagues who have been examining the healing potential of vitamin C for the last 30 years, have recently found that a mixture of vitamin C and copper compound has lethal effects on cancer.

According to several studies, vitamin A exerts an inhibiting effect on carcinogenesis. It is one of the most important aids to the body's defence system to fight and prevent cancer. Dr. Leonida Santamaria and his colleagues at the University of Pavia in Italy have uncovered preliminary evidence suggesting that beta-carotene, a precursor of vitamin A may actually inhibit skin cancer by helping the body thwart the cancer-causing process known as oxidation.

Prevention

It is more important to prevent the disease than to

treat it, as measures to treat the disease bring only temporary results in view of the poor survival rate after the use of such treatment. The best way to prevent cancer is to build up the body's defences through excellent nutrition. The tissues, cells and organs should be kept in such a healthy state that cancer cannot take hold. This can be achieved by completely avoiding all refined, synthetic and processed foods as also white flour, white sugar and foods with chemicals additives. The foods which build up the body are natural, whole foods, raw vegetables and fruits, protein from vegetable sources, raw milk, whole grains and vitamins and minerals in their natural form.

Recent studies from all over the world suggest that the liberal use of green and yellow vegetables and fruits can prevent cancer. The 20-year old, ongoing Japanese study found that people who are green and yellow vegetables every day had a decreased risk of developing lung, stomach and other cancers. A Harvard University study of more than 1,200 elderly Massachusetts residents found that those who reported the highest consumption of carrots, squash, tomatoes, salads or leafy green vegetables, dried fruits, fresh strawberries or melon had a decreased risk of cancer. The other preventive measures are plenty of rest, complete freedom from worries and mental stress and plenty of fresh air.

TREATMENT CHART FOR CANCER

A - DIET

I. Raw juice diet for three to five days. Take a glass of fresh fruit or vegetable juice, diluted with water on 50:50 basis, every two hours. Use warm-water enema daily during this period.

II. An all-fruit diet for further three to five days, taking three meals a day of fresh juicy fruits at five-hourly intervals.

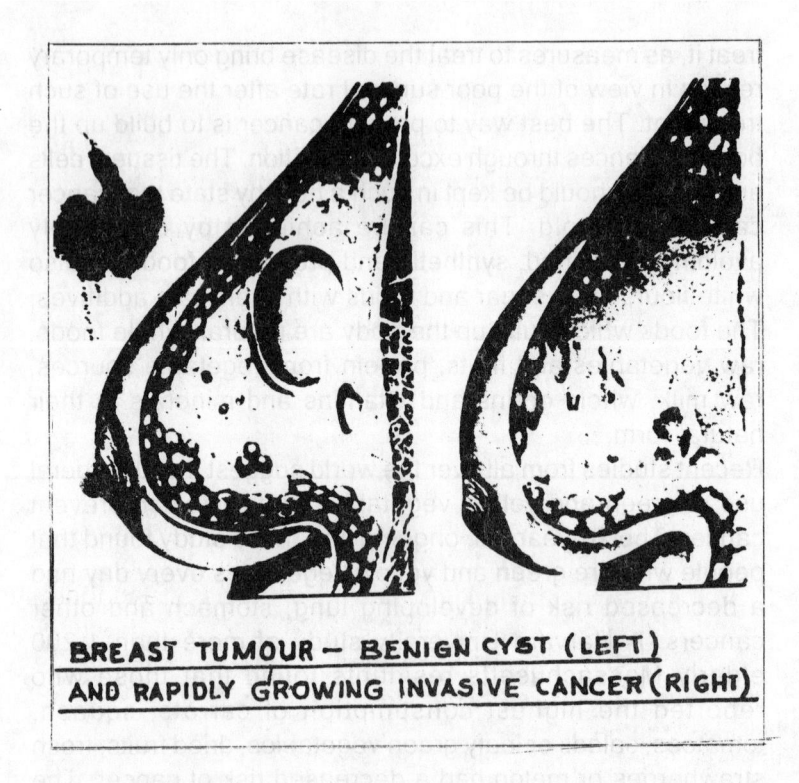

BREAST TUMOUR — BENIGN CYST (LEFT) AND RAPIDLY GROWING INVASIVE CANCER (RIGHT)

III. Thereafter, adopt a well-balanced diet on the following lines:-
1. *Upon arising:* A glass of lukewarm water with half a freshly squeezed lime and a teaspoon of honey.
2. *Breakfast:* Fresh fruit and a glass of milk, preferably goat's milk, sweetened with honey and some seeds or nuts.
3. *Lunch:* A bowl of freshly-prepared steamed vegetables, two or three whole wheat chappatis and a glass of butter milk.
4. *Mid-afternoon:* A glass of fresh fruit or vegetable juice.
5. *Dinner:* A good-sized raw vegetable salad and sprouts, with lime juice dressing, followed by a hot course if desired.
6. *Bedtime snack:* A glass of milk or one apple.

DIET CURE FOR COMMON AILMENTS

NOTE: Repeat the short juice fast followed by an all-fruit diet at monthly intervals.

AVOID: Tea, coffee, sugar, white flours and products made from them, refined foods, fried foods, flesh foods, condiments, pickles, alcohol and smoking. Take salt in a vey minute quantity.

Especially Beneficial: Garlic, cabbage, Red beet, red beet juice, lemon, ginger, liquorice, turmeric, citrus fruits, soyabean, cucumber and tomato.

B - OTHER MEASURES

1. Fresh air, breathing and other light exercises.
2. Proper sleep and adequate rest.
3. Avoid all carcinogenic chemicals in air, water and food.

CHAPTER 14

Cataract

Cataract is one of the most common eye diseases. The word literally means a waterfall. It refers to an opacity in the lens of the eye which obscures the vision. Blindness ensues when no light rays can enter the eye through the opacity of the lens.

Symptoms

The first sign of cataract is blurred vision. The patient finds it difficult to see things in focus. As the cataract progresses, the patient may get double vision or spots or both. There is gradual increase in blindness. At first, vision in twilight may be better than in full daylight since light is admitted round the more widely-dilated pupil in the dark. In the advance stage, objects and persons may appear merely blobs of light. In the final stage, there is a grayish-white discoloration in the pupil.

Causes

Cataract is often found in association with other defects of the eye. There are four factors which contribute to the loss of transparency of the lens. These are, stagnation of the fluid current in the lens resulting from bad blood condition; deterioration in the nutrition of the lens which diminishes the vitality and resistance of the delicate lens fibres; acid and salt deposits between the lens fibres which have an irritating effect on the lens tissues and exert an increasing pressure on its delicate fibres, gradually destroying them; and disintegration of the lens fibres, clouding the whole lens in the absence of appropriate measures.

As in case of most diseases, poisons in the blood stream due to dietetic errors and faulty style of living is the real cause of cataract. The toxic matter in the blood stream spreads throughout the body to find shelter in any available weak spot. It strikes the lens if that part has become weak through strain, excessive use of the eyes or local irritation. The condition becomes worse with the passage of time and then a cataract starts developing. Other causes of cataract are stress and strain, excessive intake of alcoholic drinks, sugar, salt, smoking, certain physical ailments such as gastro-intestinal or gall-bladder disturbances, diabetes, vitamins deficiencies, especially of vitamin C, fatty acid intolerances, ageing, radiation and side-effects of drugs prescribed for other diseases.

Some specialists believe that the most important cause of many cataracts is poor nutrition. This may be true even in case of the type of cataract commonly called senile or ageing cataract. The cause may be a lifetime of malnutrition. Dr. Morgan Raiford, opthalmologist who has studied cataracts for many years, considers faulty nutrition to be a basic factor in cataract. He has found by experience that prevention of cataract is initiated by improving nutrition.

Dietary Treatment

Cataract is a most stubborn condition to deal with. If it has become deep-seated, nothing short of a surgical operation will help in overcoming the trouble. If, however, the cataract is in the early stages, there are good chances of getting over the ailment by natural means. Even advanced cases can be prevented from becoming worse.

A thorough course of cleansing the system of the toxic matter is essential. To start with, it will be beneficial to undergo a fast for three to four days on orange juice and water. A warm water enema may be taken during this period. After this initial fast, a diet of a very restricted nature should be followed for two weeks. In this regimen, breakfast may consist of oranges or grapes or any other juicy fruit in season. Raw vegetable salads in season, with olive oil and lemon juice dressing, and soaked raisins, figs or dates should be taken during lunch. Evening meals may consist of vegetables such as spinach, cabbage, cauliflower, carrot or turnips steamed in their own juices, and a few nuts or some fruits, such as apple, pears and grapes. Potatoes should not be taken. No bread or any other article of food should be added to this list.

After two weeks on this diet, the cataract patient may start on a fuller diet on the following lines.
Breakfast: Any fresh fruits in season, except bananas.
Lunch: Large mixed raw vegetable salad with wholemeal bread or chappatis and butter.
Dinner: Two or three steamed vegetables, other than potatoes, with nuts and fresh fruits.

The short fast followed by a restricted diet should be repeated after three months of the commencement of the treatment and again three months later, if necessary. The bowels should be cleansed daily with a warm water enema during the fast, and afterwards as necessary.

The patient should avoid white bread, sugar, cream, refined cereals, rice, boiled potatoes, puddings, and pies, strong tea or coffee, alcoholic beverages, condiments, pickles, sauces, or other so-called aids to digestion.

There is increasing evidence to show that in several cases cataracts have actually been reversed by proper nutritional treatment. However, the time needed for such treatment may extend from six months to three years. Adelle Davis, one of America's best-known nutritionists, has pointed out that animals develop cataracts if deprived of pantothenic acid and amino acid, tryptophane and vitamin B6 needed for tryptophane assimilation. She states that the diet of the cataract patient should be high in B2, B6, as well as whole B complex, pantothenic acid, Vitamin C, D, E and other nutrients.

Along with the dietary treatment, the patient should adopt various methods of relaxing and strengthening the eyes. These include moving the eyes gently up and down, from side to side and in a circle, clock-wise and anti-clockwise; rotating the neck in circles and semi-circles and briskly moving the shoulders clock-wise and anti-clockwise.

Palming is highly beneficial in removing strain and relaxing the eyes and its surrounding tissues. The procedures is as follows: sit in a comfortable position and relax with your eyes closed. Cover the eyes with the palms, right palm over the right eye and the left over the left eye. Do not press on the eyes themselves. Then allow your elbow to drop to your knees, which should be fairly close together. Try to imagine blackness, which grows blacker and blacker.

Fresh air and gentle outdoor exercise, such as walking, are other essentials to the treatment.

TREATMENT CHART FOR CATARACT

A - DIET

I. A fast on orange juice for three days. During this period, orange juice diluted with water should be taken every two hours from 8 a.m. to 8 p.m. and bowels cleansed with warm water enema.

II. After the juice fast, the following restricted diet should

Early cataract showing lens striae.

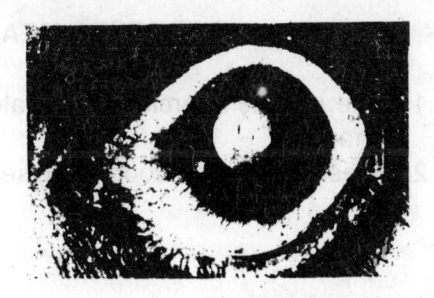

Mature cataract.

Early cataract showing lens striae (left). Mature cotaract (Right)

be taken for 10 to 15 days:-
1. *Breakfast:* Juicy fruits.
2. *Lunch:* Raw vegetable salad with olive oil and lime juice dressing and cooked raisins, dates or figs.
3. *Dinner:* Steamed vegetables and a few nuts or fruits.

II. Thereafter, adopt a well-balanced diet on the following lines:-
1. *Upon arising:* 25 black raisins soaked overnight in water along with water kept overnight in a copper vessel.
2. *Breakfast:* Fresh fruits, a glass of milk, sweetened with honey and few almonds.
3. *Lunch:* Steamed vegetables, two or three whole wheat chappatis and a glass of buttermilk.
4. *Dinner:* A large bowl of fresh salad of green vegetables, with sprouted mung beans and cottage cheese or buttermilk.
5. *Before retiring:* A glass of fresh milk with few dates.

AVOID: White bread, sugar, cream, refined cereals, rice, boiled potatoes, pudding and pies, strong tea or coffee, alcoholic beverages, condiments, pickles and sauces.

NOTE: The short juice fast followed by restricted diet should be repeated every two months.

B - OTHER MEASURES

1. Eye muscle exercises and palming as explained in the chapter.
2. Fresh air and outdoor exercise, especially Brisk walks.

CHAPTER 15

Cholera

Cholera is an acute inflammatory disorder of the intestines, caused by bacteria. It is a serious infection, involving the lower part of the small bowel. It is a waterborne disease and is common during mansoon. The disease is predominant in endemic areas like India and other countries of South east and Mid east Asia.

Cholera strikes suddenly. The intestinal canal is filled with bacilli. These bacilli die rapidly and leave the person quickly, alive or dead. This disease comes as a epidemic and creates havoc, but subsides quickly in the locality. Those who are susceptible to it are carried away and those who are left alive become immuned to it.

Symptoms

The first symptom of cholera is mild diarrhoea. This is followed by sudden violent purging and lack of proper control of the bowel. The patient feels pain and muscle cramps in the lower abdomen. He suffers from nausea and vommitting. The stools are loose, watery, and greyish-brown in colour.

The sudden loss of fluid causes severe dehydration, and soon the patient begins to feel intense thirst. His tongue becomes white and dry. His skin is wrinkled, the eyeballs sunken and cheeks hollow. Breathing becoms somewhat laboured and difficult. The blood pressure may fall due to the lack of fluids in the body. The temperature may come down to subnormal, although the pulse rate will be rapid. Unless the fluid is quickly replaced, death may result from complete collapse of the circulation.

Causes

Cholera is caused by a short curved, rod-shaped germs known as vibrio cholerate. This germ produces a powerful poison. It is spread by flies and water contaminated by the germs. The real cause of the disease, however, is the toxic and devitalised condition of the system brought by incorrect feeding habits and faulty style of living. This condition facilitates invasion of cholera germs.

Dietary Treatment

Before the onset of dehydration, the treatment should aim at combating the loss of fluids and salts from the body. To allay thirst, the patient should sip water, soda water or green coconut water. Even these may be thrown out by vomitting. Therefore only small quantities of water should be given repeatedly, as these may remain for sometime within the stomach, and a stay of every one minute means some absorption. Ice may be given for sucking. This will redue internal temperature and restrict the tendency to vomit. Once the patient is dehydrated, intravenous infusions of saline solution should be given to compensate for the loss of fluids and salts from the body. The patient may require two litres or more a day. Care should, however, be taken to avoid water logging. Potassium may be added to the fluids, if there are signs of loss of this mineral.

After the acute stage of cholera is over, the patient may be given green coconut water and barley water in very thin form. When the stools begin to form, he should be given buttermilk. As he progresses towards recovery, rice softened to semi-solid form, mixed with curd, may be given.

The patient should not be given solid food till he has fully recovered. Liquid and bland foods are the best which he can ingest without endangering a reoccurance of the disease. Lemon, onion, green chillies, vinegar and mint should be included in the daily diet during an epidemic of cholera.

Certain food remedies have been found beneficial in the treatment of cholera. The foremost among these is the use of lemon (bara nimbu). The juice of this fruit can kill cholera bacilli within a very short time. It is also a very effective and reliable preventive food item against cholera during the epidemic. It can be taken in the form of sweetened or salted beverages for this purpose. Taking of this fruit with meals daily also serves as an effective preventive against cholera.

The root bark of guava (amrud) is another valuable remedy. It is rich in tannins and can be successfully used in the form of concentrated decoction in cholera. About 30 grams of the root bark should be used in 500 ml. of water to make the decoction. The water should be boiled till it is reduced by one-third. It can be taken twice daily. It will arrest vomiting and symptoms of diarrhoea.

Another effective remedy for cholera is the use of the leaves and flowers of peach (arhu). They should be taken in the form of syrup or conserve. The leaves of drumstick (sanjana) tree are also useful in this disease. Half a teaspoon of fresh leaf-juice, mixed with equal quantity of honey and half a glass of tender coconut water, can be given two or three times as a medicine in the treatment of cholera.

Onion is very useful in cholera. About 15 grams of this vegetable and four black peppers should be finely pounded in a pestle and given to the patient. It allays thirst and restlessness and the patient feels better. The fresh juice of bitter gourd (karela) is another effective medicine in early stages of cholera. A teaspoon of this juice, mixed with equal quantity of white onion juice and half a teaspoon of lime juice, should be given.

Other Measures

The intense visceral congestion can be relieved by maintaining warmth and activity of the skin. This can be achieved by applying hot-blanket pack or by taking hot full-bath followed by vigorous cold rubbing with towel until surface is red. To check vomiting, ice-bag should be applied over stomach, throat and spine. Cold compresses can also be applied over the abdomen with beneficial results. They should be changed every 15 or 20 minutes.

Cholera can be controlled only by rigid purification of water supplies and proper disposal of human wastes. In cases of slightest doubt about contamination of water, it must be boiled before use for drinking and cooking purposes. All foodstuffs must be kept covered and vegetables and fruits washed with a solution of potassium permaganate before consumption. Othe precautions against this disease include avoiding all uncooked vegetables, thorough washing of hands by all who handle food, and the elimination of all contacts with the disease.

TREATMENT CHART FOR CHOLERA

A - DIET

I. Water, soda water or green coconut water should be sipped to compensate for loss of fluids. Ice may be sucked to reduce temperature and prevent vomitting. Intravenous infusions of saline solution in case of dehydration.

II. Green coconut water, barley water and buttermilk may be given after the acute stage. Softened rice mixed with

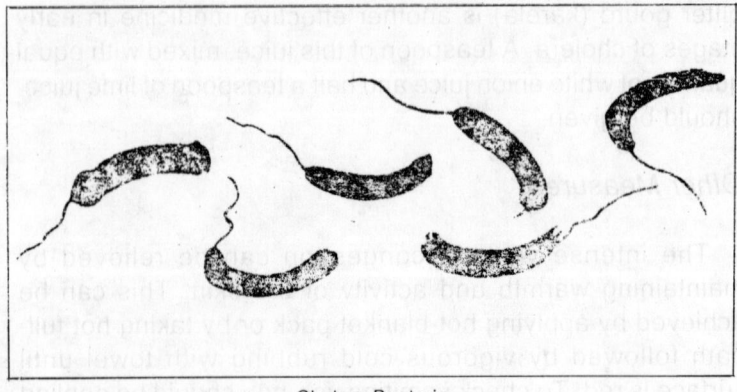

Cholera Bacteria

curd may be given after progress towards recovery. More liquid and bland foods may be introduced gradually.

III. After complete recovery, gradually embark upon a well-balanced diet on the following lines:-
1. *Upon arising:* A glass of lukewarm water with half a freshly-squeezed lime and a teaspoon of honey.
2. *Breakfast:* Fresh fruits such as apple, orange, grapes, papaya, mangoes, a cup of fresh milk, sweetened with honey or buttermilk.
3. *Lunch:* A bowl of steamed vegetables, whole wheat chappatis with butter and a glass of buttermilk.
4. *Mid-afternoon:* A glass of fresh fruit or vegetable juice or sugarcane juice.
5. *Dinner:* A bowl of fresh green vegetable salad, with lime juice dressing, sprouted seeds and fresh home-made cottage cheese or a glass of buttermilk.

Especially Beneficial: Lemon (Bara Nimbu) juice, Leaves and Flowers of Peach (Arhu), Onion and Root Bark of Guava (*Amrud*).

B - OTHER MEASURES

1. Apply hot-blanket pack or take hot-full bath followed by vigorous cold rubbing with towel.
2. Apply ice-bag or cold compress over stomach, throat and spine.
3. Ensure rigid purification of water supplies and proper disposal of human wastes.

CHAPTER 16

Cirrhosis of the Liver

Cirrhosis of the liver refers to all forms of liver disease characterised by a significant loss of cells. It is one of the most serious hepatic diseases. The liver gradually contracts in size and becomes hard and leathery.

The liver is one fo the most important glandular organs in the body. It is located high up on the right side of the abdomen just under the diaphragm. It is a vast chemical laboratory which performs many important functions. It produces bile, cholesterol, lecithin, blood albumin which is vital to the removal of tissue wastes, prothrombin necessary for the clotting of blood and numerous enzymes. It inactivates hormones no longer needed, synthesises many amino acids used in building tissues and breaks proteins into sugar and fat when required for energy. It stores vitamins and minerals. It also destroys harmful substances and detoxifies drugs, poisons, chemicals and toxins from bacterial infections. Liver damage interferes with all of these functions.

In cirrhosis of the liver, although regenerative activity continues, the loss of liver cells exceeds cell replacement. There is also distortion of the vascular system which interferes with the portal blood flow through the liver. The progressive degeneration of liver structure and function may ultimately lead to hepatic failure and death. The most common of several form of cirrhosis is portal cirrhosis, also known as haennoc's cirrhosis.

Symptoms

In the early stages of the disease, there may be nothing more than frequent attacks of gas and indigestion, with occasional nausea and vomiting. There may be some abdominal pain and loss of weight. In the advanced stage, the patient develops a low grade fever. He has a foul breath, jaundiced skin and distended veins in the abdomen. Reddish hairlike markings, resembling small spiders, may appear on the face, neck, arms and trunk. The abdomen becomes bloated and swollen, the mind gets clouded and there may be considerable bleeding from the stomach.

Causes

Excessive use of alcohol over a long period is the most potent cause of cirrhosis of the liver. It has been estimated that 1 out of 12 chronic alcoholics in the United States develops cirrhosis. The disease can progress to the end-stage of hepatic failure, if the person does not abstain from alcohol. Cirrhosis appears to be related to the duration of alcohol intake and the quantity consumed daily. Recent research indicates that the average duration of alcohol intake to produce cirrhosis is 10 years and the dose is estimated to be in excess of 16 ounces of alcohol daily.

Poor nutrition can be another causative factor in the development of cirrhosis and a chronic alcoholic usually suffers from a severe malnutrition too, as he seldom eats. Other causes of cirrhosis are excessive intake of highly seasoned food, habitual taking of quinine for a prolonged period in tropical climate and drug treatments for syphilis, fever and other diseases. It may also result from a highly toxic condition of the system in general. In fact, anything which continually over-burdens the liver cells and leads to their final breakdown can be a contributing cause of cirrhosis.

Dietary Treatment

The patient should be kept in bed. He must abstain completely from alcohol in any form. He should undergo an initial liver cleaning programme with a juice fast for seven days. Freshly-extracted juices from red beets, lemon, papaya and grapes may be taken during this period. This may be followed by the fruit and milk diet for two to three weeks. In this regimen, the patient should have three meals a day of fresh juicy fruits and milk. The fruits may include apples, pears, grapes, grapefruits, oranges, pineapples and peaches. Two pints of milk may be taken on the first day. It should be increased by half a pint daily upto four or five pints a day. The milk should be fresh and unboiled, but may be slightly warmed, if desired. It should be sipped very slowly.

After the fruit and milk diet, the patient may gradually embark upon a well-balanced diet of three basic food groups, namely, seeds, nuts and grains vegetables and fruits, with emphasis on raw organically-grown foods. Adequate high quality protein in necessary in cirrhosis. The best complete proteins for liver patients are obtained from raw goat's milk, home-made raw cottage cheese, sprouted seeds and grains and raw nuts, especially almonds. Vegetables such as beets, squashes, bitter gourds, egg-plants, tomatoes, carrots, radishes and papayas are useful in this condition. All fats and oils should be excluded from the diet for several weeks.

The patient should avoid all refined, processed and canned foods, sugar in any form, spices and condiments, strong tea and coffee, fried foods, all preparations cooked in ghee, oil or butter and all meats rich in fat. The use of salt should be restricted. The patient should also avoid all chemical additives in food and poisons in air, water and environment as far as possible.

A warm water enema should be used during the treatment to cleanse the bowels. If constipation is chronic, all steps should be taken for its eradication. Application of alternate compress to liver area followed by general wet sheet rub will be beneficial. The morning dry friction and breathing and other exercises should form a regular daily feature of the treatment.

TREATMENT CHART FOR CIRRHIOSIS OF THE LIVER

A - DIET

I. Raw juice diet for three to five days. During this period a glass of fresh fruit or vegetable juice diluted with water should be taken every two hours from 8 a.m. to 8 p.m. and bowels cleansed daily with warm water enema.

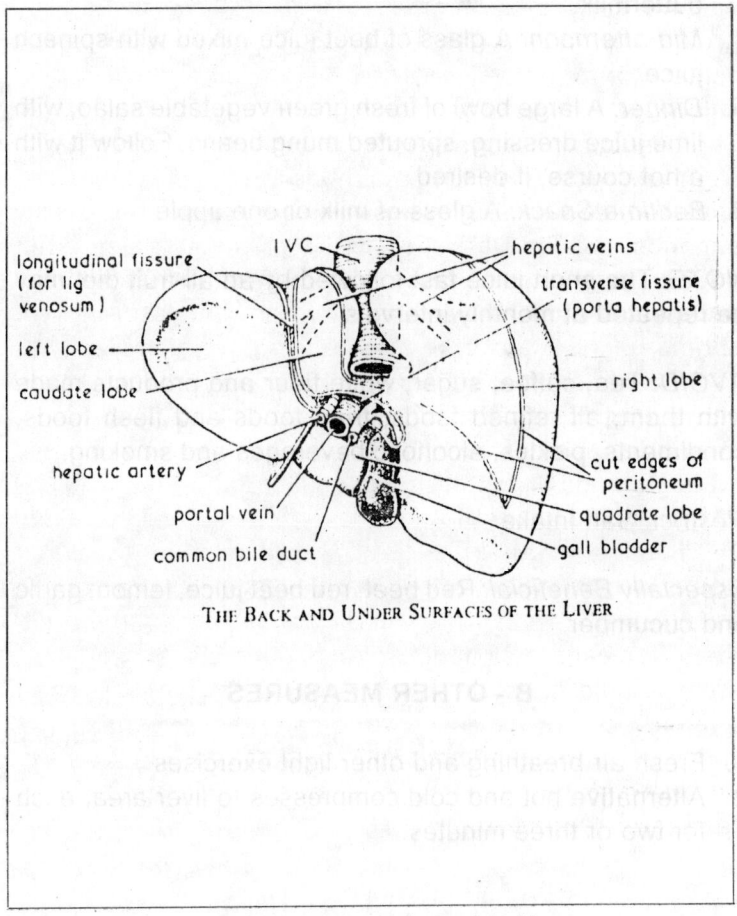

The Back and Under Surfaces of the Liver

II. An all-fruit diet for further three to five days.

III. Thereafter, adopt a well-balanced diet on the following lines:-
1. *Upon arising:* A glass of lukewarm water with half a freshly-squeezed lime and a teaspoon of honey.
2. *Breakfast:* Fresh fruits, a glass of milk, sweetened with honey and some seeds or nuts, especially almonds or sesame seeds.
3. *Lunch:* A bowl of freshly-prepared steamed vegetables, two or three whole wheat chappatis and a glass of buttermilk.
4. *Mid-afternoon:* A glass of beet juice mixed with spinach juice
5. *Dinner:* A large bowl of fresh green vegetable salad, with lime juice dressing, sprouted mung beans. Follow it with a hot course, if desired.
6. *Bedtime Snack:* A glass of milk or one apple.

NOTE: The short juice fast followed by an all-fruit diet may be repeated at monthly intervals.

AVOID: Tea, coffee, sugar, white flour and products made with them, all refined foods, fried foods and flesh foods, condiments, pickles, alcoholic beverages and smoking.

Restrict: Salt Intake

Especially Beneficial: Red beet, red beet juice, lemon, garlic and cucumber.

B - OTHER MEASURES

1. Fresh air breathing and other light exercises
2. Alternative hot and cold compresses to liver area, each for two or three minutes.

CHAPTER 17

Colitis

Chronic ulcerative colitis is a severe prolonged inflammation of the colon or large bowel in which ulcers form on the walls of the colon. In severe cases, ulceration leads to bleeding and the patient passes bloody stools with pus and mucus. The disease results from prolonged irritation of the delicate membrane which lines the walls of the colon. It affects all age groups from very young children to the elderly.

Normally, it is the function of the colon to store waste material until most of the fluids have been removed to enable well-formed soft stools, consisting of non-absorbable food materials to be passed. Persons who suffer from an irritable colon have irregular and erratic contractions which are specially noticeable on the left side.

Symptoms

Chronic ulcerative colitis usually begins in the lower part of the bowels and spreads upwards. The first symptom is an increased urgency to move the bowel, followed by cramping pains in the abdomen and bloody mucus in the stools. As the disease spreads upwards, the stools become watery and more frequent and are characterised by rectal straining. All this loss of blood and fluid from the bowels results in weakness, fever, nausea, vomiting, loss of appetite and anaemia.

The patient may develop a bloated feeling because the gas is not obsorbed or expelled normally. Some patients suffer from constipation alternating with periods of loose bowel movements. Still others may suffer from persistent diarrhoea for years together. The patient is usually malnourished and may be severely underweight. He may suffer from frequent insomnia.

Ulcerative colitis in its severe form may also lead to nutritional problems. The improper assimilation of food due to inflammatory conditions may cause deficiency diseases. This may gradually result in nervous irritability, exhaustion and depression. In very severe cases, the patient may even develop suicidal tendencies.

Causes

The main cause of colitis is chronic constipation and the use of purgatives. Constipation causes an accumulation of the hard faecal matter which is never properly evacuated. The use of purgatives only increases irritation. Often, colitis is caused by poorly-digested roughage, especially of cereals and carbohydrates, which causes bowel irritation. It may also result from an allergic sensitivity to certain foods, especially milk, wheat and eggs. Often, the intake of antibiotics may upset the bacterial flora in the intestines and interfere with proper digestion.

Severe stress may also produce ulcerative colitis. During any form of severe stress, outpouring of adrenal hormones causes such destruction of body protein that at times parts of the walls, lining the intestines, are literally eaten away. Such stress also depletes the body of pantothenic acid. Experiments on animals have shown that they can develop ulcerative colitis when they are kept on diets deficient in pantothenic acid.

Dietary Treatment

Diet plays an important part in the treatment of colitis. It is advisable to observe a juice fast for five days or so in most cases of colitis. The juices may be diluted with a little boiled water. Papaya juice and raw cabbage or carrot juice is especially beneficial. Citrus juices should be avoided. The bowels should be cleansed daily with a warm water enema.

After the juice fast, the patient should gradually adopt a diet of small, frequent meals of soft cooked or steamed vegetables, rice, *dalia* (coarsely broken wheat) and well-ripened fruits like banana and papaya, yogurt and home-made cottage cheese. Sprouted seeds and grains, whole meal bread and raw vegetables may be added gradually to this diet after about 10 days. Tender coconut water is highly beneficial as it is soothing to the soft mucosa of the colon. Cooked apples also aid the healing of ulcerative conditions because of its ample concentration of iron and phosphorus. All food must be eaten slowly and chewed thoroughly.

Foods which should be excluded from the diet are white sugar, white bread and white flour products, highly seasoned foods, highly salted foods, strong tea, coffee and alcoholic beverages and foods cooked in aluminum pans.

The following menu may serve as the guideline and should be adopted for at least three months:

Breakfast: Ripe bananas or papaya and milk. Butter-milk may be taken if milk is not tolerated.

Mid-morning: Carrot or raw cabbage juice.

Lunch: Steamed or lightly cooked vegetables, rice or *dalia,* butter and butter-milk.

Mid-afternoon: Coconut water or fruit juice.

Dinner: Salad of raw vegetables, sprouts like alfalfa and mung beans, home-made cottage cheese and nuts. Instead of raw vegetables cooked ones like carrot, beetroot, tomatoes, lettuce, cabbage may be used.

Before retiring: A glass of milk or a baked apple.

The patient should have a bowel movement at the same time each day and spend 10 to 15 minutes in the endeavour. Straining at stools should be avoided. Drinking two glasses of water first thing in the morning will stimulate a normal bowel movement. An enema may be used if no bowel movement occurs. Butter-milk enema twice a week is also soothing and helps in re-installing a healthy bacterial flora in the colon. Complete bed rest and plenty of liquids are very important. The patient should eliminate all causes of tension, adjust to his disability and face his discomfort with patience.

TREATMENT CHART FOR COLITIS

A - DIET

I. Fresh fruit or vegetable juices diluted with water for five days. Warm water enema should be taken daily during this period.

II. The following menu may be adopted for 10 days after the juice fast:-
1. *Upon arising:* 25 black raisins soaked overnight in water alongwith the water in which they are soaked and water kept overnight in copper *lota.*

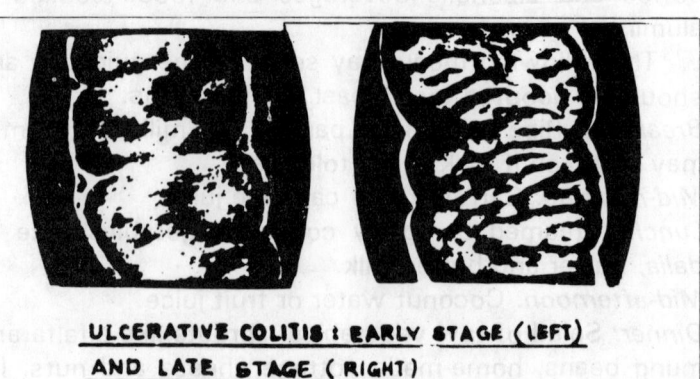

ULCERATIVE COLITIS : EARLY STAGE (LEFT) AND LATE STAGE (RIGHT)

Ulcerative colitis, a serious condition involving the large bowel.
Picture at left shows early stage, and right, late stage of the disease. Healing is usually slow and extensive scarring of the colon walls generally follows.

2. *Breakfast:* Banana or papaya and milk, sweatened with a teaspoon of honey or buttermilk.
3. *Mid-morning:* Mixed juices of carrot and cabbage.
4. *Lunch:* Steamed vegetables, rice or dalia (coarsely broken wheat), and a glass of buttermilk.
5. *Mid-afternoon:* Coconut water.
6. *Dinner:* Cooked vegetables, dates and cooked apple.
7. *Before retiring:* A glass of milk or one cooked apple.

NOTE: The following foods should be introduced gradually after 10 days:-

Apple, peaches, pears, grapes, melons, pineapple, raw vegetables, nuts, sprouts, butter, cottage cheese and whole grains.

Especially Beneficial: Banana, papaya, coconut water and raw cabbage juice, millet cereals, buttermilk and buttermilk enema.

AVOID: Meats, sugar, tea, coffee, alcohol, condiments, pickles, refined and processed foods and products made from sugar and white flour.

B - OTHER MEASURES

1. Wet abdomen pack for one hour, twice daily, morning and evening.
2. Hot fomentation to the abdominal region in case of pain.
3. Neutral immersion bath for half an hour before retiring.

CHAPTER 18

Common Cold

The common cold, also known as acute coryza, is an inflammation of the upper respiratory tract caused by infection with virus. It occurs more often than all other diseases. A person suffers from this disease three times in a year on an average. A cold usually lasts from three to ten days. The patient feels miserable for the first three days or so.

Symptoms

The first signs of a cold are a feeling of soreness of the throat and congestion of the nasal passage. Although the disease normally begins in the nose and throat, it affects all parts of the body. Its usual symptoms are a running nose, sneezing, a rise in temperature, headache, sore throat, chill, aches and pains in the body and loss of appetite. The skin around the nostrils may become sore.

Causes

The common cold results from exposure to the virus. Its intensity will, however, depend upon the state of health of the person and environmental factors. Lowered vitality, allergic disorders of the nose and throat, chilling of the body, lack of sleep, depression, fatigue and factors such as sudden changes in temperature, dust and other irritating inhalations are important causes contributing to the development of a cold.

The real cause of a cold, however, is the toxic condition of the body brought about by wrong food habits such as an excessive intake of starch, carbohydrates, proteins and other acid-forming foods. A cold, is, therefore, nature's simplest way of expelling toxic waste from the human system. The duration of the cold will depend on the amount of poisons accumulated in the body and the rapidity with which they are expelled.

Dietetic Treatment

To treat a cold by means of customary suppressive drugs like aspirin, codeine, etc., will only pave the way for future trouble of a more serious nature. For, such a treatment puts a sudden stop to the eliminative process then taking place and forces the toxic matter back into the tissues again. Moreover, drugs have no effect on the duration of the cold. It has been aptly said that a cold can be cured in a week by taking medicines; otherwise it will subside in seven days.

The only real treatment for colds is a proper diet. The best way to begin the treatment is to put the patient on a fast for two days. Nothing should be taken during this period except warm water mixed with lemon juice and honey or fruit juice and hot water. A liquid diet of fruit juice in large amounts is necessary to neutralise the acid condition of the blood and hot drinks are needed to help clear and kidneys. Pineapple juice in particular is highly beneficial. A warm water enema should be used daily to cleanse the bowels during this period.

The short juice fast may be followed by an exclusive fresh fruit diet for three days. In this regimen, the patient should have three meals a day of fresh, juicy fruits such as apples, pears, grapes, grapefruits, oranges, pineapples, peaches, melons or any other juicy fruit in season. Bananas, dried or stewed or tinned fruits, should not be taken. No other foodstuff should be added to the diet as otherwise the whole value of the treatment will be lost.

After the exclusive fruit diet, the patient may gradually embark upon a well-balanced diet of three basic food groups, namely seeds, nuts and grains, vegetables and fruits. It is advisable to avoid, meat, fish, eggs, cheese and starchy foods for few days.

The patient should strengthen the system as a whole by taking a diet which should supply all the vitamins and minerals the body needs. Vitamin C, however, heads the list of these nutrients. It protects the person from infection and acts as a harmless antibiotic. It is found in citrus fruits, green leafy vegetables, sprouted Bengal gram and green gram.

According to Dr. Linus Pauling, a noble prize-winning scientist, the regular use of this vitamin in the optimum daily amount will prevent the common cold and if a cold has already appeared, large doses of this vitamin will relieve the symptoms and shorten its duration. He estimates that one to two grams or 1000 mg. to 2000 mg. per day is approximately the optimum amount of this vitamin. His advice is to swallow one or two 500 mg. tablets of vitamin C at the appearance of first sign of the cold and continue the treatment by taking an additional tablet every hour.

Garlic oil combined with onion juice, diluted with water and drunk several times a day, has been found, in several studies to be extremely effective in the treatment of common cold. Steam inhalation will help relieve the congestion of the nasal tissues. Gargling with hot water mixed with salt is beneficial for a sore throat. Cold chest packs should be applied two or three times a day as they will relieve congestion of lungs and help in eliminating the accumulated mucus.

Other useful measures in the treatment of common cold are a mild sunbath, fresh air and deep breathing, brisk walks, sound sleep, adjustment of one's clothes and habits to the requirements of the season, so as to nullify the effect of weather fluctuations.

TREATMENT CHART FOR COMMON COLD

A - DIET

I. Fast on raw juices for three to five days. Taka a glass of fresh fruit or vegetable juice, diluted with water on 50:50 basis, every two hours. Use warm-water enema daily during this period.

The juice from Pineapple is highly beneficial in the treatment of Common Cold.

II. All all-fruit diet for further three to five days, taking three meals a day of fresh juicy fruits at five-hourly intervals.

III. Therefore, adopt a well-balanced diet as follows:-

1. *Upon arising:* A glass of lukewarm water with half a freshly-squeezed lime and a teaspoon of honey.
2. *Breakfast:* Fresh fruit, a glass of milk, sweetened with honey and some seeds or nuts.
3. *Lunch:* A bowl of freshly-prepared steamed vegetables, two or three whole wheat chappatis and a glass of butter milk.
4. *Mid-afternoon:* A glass of fresh fruit or vegetable juice.
5. *Dinner:* A good-sized raw vegetable salad and sprouts with lime juice dresing, followed by a hot course if desired.

Home remedies: Lime, Garlic soup, ginger, lady's fingers, turmeric and vitamin C.

AVOID: Tea, coffee, sugar, white flour and products made from them, refined foods, fried foods, flesh foods, condiments, pickles, alcohol and smoking.

B - OTHER MEASURES

1. Wet chest pack for one hour every morning on an empty stomach.
2. A hot-Epsom salts bath twice a week in the night.
3. Fresh air, brisk walks and yogasanas.
4. Massage once a week.

CHAPTER 19

Conjunctivitis

Conjunctivitis refers to an inflammation of the conjunctiva, the thin transparent membrane covering the front of the eye. It is also known as sore eyes and is a very common form of eye trouble. It spreads from person to person through direct contact. Overcrowding, dirty surroundings and unhealthy living conditions can cause epidemics of this ailment.

Symptoms

The eyeball and under side of the eyelids become inflamed. At first, the eyes are red, dry and burning. Later, there may be a watery secretion. In more serious cases, there is pus formation. During sleep, this material dries, making the lashes stick together.

Causes

Medical science believes that conjunctivitis results from bacterial infection, viruses or eye-strain. Prolonged work under artificial light and excessive use of the eyes in one way or the other no doubt contributes towards the disease. But its real cause can be traced to a catarrhal condition of the system resulting from general toxaemia due to dietetic errors and faulty style of living. The patient generally suffers from colds or other ailments indicative of a general catarrhal condition.

Dietetic Cure

The treatment of conjunctivitis through salves and ointments does not cure the disease. To be effective, treatment must be constitutional. A thorough cleansing of the system and adoption of natural laws in diet and general living alone can help eliminate conjunctivitis.

The best way to commence the treatment is to adopt an exclusive fresh fruit diet for about seven days. The diet may consist of fresh, juicy fruits in season such as apples, oranges, pears, grapes, pineapples and grapefruits. Bananas should, however, not be taken. No other foodstuff should be added to this diet.

Those who have a serious trouble should undertake a juice fast for three or four days. The procedure is to take the juice of an orange, in a glass of warm water, if desired, every two hours from 8 a.m. to 8 p.m. Nothing else should be taken, as otherwise, the value of the fast will be lost. If orange juice is not liked, carrot juice may be substituted. A warm water enema should be taken daily during the period of fasting.

The short, juice fast may be followed by an all-fruit diet for further seven days. Thereafter, the patient may adopt a general diet scheme as outlined in Chapter 12 on Cataract. The eye muscle exercises for relaxing and strengthening the eyes as mentioned therein will also be beneficial in the treatment of conjunctivitis.

The patient should avoid an excessive intake of starchy and sugary foods in the form of white bread, refined cereals, potatoes, puddings, pies, pastry, sugar, jams and confectionery, which cause the general catarrhal condition as well as conjunctivitis. He should also avoid the intake of excessive quantities of meat and other protein and fatty foods, strong tea and coffee, too much salt, condiments and sauces.

Raw juices of certain vegetables, especially carrots and spinach, have been found valuable in the treatment of conjunctivitis. The combined juices of these two vegetables have proved very effective. Six ounces of spinach juice should be mixed with ten ounces of carrot juice in this combination.

Vitamin A and B2 have also been found valuable in the treatment of conjunctivitis. The patient should take liberal quantities of natural foods rich in these two vitamins. The valuable sources of vitamin A are whole milk, curds, butter, carrots, pumpkins, green leafy vegetables, tomatoes, mangoes and papayas. Foods rich in vitamin B2 are green leafy vegetable, milk, almonds, citrus fruits, bananas and tomatoes.

As regards local treatment to the eyes themselves, a cold foment renders almost immediate relief by chasing away an overactive local blood supply. The procedure is as follows:-

Fold a small hand towel. Saturate it with cold water. Squeeze out excess water and mould towelling gently over both eyes. Repeat the process as soon as the foment gets warned.

A daily exercise routine, including breathing exercises and fresh air will be most beneficial. The eyes should be looked after carefully and excessive reading or close work under artificial light must be avoided.

TREATMENT CHART FOR CONJUNCTIVITIS

A - DIET

I. An exclusive diet of fresh juicy fruits for five days. During this period, take three meals a day of fresh juicy fruits at five-hourly intevals and use warm water enema daily.

II. Thereafter, adopt a well-balanced diet on the following lines:-

1. *Upon arising:* A glass of lukewarm water mixed with half a freshly-squeezed lime and a teaspoon of honey.
2. *Breakfast:* Fresh fruits, a glass of milk, sweetened with honey and few almonds.
3. *Lunch:* Steamed vegetables, two or three whole wheat chappatis, and a glass of buttermilk.
4. *Dinner:* A large bowl of fresh salad of green vegetables with mung sprouts and cottage cheese or buttermilk.
5. *Before retiring:* A glass of fresh milk with few dates.

AVOID: White bread, refined cereals, potatoes, puddings, pies and sugary foods, meats and excessive quantities of protein and fatty foods, too much salt, tea and coffee.

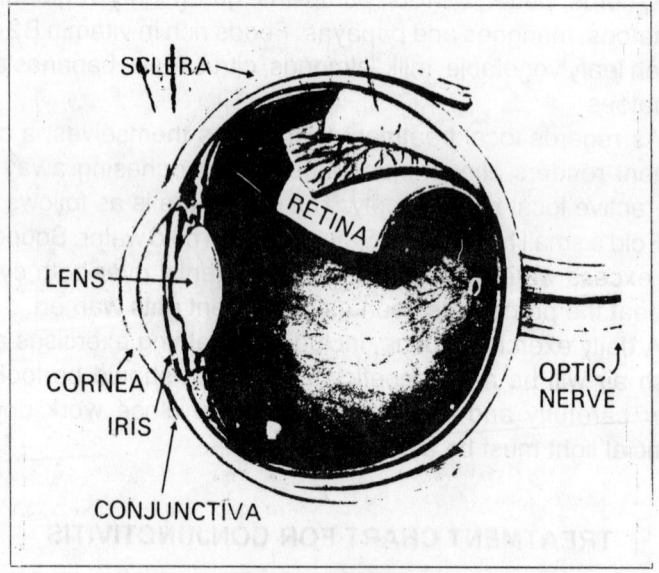

Structure of the Eye

B - OTHER MEASURES

1. Apply cold packs over the eyes.
2. Breathing and other exercises and fresh air.
3. Eye muscle exercises as explained in the Chapter on Cataract.
4. Avoid excessive reading and close work under artificial light.

CHAPTER 20

Constipation

Constipation is a common disturbance of the digestive tract. In this condition, the bowels do not move regularly, or are not completely emptied when they move.

Constipation is the chief cause of many diseases because such a condition produces toxins which find their way into the blood stream and are carried to all parts of the body. This results in weakening of the vital organs and lowering of the resistance of the entire system. Appendicitis, rheumatism, arthritis, high blood pressure, cataract and cancer are only a few of the diseases in which chronic constipation is an important predisposing factor.

The number of motions required for normal health varies from person to person. Most people have one motion a day, some have two a day, while others have one every other day. However, for comfort and health, at least one clear bowel movement a day is essential and considered normal.

Symptoms

The most common symptoms of constipation are infrequency, irregularity or difficulty of elimination due to hard faecal matter. Among the other symptoms are coated tongue, foul breath, loss of appetite, headache, dizziness, dark circles under the eyes, depression, nausea, pimples on the face, ulcer in the mouth, constant fullness in the abdomen, diarrhoea alternating with constipation, varicose veins, pain in the lumbar region, acidity, heart burn and insomnia.

Causes

The most important causes for chronic constipation are an unsuitable diet and a faulty style of living. All foods in their natural state contain a good percentage of 'roughage' which is most essential in preserving natural balance of foods and also in helping peristalsis — the natural rhythmic action by means of which the food is passed down the alimentary canal. Much of the food we eat today is deficient in natural bulk or roughage and this results in chronic constipation.

Intake of refined and rich food lacking in vitamins and minerals, insufficient intake of water, consumption of meat in large quantities, excessive use of strong tea and coffee, insufficient chewing, overeating and a wrong combination of food, irregular habits of eating and drinking may all contribute to poor bowel function. Other causes include faulty and irregular habit of defecation, frequent use of purgatives, weakness of abdominal muscles due to sedentary habits, lack of physical activity and emotional stress and strain.

Diseases such as tumours or growths, sluggish liver, colitis, spastic condition of the intestines, hyperactivity, diseases of the rectum and colon, bad teeth, uterine disease, diabetes, use of certain drugs for treating other ailments, abnormal condition of the lower spine and enlargement of the prostate gland can also cause chronic constipation. Elderly patients may suffer from constipation due to relaxed muscle tone, inadequate dietary intake for nutritional needs and diminished activity.

Dietary Treatment

The purgatives and laxatives give only temporary relief. They unnecessarily irritate the stomach and intestines, weakening the colon. Laxative abuse may also lead to low blood potassium and long term chronic ill-health. The natural way to treat constipation is to re-educate the bowels and give up all artificial aids. The observance of regular hours for meals, elimination and sleep, a balanced diet, sufficient exercise, and a high standard of general health with good muscular tone are essential in the treatment of constipation.

The most important factor in curing constipation is a natural and simple diet. This should consist of unrefined foods such as whole grain cereals, bran, honey, molasses and lentils; green and leafy vegetables, especially spinach, french beans, tomatoes, lettuce, onions, cabbage, cauliflower, brussels sprouts, celery, turnip, pumpkin, peas, beets, asparagus and carrots; fresh fruits, especially pears, grapes, figs, papayas, mangoes, grapefruits, gooseberries, guavas and oranges; dry fruits such as figs, raisins, apricots and dates; milk products in the form of butter, ghee and cream.

The diet alone is not enough. Food should be properly chewed — each morsel for at least 15 times. Hurried meals and meals at odd times should be avoided. Sugar and sugary foods should be strictly avoided because sugar steals B vitamins from the body, without which the intestines cannot function normally. Foods which constipate are all products made of white flour, rice, bread, pulses, cakes, pastries, biscuits, cheese, fleshy foods, preserves, white sugar and hard boiled eggs.

Drinking lots of water is beneficial not only for constipation but also for cleaning the system, diluting the blood, and washing out poisons. Normally, six to eight glasses of water should be taken daily as it is essential for digesting and dissolving food nutrients so that they can be absorbed and utilised by the body. Water should, not however, be taken with meals as it dilutes the gastric juices essential for proper digestion. Water should be taken either half an hour before or an hour after meals.

Grapes have proved highly beneficial in overcoming constipation. The combination of the properties of the cellulose, sugar and organic acid in grapes make them a laxative food. Their field of action is not limited to clearing the bowels only. They also tone up the stomach and intestines and relieve the most chronic constipation. One should take at least 350 grams of grapes daily to achieve the desired results. When fresh grapes are not available, raisins soaked in water can be used. Raisins should be soaked in a tumberful of drinking water for 24 to 48 hours. This would swell them to the original size of the grapes. The raisins should be eaten early in the morning. The water in which raisins are soaked should also be drunk.

Drinking hot water with sour lime juice and half a tea-spoon of salt is also an effective remedy for constipation. Drinking water which has been kept overnight in a copper vessel, first thing in the morning, will bring good results. Linseed is extremely useful in difficult cases of constipation. A tea-spoon of linseed swallowed with water before each meal provides both bulk and lubrication.

In all ordinary cases of constipation, an exclusive fruit diet for about seven days would be the best way to begin the treatment. For long-standing and stubborn cases, it would be advisable to have a short fast for four or five days. This will drive out the packed contents of the bowels, eliminate toxins and purify the blood stream. The weak patients may take orange juice during the period of fasting. After the all-fruit diet or the short fast, as the case may be, the patient should gradually embark upon a balanced diet comprising adequate raw foods, ripe fruits and whole grain cereals. In some cases, further short periods on fruits or short fasts may be necessary at intervals of two months or so, depending on the progress being made. The bowels should be cleansed daily through warm water enema for few days at the commencement of the treatment.

TREATMENT CHART FOR CONSTIPATION

A - DIET

I. An all-fruit diet for five days. Take fresh juicy fruits at five-hourly intervals during the day and use warm water anema to cleanse the bowels.

II. Thereafter, gradually adopt a well-balanced diet on the following lines:-
1. *Upon arising:* 25 black raisins soaked overnight in water along with water in which they are soaked and water kept overnight in copper vessel.

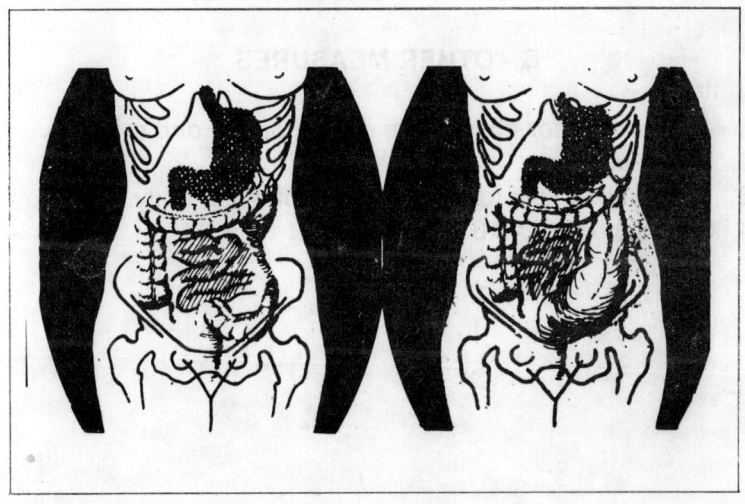

Spastic colon, left, causes severe constipation and pain. Greatly enlarged colon, right, has lost its "tone," The result is chronic constipation.

2. *Breakfast:* Fresh fruit and a glass of milk, sweetened with honey.
3. *Lunch:* A bowl of freshly prepared steamed vegetables, two or three whole wheat chappatis and a glass of buttermilk.
4. *Mid-afternoon:* A glass of carrot juice or coconut water.
5. *Dinner:* A large bowl of fresh green vegetable salad, with lemon juice dressing, mung bean sprouts, cottage cheese

or a glass of buttermilk. Follow it with a hot course, if desired.
6. *Bedtime Snack:* A glass of milk or one apple.

III. Always follow the undermentioned rules regarding eating:

1. Never eat and drink together.
2. Never hurry through a meal.
3. Never eat to full stomach

AVOID: Tea, coffee, sugar, white flour, all products made with sugar and white flour, all refined foods, fried foods and flesh foods as well as condiments and pickles.

B - OTHER MEASURES

1. Brisk walks for 45 minutes daily morning and evening.
2. Yogic asanas.
3. Drink atleast six to eight glasses of water daily.
4. Cold hip bath for 10 minutes daily.

CHAPTER 21

Cough

Coughing is the action by which excess mucus is driven out. It is a vital body defense mechanism, which ejects every thing from germs to foreign bodies from the lungs and windpipe. When a person is unable to cough, as for instance, following surgery or a chest injury, pneumonia may develop and cause a serious threat.

The air passages of the lungs are lined with cells secreting mucus. They normally trap particles of dust. When the membranes the lining of air passages is irritated. Coughing helps eliminate this excess mucus. In the process a dry hacking sound is produced. It is a very common condition affecting persons of all ages.

Symptoms

A person who is going to cough first draws a deep breath in. He then closes his glottis and contracts his muscles. This builds up pressure in the chest. Then, he suddenly opens his glotis so that there is an explosive discharge of air which sweeps through the air passages and carries with it the excess secretions or, in some cases, foreign matter which has irritated the larynx, trachea or bronchi.

Causes

Cough may be caused by inflammation of the larynx or the pharynx. It may also result from digestive disturbance. A cough can develop in the chest due to weather condition or seasonal changes. The real cause of this disorder, however, is clogging of the bronchial tube with waste matter. This has been brought about by wrong feeding habits. The reason for higher incidence of cough during winter than in other seasons is that an average person usually eats more of the catarrh-forming foods such as white bread, meat, sugar, porridge, puddings and pies in the colder months of the year. Over clothing with heavy-under-garments during this period also prevents proper aeration of the skin.

Dietary Treatment

In case of severe cough, the patient should take only orange juice and water till the severity is reduced. The procedure is to take the juice of an orange diluted in warm water every two hours during the day. The warm water enema should be used daily to cleanse the bowels. After the juice diet, the patient should adopt an all-fruit diet for further two or three days.

In case of mild cough, the patient can begin with an all fruit diet for five days or so, taking three meals a day of fresh juicy fruits such as apple, pear, grapes, grape-fruit, orange, pineapple, peaches and melon. For drinks, unsweetened lemon water or cold or hot plain water may be taken. After the all fruit diet, the patient should follow a well-balanced diet, with emphasis on whole grain cereals, raw or lightly-cooked vegetables and fresh fruits.

The patient should drink hot water freely. This will make the secretion thinner and less viscid, thereby loosing the cough. The quantity of water should be considerable so as to cause a feeling of warmth and perspiration. When the skin becomes moist by sweating, the mucous membrance also pours out watery secretion giving much relief.

The patient should avoid meats, sugar, tea, coffee, condiments, pickles, refined and processed foods. He or she should also avoid soft drinks, candies, ice-cream and all products made from sugar and white flour.

Several food remedies have been found beneficial in the treatment of cough. One of the most effective of these is the use of grapes. They tone up the lungs and act as an expectorant. Simple cold and cough are relieved through its use in a couple of days. A combination of honey with grape juice is a specific for cough.

Almonds (*badam*) are useful in dry coughs. They should be soaked in water for about an hour or so and the brown skin removed. They should then be ground will to form a fine paste and 20 grams each of butter and sugar added to it. This paste should be given in the morning and evening.

Onion (*piyaz*) is valuable in cough. This vegetable should be chopped fine and juice extracted from it. This juice, mixed with honey and kept for four or five hours, will make an excellent cough syrup. It is also useful in removing phelgm. A medium size onion should be crushed, the juice of one lemon should be added to it and then one cup of boiling water should be poured on it. Some honey should be added to taste and it should be taken two or three times a day.

The root of turmeric (*haldi*) plant is useful in dry cough. The root should be roasted and powdered This powder should be taken in three grams doses twice daily in the morning and evening.

A sauce made from raisins (*munaqqa*) is valuable in cough. This sauce is prepared by grinding 100 grams of raisins with water. About 100 grams of sugar should be mixed with it and the mixture should be heated and preserved when the bulk has turned saucy. This sauce should be taken in 20 grams dose at bed time daily.

Aniseed (*vilaiti saunf*) is also useful in hard dry cough with difficult expectoration. It breaks up mucus. A tea made from this spice should be taken regularly for treating this condition.

Other Measures

Other useful measures in the treatment of cough are hot fomentations to the chest and throat and application of frequent chest packs. If the cough is checked while the secretion is abundant, the patient should be made to sit in the tub with a small amount of hot water, and cold water should be poured over his head, spine and chest to induce cough. This should be followed by vigorous rubbing. The patient should be dried thoroughly and then wrapped in dry blankets in the bed.

TREATMENT CHART FOR COUGH

A - DIET

I. Fast on fruit juice for five days in case of severe cough. Take a glass of fresh fruit juice, diluted with water on 50:50 basis, every two hours. Use warm-water enema daily during this period.

Grapes are very effective remedy in cough

II. An all-fruit diet for five days in case of mild cough, taking three meals a day of fresh juicy fruits, at five-hourly intervals.

III. Thereafter, adopt a balanced diet, on the following lines:-

COUGH

1. *Upon arising:* 25 black raisins soaked overnight in water along with the water in which they are soaked and water kept overnight in a copper vessel.
2. *Breakfast:* Fresh fruit, a glass of milk, sweetened with honey and some seeds or nuts.
3. *Lunch:* Freshly-prepared steamed or lightly-cooked vegetables, whole wheat chappatis and a glass of buttermilk.
4. *Mid-afternoon:* A glass of fresh fruit or vegetable juice.
5. *Dinner:* Raw green vegetable salad and sprouts, with lime juice dressing, followed by a hot course, if desired.
6. *Home Remedies:* Grapes, almonds, onion juice, turmeric, a sauce made from raisin and aniseed.

AVOID: Meats, sugar, tea, coffee, soft drinks, ice cream, condiments, pickles refined and processed foods, white flour and products made from white flour and sugar.

B - OTHER MEASURES

1. Hot foementations to the chest and throat.
2. Application of frequent chest packs.
3. Hot tub bath with cold compress on the head in case of checked cough with abundance of secretion.

CHAPTER 22

Depression

Depression is the most common of all emotional disorders. This may vary from a feeling of slight sadness to utter misery and dejection. It stems from a variety of physical and psychological symptoms which together constitute a syndrome.

Depression is the most unpleasant experience a person can go through. It is far more difficult to cope with than physical ailments. The growing complexities of modern life and resultant crises, as well as mental stress and strain in day-to-day life usually lead to this disorder. Suicide is the major risk in depression.

Symptoms

It is not always easy to diagnose depression clinically. The most striking symptoms of depression are feelings of an acute sense of loss and inexplicable sadness, loss of energy and loss of interest. The patient usually feels tired and lacks interest in the world around him. Sleep disturbance is frequent. Usually, the patient wakes up depressed at 4 or 5 in the morning and is unable to go back to sleep. Other disturbed sleep patterns are, difficulty in falling asleep, nightmares and repeated waking from midnight onwards.

The patient often suffers from guilt, oppressive feelings and self-absorption. Other symptoms of depression are: loss of appetite, giddiness, itching, nausea, agitation, irritability, impotence or frigidity, constipation, aches and pains all over the body, lack of concentration and lack of power of decision. Some persons may lose interest in eating and suffer from rapid loss of weight while others may resort to frequent eating and as a result gain in weight.

Cases of severe depression may be characterised by low body temperature, low blood pressure, hot flushes and shivering. The external manifestations represent a cry for help from the tormented mind of the depressed persons. The severely depressed patients feels worthless and is finally convinced that he himself is responsible for his undoing and his present state of hopeless despair.

Causes

Depleted functioning of the adrenal glands is one of the main causes of mental depression. Irregular diet habits cause digestive problems and lead to the assimilation of fats. An excess of carbohydrates like cereals, white sugar, coffee, tea, chocolates and comparatively less quantities of vegetables and fruits in the diet may result in indigestion. Due to indigestion gases are produced in the digestive tract, causing compression over the diaphragm in the region of the heart and lungs. This in turn, reduces the supply of oxygen to the tissues which raises the carbon dioxide level, causing general depression. The excessive and indiscriminate use of drugs also leads to faulty assimilation of vitamins and minerals of the body and ultimately causes depression. The use of aspirin leads to deficiencies of vitamin C and antacids can cause deficiencies of calcium and vitamin B. Diabetes, low blood sugar (hypoglycemia) and weakness of the liver, resulting from the use of refined or processed foods, fried foods and an excessive intake of fats may also lead to depression.

Dietetic Treatment

The modern medical system treats depression with anti-depression drugs which provide temporary relief but have harmful side-effects and do not remove the causes or prevent its recurrence. The harmful side-effects include gross liver damage, hypersensitivity, insomnia, hallucinations, a confused state, convulsions and a fall in blood pressure.

DEPRESSION

In nature cure, emphasis is placed on diet which has a profound effect on the mental health of a person. Even a single nutritional deficiency can cause depression in susceptible people. Dr. Priscilla, associate clinical professor at the University of California, prescribes nutritional therapy to build up brain chemicals, such as serotonin and norepinephrine, that affect one's moods and are often lacking in depressed people. She recommends eating foods rich in B vitamins, such as whole grains, green vegetables, eggs and fish.

The diet of persons suffering from depression should completely exclude tea, coffee, alcohol, chocolate and cola, all white flour products, sugar, food colourings, chemical additives, white rice and strong condiments. The diet should be restricted to three meals. Fruits can be taken in the morning for breakfast with milk and a handful of nuts and seeds. Lunch may consist of steamed vegetables, whole wheat chappatis and a glass of butter-milk. For dinner, green vegetable salad and all available sprouts such as alfalfa seeds, mung, cottage cheese or a glass of butter-milk would be ideal.

The depressive mood can be overcome by activity. Those who are depressive will forget their misery by doing something. Exercise also plays an important role in the treatment of depression. It not only keeps the body physically and mentally fit but also provides recreation and mental relaxation. It also gives a feeling of accomplishment and thus reduces the sense of helplessness. The patient must also learn the art of scientific relaxation and meditation which will go a long way in curing depression.

TREATMENT CHART FOR DEPRESSION

A - DIET

I. Fast on juices for three days. Take a glass of fruit or vegetable juice every two hours, diluted with water during the day and cleanse the bowels with warm-water enema.

II. All-fruit diet for three further days. Take fresh juicy fruits at five-hourly intervals during this period.

Meditation is a simple and effective self-treatment for mental depression.

III. Thereafter, the following diet may be adopted:-
1. *Upon arising:* 25 black raisins soaked overnight in water alongwith water in which they are soaked and the water kept overnight in a copper vessel.
2. *Breakfast:* Fresh fruit, a glass of milk and a handful of raw nuts,
3. *Lunch:* A bowl of freshly-prepared steamed vegetables, two or three whole wheat chappatis and a glass of buttermilk.
4. *Mid-afternoon:* A glass of vegetable or fruit juice or sugarcane juice.
5. *Dinner:* A large bowl of fresh green vegetable salad and mung bean aprouts.

AVOID: Meats, sugar, white flour, tea, coffee, condiments, pickles refined and processed foods, fried foods and products made from sugar and white flour.

B - OTHER MEASURES

1. Drink eight to ten glasses of water daily.
2. Cool water bath twice daily.
3. Neutral immersion bath for one hour daily, before retiring.
4. Wet abdomen pack once daily.
5. Exercise, especially yogic asanas and brisk walks for 45 minutes daily, morning and evening.
6. Cultivate some good hobby and spend some time on it.
7. Meditation every morning.
8. Adequate rest and sleep.

CHAPTER 23

Diabetes

Diabetes mellitus is a nutritional disorder, characterised by an abnormally elevated level of blood glucose and by the excretion of the excess glucose in the urine. It results from an absolute or relative lack of insulin which leads to abnormalities in carbohydrate metabolism as well as in the metabolism of protein and fat.

Diabetes is a disease known to the medical world since time immemorial. Its incidence is, however, much higher at present than ever in the past. This is especially true in case of more advanced countries of the world due to widespread affluence and more generous food supply

The most commonly used screening tests are the determination of the fasting blood glucose level and the two-hour post-prandial, that is after a meal. The normal fasting blood sugar content is 80 to 120 mg. per 100 ml. of blood and this can go up to a level of 180 mg. per 100 ml. of blood two hours after meals. Anything above these norms can be termed diabetic levels.

Diabetes occurs in all age groups, from young infants to the elderly. The greatest incidence occurs in middle or older aged persons. It is estimated that 80 to 85 per cent of all individuals with diabetes mellitus are 45 years of age or older.

Symptoms

The word diabetes is derived from the Greek word meaning "to siphon; to pass through," and mellitus comes from the latin word "honey". Thus two characteristic symptoms, namely, copious urination and glucose in the urine give the name to the disease. The normal volume of urine passed daily is about three pints, but in the diabetic condition it can vary from eight to forty pints. The urine is of a pale colour, has an acidic reaction and sweetish odour. The quantity of sugar present in it varies from two to forty grams per ounce, the total per day in many cases reaching as much as two lbs. in 30 pints of urine.

A diabetic feels hungry and thirsty most of the time, does not put on weight, though he eats every now and then, and gets tired easily, both physically and mentally. He looks pale, may suffer from anaemia, constipation, intense itching around the genital organs, palpitations and general weakness. He feels drowsy and has a lower sex urge than a normal person.

Causes

Diabetes has been described by most biological doctors as a "prosperity" disease, primarily caused by systematic overeating and consequent obesity. Not only is the overeating of sugar and refined carbohydrates harmful but also of proteins and fats, which are transformed into sugar if taken in excess and may result in diabetes. Too much food taxes the pancreas and eventually paralyses its normal activity. It has been estimated that the incidence of diabetes is four times higher in persons of moderate obesity and 30 times higher in persons of severe obesity.

Grief, worry and anxiety also have a deep influence on the metabolism and may cause sugar to appear in the urine. The disease may be associated with some other grave organic disorders like cancer, tuberculosis and cerebral disease. Heredity is also a major factor in the development of the disease. It has been rightly said, "Heredity is like a cannon and obesity pulls the trigger."

Dietary Treatment

Any successful method of diabetes treatment should aim at removing the actual cause of the disease and building up the entire health-level of the patient. Diet therapy is the basis of such a treatment. The primary dietary consideraton for a diabetic patient is that he should be a strict lacto-vegetarian and take a low-caloric, low-fat, alkaline diet of high quality, natural foods. Fruits, nuts and vegetables, whole meal bread and dairy products form a good diet for the diabetic. These foods are best eaten in as dry a condition as possible to ensure thorough ensalvation during the first part of the process of digestion.

Cooked starchy foods should be avoided as in the process of cooking the cellulose envelops of the starch granules burst and consequently the starch is far too easily absorbed in the system. The excess absorbed has to be got rid of by the kidneys and appears as sugar in the urine. With raw starchy foods, however, the saliva and digestive juices in the small intestine regulate the quantities required to be changed into sugar for the body's needs. The unused and undigested portion of raw starchy foods does not become injurious to the system, as it does not readily ferment.

The diabetic should not be afraid to eat fresh fruits and vegetables which contain sugar and starch. Fresh fruits contain sugar (fructose) which does not need insulin for its metabolism and is well tolerated by diabetics. Fats and oils should be taken sparingly, for they are apt to lower the tolerance for proteins and starches. Emphasis should be on raw foods as they stimulate and increase insulin production. For protein, home-made cottage cheese, various forms of soured milk and nuts are best. The patients should avoid overeating and take four or five small meals a day rather than three large ones.

The following diet should serve as a guideline.

Upon arising: A glass of lukewarm water with freshly squeezed lemon juice.

Breakfast: Any fresh fruit with the exception of bananas, soaked prunes, a small quantity of whole meal bread with butter and fresh milk.

Lunch: Steamed or lightly cooked green vegetables such

as cauliflower, cabbage, tomatoes, spinach, turnip, asparagus and mushrooms, two or three whole wheat chappatis according to appetite and a glass of butter-milk or curd.

Mid-afternoon: A glass of fresh fruit or vegetable juice.

Dinner: A large bowl of salad made up of all the raw vegetables in season. The salad may be followed by a hot course, if desired, and fresh home-made cottage cheese.

Bedtime snack: A glass of fresh milk.

Flesh foods find no place in this regime, for they increase the toxaemic condition underlying the diabetic state and reduce the sugar tolerance. On the other hand, a non-stimulating vegetarian diet, especially one made up of raw foods, promotes and increases sugar tolerance. Celery, cucumbers, string beans, onion and garlic are especially beneficial. Cucumbers contain a hormone needed by the cells of the pancreas for producing insulin. Garlic has proved beneficial in reducing blood sugar in diabetes.

Recent scientific investigations have estabilshed that bitter gourd *(karela)* is highly beneficial in the treatment of diabetes: It contains an insulin-like principle, known as plant-insulin which has been found effective in lowering the blood and urine sugar levels. The diabetic patient should take the juice of three or four bitter gourds daily in between meals for positive results.

The patients should avoid tea, coffee and cocoa because of their adverse influence on the digestive tract. Other foods which should be avoided are white bread, white flour products, sugar, tinned fruits, sweets, chocolates, pastries, pies, puddings, refined cereals and alcoholic drinks.

The most important nutrient in the treatment of diabetes is manganese which is vital in the production of natural insulin. It is found in citrus fruits, in the outer covering of nuts, grains and in the green leaves of edible plants. Other nutrients of special value are zinc, B-complex vitamins and poly-unsaturated fatty acids.

TREATMENT CHART FOR DIABETES

A - DIET

1. *Upon arising:* Bitter gourd (*karela*), juice and a glass of lukewarm water with half a freshly-squeezed lime.
2. *Breakfast:* Any fresh fruit with the exception of bananas, a small quantity of whole meal bread with butter and fresh milk.

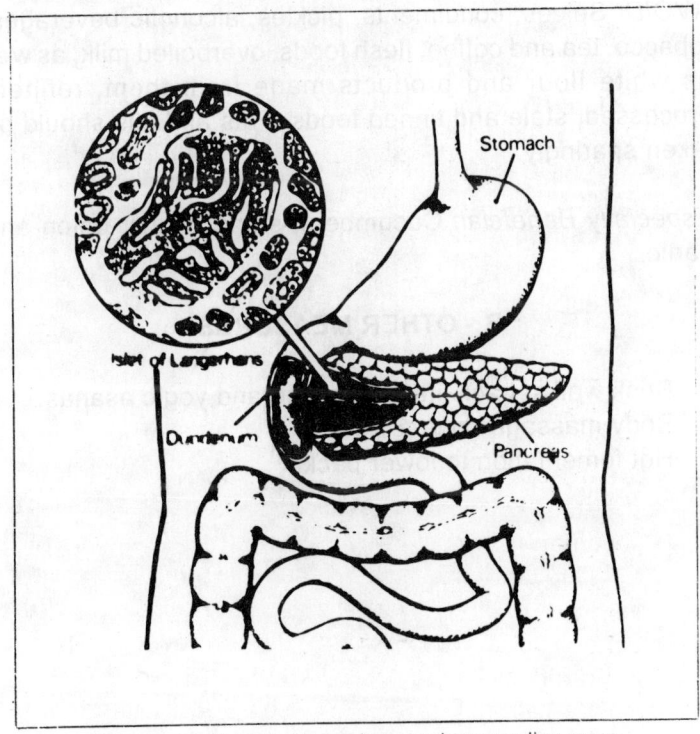

Pancreas with islet of langerhans and surrounding areas.

3. *Lunch:* A bowl of freshly-prepared steamed vegetables, one or two whole wheat chappatis, butter and a glass of buttermilk.
4. *Mid-afternoon:* A glass of fresh fruit or vegetable juice.
5. *Dinner:* A large bowl of raw vegetable salad, with lime juice dressing, sprouted mung beans and cottage cheese.

6. *Bedtime snack:* A glass of fresh milk or fresh fruit.

NOTE:
1. Fresh fruits contain sugar fructose, which does not need insulin for its metabolism and is well tolerated by diabetics.
2. Raw foods should be taken liberally as they stimulate and increase insulin production.

AVOID: Spices, condiments, pickles, alcoholic beverages, tobacco, tea and coffee, flesh foods, overboiled milk, as well as white flour and products made from them, refined, processed, stale and tinned foods. Fats and oils should be taken sparingly.

Especially Benefcial: Cucumbers, string beans, onion and garlic.

B - OTHER MEASURES

1. Brisk walks, back lifting exercise and yogic asanas.
2. Body massage once a week.
3. Hot fomentation to lower back.

CHAPTER 24

Diarrhoea

Diarrhoea refers to the frequent passage of loose or watery unformed stools. It may be acute or chronic. Commonly known as "loose motions", it is perhaps the most common disease in India.

The intestines normally get more than 10 litres of liquid per day which comes from the diet and from the secretions of the stomach, liver, pancreas and intestines. In the case of diarrohea, water is either not absorbed or is secreted in excess by the organs of the body. It is then sent to the colon where the water holding capacity is limited. Thus, the urge to defecate comes quite often.

Causes

There are many and varied causes of diarrhoea. The chief causes are overeating or eating of wrong foods, putrefaction in the intestine tract, fermentation caused by incomplete carbohydrate digestion, nervous irritability and excessive intake of laxatives. Other causes include infection by parasites, germs, virus, bacteria or a poison which has entered into the body through food, water or air, allergies to certain substances or even common foods such as milk, wheat, eggs and sea foods and emotional strain or stress in adults and fright in children.

It may also result from the use of antibiotic drugs. This is due to the destruction of the beneficial bacteria in intestines along with pathogenic bacteria at which the antibiotic treatment was aimed.

Diarrhoea may be a prominent feature of organic diseases affecting the small or large intestine such as the sprue syndrome, malignant disease and ulcerative colitis. It may also result from operations on the gastro-intestinal tract. Diarrhoea may alternate with constipation. This may be a result of the irritation of the mucous membrane by impacted hard faeces.

Diarrhoea for prolonged periods can lead to certain complications. These may include general weakening of health due to loss of vitamins like A, D, E and K and other nutrients as food is rushed through the body without giving the nutrients a chance of being absorbed, dehydration due to loss of body fluids and washing out of minerals from the body and nervous conditions.

Among the various complications, dehydration poses a serious problem, especially when diarrhoea is accompanied by vomiting. It can even be fatal if unchecked. Dehydration is characterised by hot, dry skin over the abdomen, sunken eyes, dry mouth, intense thirst and reduced flow of urine. This can usually be prevented, if the patient suffering from diarrhoea, with or without vomiting, is given plenty of liquids. The patient should be given about 150 to 200 ml. of fluid every hour from 6 a.m. to 10 p.m.

Dietary Cure

In severe cases of diarrhoea, it is advisable to observe a complete fast for two days to give rest to the gastro-intestinal tract. Warm water only may be taken during the period to compensate for the loss of fluids. An enema with water temperature of 95°F, may be taken daily during this period. Juices of fruits like orange or pomegranate, butter-milk, or coconut water may be taken after the acute symptoms are over. Barley water mixed with an equal quantity of milk, with added sugar, can also be given. In mild cases, well-boiled rice or *khichdi* (rice and mung dal cooked with a pinch of salt), with curd and ripe bananas are permitted.

Foods which should be avoided in diarrhoea are milk and milk-drinks, whole grain breads and cereals, cheese, fruits except banana, nuts, meats, fatty soups, sweets and all vegetables except tomato juice.

After the condition improves, meals can be enlarged grdually to include raw juices like papaya juice, lemon juice and fresh pineapple juice, cooked vegetables, whole rice, soured milks such as yogurt and butter-milk. Raw foods should be taken only after the patient completely recovers.

Certain natural remedies have been found effective in curing diarrhoea and these are carrot soup, banana, turmeric powder, the cultured or sour milk and garlic. Carrot soup supplies water to combat dehydration, replenishes sodium, potassiu, phosphorus, calcium, sulphur and magnesium, supplies pectin and coats the intestine to allay inflammation. It checks gthe growth of harmful intestinal bacteria and prevents vomiting. One pound of carrot may be cooked in five ounces of water until it is soft. The pulp should be strained and boiled water added to make a quart. Three-quarter tablespoon of salt may be mixed. The soup should be given in small amounts to the patient every half an hour.

Bananas congtain pectin and encourage the growth of beneficial bacteria. Turmeric, a yellow vegetable powder used as a condiment has proved beneficial. Acidified milk such as yogurt or butter-milk help ovecome the harmful intestinal flora and re-establish the benign or friendly flora. The acid in the soured milk also fights germs and bacteria. Garlic is yet another natural remedy which fights diarrhoea and routs parasites. It is a powerful, effective and harmless antibiotic and aids digestion.

TREATMENT CHART FOR DIARRHOEA

A - DIET

I. Complete fast for two days in severe cases, taking only warm water. Use warm-water enema daily during this period.

II. Take juices of orange, pomegranate, butter milk, coconut water and barley water, after acute symptom subside.

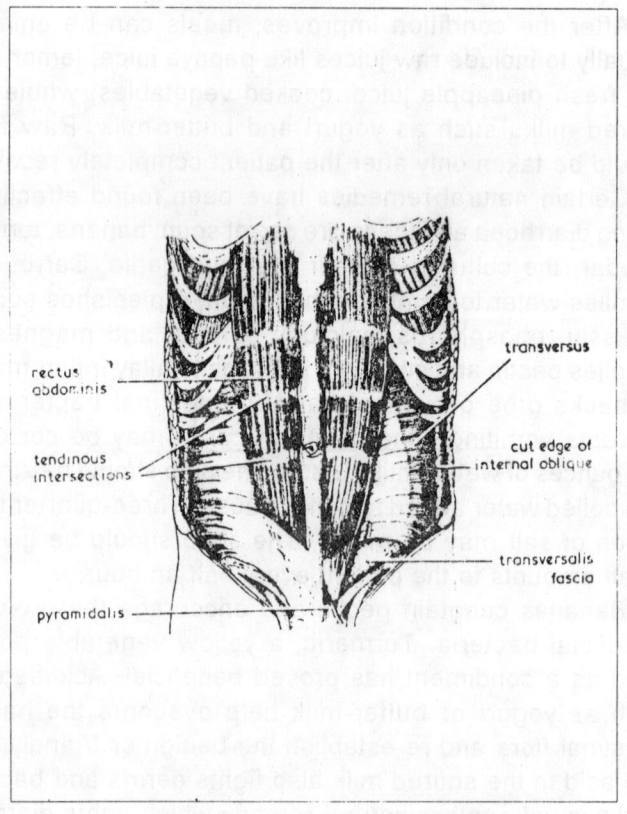

Deep Layer of Abdominal Muscles

III. Take well-boiled rice with curd and ripe bananas in mild cases.

IV. Thereafter, take fruit juices, cooked vegetables, whole rice and soured milks.

V. *Home Remedies:* Carrot soup, banana, turmeric powder, soured milks and garlic.

VI. *Avoid:* Milk and milk-drinks, whole grain breads and cereals, cheese, fruits except banana, nuts, meats, fatty soups, sweets and all vegetable except tomato juice till complete recovery.

B - OTHER MEASURES

1. Abdominal compress at 60° F renewed every 15-20 minutes.

2. Cold hip bath at 40° F-50° F.

3. Abdominal fomentations every two hours in case of pain.

CHAPTER 25

Dysentery

Dysentery refers to a serious condition affecting the large intestine. It is characterised by inflammation and ulceration of the bowel, a colic pain in the region of the abdomen and passing of liquid or semi-formed stools with mucus and blood. The disease is prevalent all over the world, except in very cold countries.

Dysentery is caused by two organisms, protozoa and bacilli. The former is generally known as amoebic dysentery and the later as bacillary dysentery. An attack of amoebic dysentery is milder in comparison with bacillary dysentery. But while bacillary dysentery can respond quickly to treatment, amoebic dysentery does not leave the patient easily, unless he is careful.

Symptoms

Dysentery may be acute or chronic. The acute form is characterised by pain in the abdomen, diarrhoea and dysenteric motions. The patient passes yellowish white mucus and sometimes only blood with stools. He feels a constant desire to evacuate, although there may be nothing to throw off except a little mucus and blood. As the disease advances, the quantity of mucus and blood increases. Occasionally, casts or shread of skin-like mucous membrane, from small fragments to 12 inches or so long and an inch wide, are seen to pass out with motions. Often the smell of the stools becomes very foetid. All the digestive processes are upset and the stomach loses power to digest and absorb food.

Chronic cases are after-effects of acute attacks. The patient does not recover completely. Stool remains putried and may contain blood, while diarrhoea and constipation may alternate, and general health is disturbed. In severe cases, the temperature may rise to 104-105°F. It may occasionally become subnormal also.

Causes

The cause of dysentery is said to be germ infection. The germs, which are supposed to cause this disease develop in the colon only as a result of putrefaction there of excessive quantities of animal protein food, fried substances, too-spiced foods and hard-to-digest fatty substances. The real cause of dysentery is thus dietary indiscretion and eating of excessive amounts of flesh food in hot weather or tropical climate unsuited to the digestion of such foods. Other causes include debility, fatigue, chill, lowered vitality, intestinal disorders and overcrowding under insanitary conditions.

Dietary Cure

The treatment of dysentery should aim at removing the offending and tonic matter from the intestine. It should help in alleviating painful symptoms, stopping the virulence of the bacteria and promoting healing of the ulcer.

To begin with, the patient should fast as long as acute symtoms are present. During this period, he should take only orange juice and water or buttermilk. The latter combats offending bacteria and helps in the establishment of beneficial micro-organisms in the intestines.

The patient may be given small doses of castor oil in the form of emulsion. This acts as a mild aperient and facilitates quicker removal of offensive matter, minimises the strain during motion and also acts as a lubricant to the ulcerated surfaces. The patient should also be given very low pressure warm water enema, admitting as much water as he can tolerate.

After the acute symptoms are over, the patient may be allowed rice, curd, fresh ripe fruits, especially, bael, banana and pomegranate and skimmed milk. Solid foods should be introduced very carefully and gradually according to pace of recovery. Flesh foods of all kinds should be avoided in future. Other foods, which should be avoided, are tea, coffee, white sugar and white flour and products made from them as well as alcohol in all forms. Foods which have a detoxyfying and cleansing effect upon the intentines such as fruits and vegetables, are most essential to the future dietary.

Among specific food remedies, bael fruit is perhaps the most efficacious in the treatment of dysentery of both the varieties. Pulp of the fruit mixed with jaggery should be given thrice daily. To deal with a chronic case of dysentery, the unripe fruit should be roasted over the fire and the pulp mixed with water. Large quantities of the infusion so made should be administered with jaggery. The pulp of the unripe fruit mixed with an equal quantity of dried ginger can also be given with buttermilk.

The use of pomegranate rind is another effective remedy for dysentery. About 60 grams of the rind should be boiled in 250 ml. of milk. It should be removed from the fire when one-third of the milk has evaporated. It should be administered to the patient in three equal doses at suitable intervals. This will bring relief.

Lemon juice is very effective in dealing with ordinary cases of dysentary. A few lemons, peeled and sliced, should be added to 250 ml. of water and boiled for a few minutes. The strained infusion should be given thrice daily.

Other Measures

The patient should take complete be rest, as movement induces pain and aggravates distressing symptoms. Hot water bag may be applied over the abdomen. Heating compresses may also be applied at 60°F over the abdomen. These compresses may be changed every half an hour or so. Hot foot bath, once or twice daily, will also be beneficial.

TREATMENT CHART FOR DYSENTERY

A - DIET

I. Fast on orange juice or buttermilk for 3 or 4 days. Take warm water enema daily during this period.

II. After the fast, take a light diet consisting of rice, curd, buttermilk, fresh ripe fruits, especially bael, banana, pomegranate, orange and skimmed milk for a week or so.

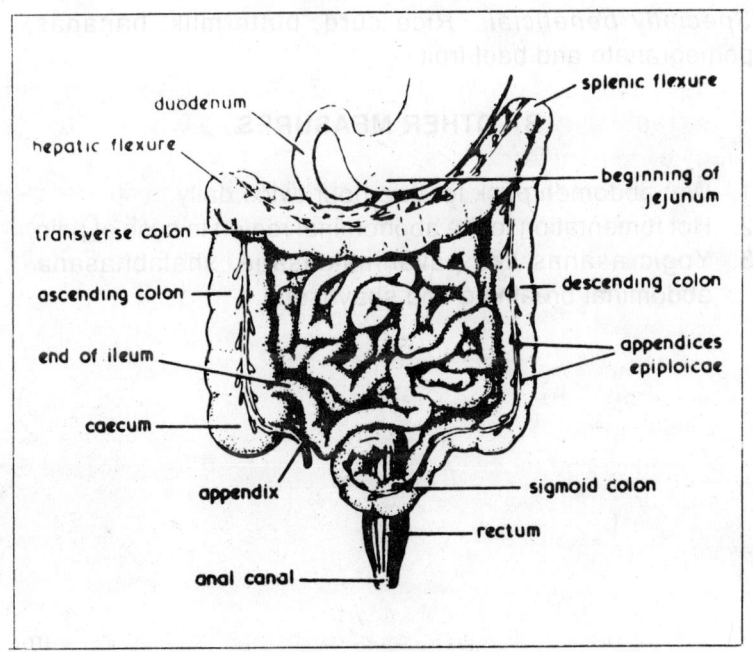

The small and large intestine

III. Thereafter gradually adopt a well-balanced diet as follows:-

1. *Upon arising:* A glass of lukewarm water with half a freshly-squeezed lime and a teaspoon of honey.
2. *Breakfast:* Fresh fruit and a glass of buttermilk.

3. *Lunch:* A bowl of freshly-prepared steamed vegetable, rice or whole wheat chappatis, curd or a glass of buttermilk.
4. *Mid-afternoon:* A glass of carrot juice or coconut water.
5. *Dinner:* A large bowl of fresh green vegetable salad, with lemon juice dressing, mung bean or alfalfa sprouts and vegetable soup.

AVOID: Flesh foods, alcohol, tea, coffee, sugar, white flour and products made from them, fried and refined foods.

Specially beneficial: Rice curd, buttermilk, bananas, pomegranate and bael fruit.

B - OTHER MEASURES

1. Wet abdomen pack for one hour twice daily.
2. Hot fomentation to the abodominal region in case of pain.
3. Yogic asanas like pavanmuktasana, shalabhasana, abdominal breathing and shavasana.

CHAPTER 26

Dyspepsia

Dyspepsia is a word of Greek origin meaning indigestion or difficulty in digestion. Any gastrointestinal symptom associated with taking of food is called dyspepsia. It is one of the most common ailments today and results from dietetic errors.

The stomach, which is the most used organ of the body, resembles a pear shaped pouch. It forms part of the digestive tract which is a tube coiled in loops, nearly 28 feet long. It varies in size and position depending on how much food it contains. An overloaded stomach prevents the diaphragm from functioning properly. It may also press on the heart.

Symptoms

Abdominal pain, a feeling of over-fullness after eating, heartburn, loss of appetite, nausea or vomiting and flatulence or gas are the usual symptoms of dyspepsia. Vomiting usually produces relief. What is vomited is intensely sour to the taste. Other symptoms are a foul taste in the mouth, coated tongue and bad breath. At times a sensation of strangling in the throat is experienced. In most cases of indigestion, the patient suffers from constipation which adds to the acidity of the system.

Causes

The main causes for dyspepsia are overeating, eating wrong food combinations, eating too rapidly and neglecting proper mastication and salivation of food. Overeating or frequent eating produces a feverish state in the system and overtaxes the digestive organs. It produces excessive acid and causes the gastric mucous membrane to become congested. Hyperacidity is the common result. Overeating makes the work of the stomach, liver, kidneys and bowels harder. When this food putrefies, its poisons are absorbed back into the blood and consequently, the whole system is poisoned.

Many persons, who gulp their food due to stress and hurry, suffer from this ailment. When food is swallowed in large chunks, the stomach has to work harder and more hydrochloric acid is secreted. Eating too fast also causes one to swallow air. These bad habits force some of the digestive fluid into the oesophagus, causing burning, a stinging sensation or a sour taste, giving an illusion of stomach acid.

Certain foods, especially if they are not properly cooked, cause dyspepsia. Some people react unfavourably to certain foods like beans, cabbage, onions, cucumber, radishes and sea-foods. Fried foods as well as rich and spicy foods often cause abdominal discomfort and gas or aggravate the existing condition. Excessive smoking and intake of alcohol can also cause stomach upset. Constipation may interfere with the normal flow through the gastrointestinal tract, resulting in gas and abdominal pain. The habit of eating and drinking together is another cause of indigestion as taking liquids with meals dilutes the digestive juices and diminishes their potency. Insomnia, emotions such as jealousy, fear and anger and lack of exercise are among the other causes of this ailment.

Dietary Cure

The only effective treatment for dyspepsia is a thorough cleansing of the digestive tract and adoption of sensible dietary habits thereafter, along with change in style of living. The best way to commence the treatment is to adopt an all-fruit diet for about five days. In this regimen, the patient should take three meals a day of fresh juicy fruits such as apples, pears, grapes, oranges, grape-fruits, pineapples, peaches and melons. Dried, stewed or tinned fruits, however, should not be taken. No other foodstuff should be added to the fruit meals, otherwise the value of the treatment will be lost.

In case of severe dyspepsia, it will be advisable to fast for two or three days before adopting an all-fruit diet. After the all-fruit diet, the patient may take a restricted diet of easily digestible foods, consisting of lightly cooked vegetables, juicy fruits and butter-milk for about ten days. He may, then gradually embark upon a well-balanced diet as outlined in Chapter 1 (Diet in health and disease).

Further short periods of two or three days on the all-fruit diet at monthly or two monthly intervals may be necessary in certain cases, depending on the progress.

Spices and condiments such as pepper, mustard, vinegar or pickles, which make food more palatable and lead to over-eating, must be avoided. Alcohol, tobacco, strong tea and coffee, highly seasoned meats, over-boiled milk, pulses, potato, rice, cheese, refined, processed, stale and tinned foods should all be avoided. Curds and cottage cheese may be used freely.

A home remedy for chronic dyspepsia is to chew about one gram of ginger with powder of rock salt before meals. For flatulence and gas, garlic is an excellent remedy. It neutralises putrefactive toxins and kills unhealthy bacteria. It also eliminates gas and helps digestion.

B vitamins are also beneficial in case of dyspepsia. B1 or thiamine is especially useful for the digestion of starches. But it should be ensured that the whole B complex group in some form is added to prevent imbalance which may be caused if only one B factor is given.

The sufferer from dyspepsia must always follow the under-mentioned rules regarding eating:

(i) Never eat and drink together. Water or other liquids should be taken half an hour before and one hour after a meal. Milk, butter-milk and vegetables soups are, however, foods and can be taken with meals.

(ii) Never hurry through a meal. Eat very slowly and

chew your food as thoroughly as possible.

(iii) Never fill the stomach completely. Always leave the table with a feeling that you could eat more.

(iv) Never sit down to a meal feeling worried, tired, excited or in a bad temper as such feelings temporarily paralyse the manufacture of digestive juices including hydrochloric acid.

(v) Do not eat if appetite is lacking. Miss a meal or two, if necessary, until real appetite returns.

(vi) Never boil vegetables, always steam them.

(vii) Do not mix too many foods at the same meal. Never eat raw vegetables and raw fruits together as they require a different set of enzymes. Take protein and starchy foods separate as far as possible.

TREATMENT CHART FOR DYSPEPSIA

A - DIET

I. Raw juice diet for three to five days. A glass of fresh fruit or vegetable juice diluted with water should be taken every two hours during the day and warm water enema used to cleanse the bowels.

II. An all-fruit diet for further three to five days

III. Thereafter, gradually adopt a well-balanced diet on the following lines:-

1. *Upon arising:* 25 black raisins soaked overnight in water along with water in which they are soaked and water kept overnight in copper vessel.
2. *Breakfast:* Fresh fruit and a glass of milk, sweetened with honey.
3. *Lunch:* A bowl of freshly-prepared steamed vegetable, two or three whole wheat chappatis and a glass of buttermilk.
4. *Mid-afternoon:* A glass of carrot juice or coconut water.
5. *Dinner:* A large bowl of fresh green vegetable salad with

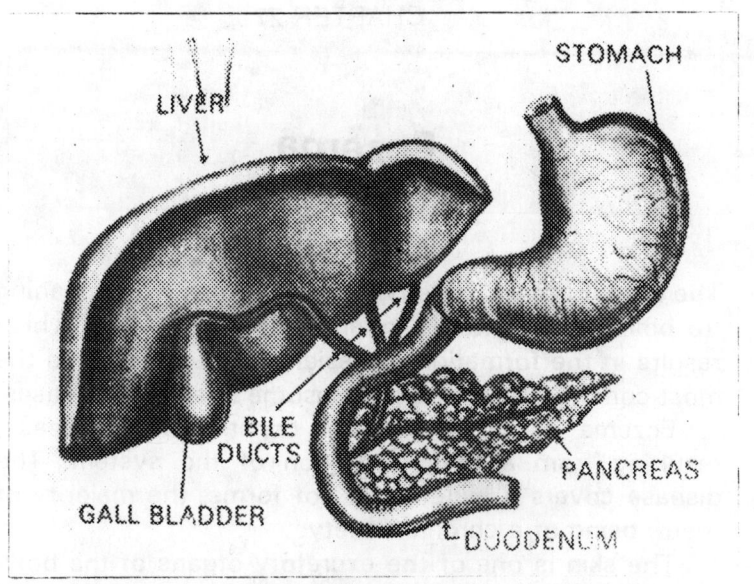

The Main Digestive Organs

lemon juice dressing, mung bean sprouts, cottage cheese or a glass of buttermilk.
6. *Bed time Snack:* A glass of milk or one apple.

NOTE: Raw juice diet for two days followed by all-fruit diet for three days should be repeated at an interval of one month till the condition improved.

AVOID: Tea, coffee, sugar, white flour, all products made from them, refined foods, flesh foods, condiments, pickles fried foods, smoking and alcohol.

B - OTHER MEASURES

1. Drink at least six to eight glasses of water daily. Water should, however, not be taken with meals, but half an hour before or an hour after a meal.
2. Cold hip bath for 10 minutes daily and wet abdomen pack for one hour daily on an empty stocmach.
3. Yogic asanas.

CHAPTER 27

Eczema

The term 'Eczema' is derived from a Greek word meaning 'to boil'. It refers to an inflammation of the skin which results in the formation of vesicles or pustules. It is the most common and most troublesome of all skin diseases.

Eczema is essentially a constitutional disease, resulting from a toxic condition of the system. The disease covers a wide variety of forms, the majority of them, being of a chronic variety.

The skin is one of the excretory organs of the body through which large quantities of toxic matter are easily eliminated. Because of its large surface, it can effectively eliminate waste matter which other organs of elimination — namely the kidneys, intestines and lungs — do not have the capacity to handle.

Symptoms

Eczema, in its acute form, is indicated by redness and swelling of the skin, the formation of minute vesicles and severe heat. If the vesicles rupture, a raw, moist surface is formed. From this, a colourless discharge oozes, which forms skin crusts when it accumulates. The disease is usually worse at night when the heat of the body is retained by the bed-clothes.

The skin itches at all stages. In the wet stage, it may become infected with bacteria. Healing of the condition is affected by scratching in response to the irritation. Scratching not only spreads infection but also lengthens the stage of drying and scaling.

Causes

Allergies play an important part in causing eczema.

Some women get eczema on their hands due to an allergy to soap or detergents used to wash clothes or dishes. Some persons develop it around the fingers when they wear rings because of allergy to metals. Researchers at the University of Texas Health Science Centre at San Antonio, in a recent study of children with atropic eczema, found that 75 per cent were allergic to a number of foods. The most common triggers for sensitive persons are eggs, peanuts, chocolate, wheat, cow's milk, chicken and potato.

The real cause of eczema is the failure of the human system to excrete the poisons from the various orifices of the body. Waste matter is excreted from the rectum through stools, from the bladder through urine, from the lungs through breath and from the pores of the skin through sweat. Sometimes the pores of the skin are overworked as waste matter is not properly eliminated from the other orifices. If the pores are not given the chance to perform their normal function, the sweat will be full of toxic matter and this will give rise to skin diseases like eczema, acne, boils and other eruptions.

Eczema can also be caused by stress. The skin is recognised as the release organ for built-up tension. Senior executives who have often to face labour problems or carry out time-bound assignments fall prey to the skin disorders known as tension or stress eczema. It manifests itself on hands and feet and behind the neck through circular oozing lesions. The condition can also be brought about by a nagging spouse, jealousy, frustration and a host of other emotions. Other causes include faulty metabolism, constipation and nutritional deficiencies. Suppressive drug treatment of former diseases is also a most potent subsidiary causative factor in many cases.

Dietary Cure

Skin applications to cure eczema may give temporary relief. If the exudation is suppressed, some other more serious disease may develop. The best way to deal with eczema is to cleanse the blood stream and the body.

The treatment should start with a fast on orange juice and water from five to ten days, depending on the severity and duration of the trouble. Juice fasting will help eliminate toxic waste from the body and lead to substantial improvement. In some cases, the condition may worsen in the beginning of the fast due to the increased elimination of waste matter through the skin. But as fasting continues, improvement will manifest itself.

Fruits, raw or steamed vegetables without salt, served with whole meal bread or chappatis may be taken after the juice fast. Coconut oil may be used instead of ghee. After a few days, curd and milk may be added to the diet. Carrot and musk melon are particularly beneficial. The patients may thereafter gradually embark upon a well-balanced diet of three basic food groups namely, seeds, nuts and grains, vegetables and fruits. A large proportion of the diet should consist of raw foods. Seeds and beans such as alfalfa, mung and soyabeans can be sprouted. This diet may be supplemented with cold-pressed vegetable oils, honey and yeast. Juice fasting may be repeated at intervals of two months or so, depending on the progress being made. In chronic and more difficult cases of eczema, the patient should fast at least once a week till he is cured.

The patient should avoid tea, coffee, alcoholic beverages and all condiments and highly flavoured dishes. He should also avoid sugar, white-flour products, denatured cereals like polished rice and pearled barley and tinned or bottled foods. He should eat only pure and wholesome foods.

Raw vegetable juices, especially carrot juice in combination with spinach juice, have proved highly beneficial in the treatment of eczema. The proportions considered helpful in this combination are carrot ten ounces and spinach six ounces to make sixteen ounces or one pint of juice.

The patient should get as much fresh air as possible. Restrictive clothing should not be worn. Two or three litres of water should be taken daily and the patient must bathe twice or thrice a day. The skin, with the exception of the parts affected with eczema, should be vigorously rubbed with the palms of the hands before taking a bath.

Coconut oil may be applied to the portions with eczema. It will help the skin to stay soft. Walking or jogging should be resorted to in order to activate the bowels. Sunbathing is also beneficial as it kills the harmful bacteria and should be resorted to early in the morning, in the first light of dawn. A light mudpack applied over the sites of the eczema is also helpful. The pack should be applied for an hour at a time. Repeat twice or thrice a day.

Eczema as a result of dyspepsia, gout or diabetes can be cured only after these diseases have been successfully treated. Children suffering from eczema due to insanitary bottle feeds can get relief if kept on fruit juices or water with a teaspoon of honey added.

TREATMENT CHART FOR ECZEMA

A - DIET

I. Raw juice diet for three to five days. A glass of fresh fruit or vegetable juice should be taken every two hours from 8 a.m. to 8 p.m. and the bowels should be cleansed daily through warm water enema, during this period.

II. An all-fruit diet for further three to five days. In this regimen, take three meals a day of fresh juicy fruits at five-hourly intervals.

III. After the all-fruit diet, a restricted diet consisting of fruits, salt-free, raw or steamed vegetables with whole meal bread or chappatis may be taken for about seven days.

IV. Thereafter, a balanced diet on the followng lines may be adopted:-

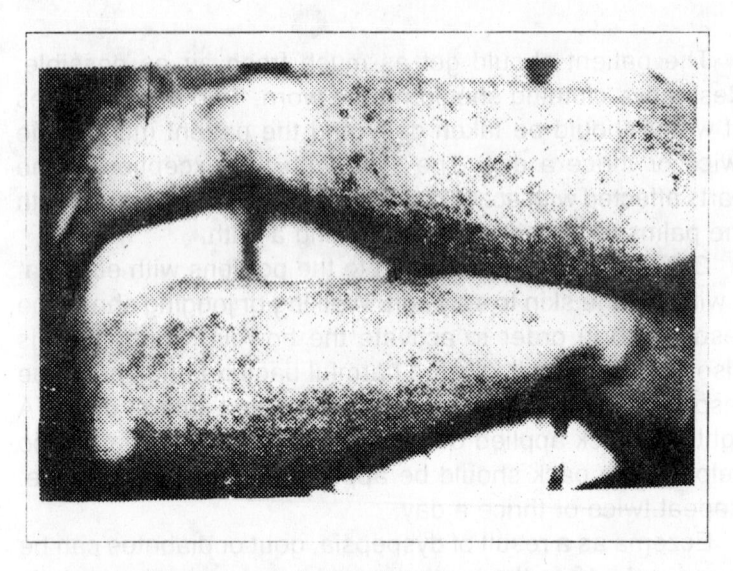

Eczema: vesicular, crusted type on forearms.

IV. Thereafter, a balanced diet on the followng lines may be adopted:-

1. *Upon arising:* A glass of lukewarm water with half a freshly squeezed lime and a teaspoon of honey.
2. *Breakfast:* Fresh fruits, a handful of raw nuts and a glass of milk.
3. *Lunch:* A bowl of freshly prepared steamed vegetables, one or two whole wheat chappatis and a glass of buttermilk.
4. *Mid-afternoon:* A glass of fresh fruit or vegetable juice.
5. *Dinner:* A large bowl of fresh green vegetable salad with lemon juice dressing, sprouts and cottage cheese or a glass of buttermilk.

AVOID: Tea, coffee, alcoholic beverages, flesh foods, condiments and highly flavoured dishes, sugar, white flouR and all products made from them and denatured cereals.

B - OTHER MEASURES

1. Sunbath everyday early morning and fresh air as much as possible.
2. Mud pack over the sites of eczema for one hour twice daily.
3. Cold compress or cold wet fomentations in case of acute eczema and hot compresses or hot fomentations in case of chronic eczema.

CHAPTER 28

Epilepsy

Epilepsy refers to a chronic condition in which repeated fits or attacks of unconsciousness occur with or without convulsions. Known as 'falling sickness' it is a serious disorder of the central nervous system. It occurs in both children and adults. Most attacks however, occur in childhood and in early adult life. Attack rates show a progressive decline in frequence with age.

Epilepsy is a very ancient disease which afflicted some of the world's greatest personalities, including Napoleon, Alexander and Julius Ceasar. The actual word "epilepsy" comes from the Greek word which means "to seize upon". The ancient people believed that evil spirts entered the body of the persons afflicted, seized upon his soul and threw his body into convulsions. The Greeks believed that the gods induced this disease. The early Christians blamed the Devil for these convulsions.

Symptoms

Epilespy is recognised by recurrent sudden attacks at irregular intervals. The patients twitch convulsively and fall unconscious to the ground during these attacks which cause tremendous nervous upheavel. There are two main types of epilepsy known as petit mal and grand mal. Each follows its own specific pattern.

In petit mal, which is a less serious form of epilepsy, an attack comes and goes within a few seconds. The patient has a momentary loss of consciousness, with no convulsions except sometimes a slight rigidity, or there may be a slight convulsive attack such as a jerk, or movement of the eyes, head, trunk or extremities, with no perceptible loss of consciousness. The patient may not fall. He may suddenly stop what he is doing and then resume it when the attack is over, without even being aware of what has happened. Petit mal attacks may occur at any time in life but are most frequent in children.

The attack in case of grand mal comes with a dramatic effect. There are violent contractions of the arms, legs and body, accompanied by a sudden loss of consciousness. Before the onset of an attack, some patients have a warning or aura in the form of strange sensations such as a current of air or a stream of water flowing over the body, noises, odours and flashes of light. In a typical attack, the patient cries out, falls to the ground, loses consciousness and develops convulsions. With the convulsions may come foaming at the mouth, twitching of the muscles, biting of the tongue, distorted fixation of limbs, rotation of the head and deviation of the eyes. The patient may lose control over his bladder rectal muscles. The attack may last several minutes and is usually followed by a deep sleep. On waking up, the patient may remember nothing of what happened to him.

People who suffer from epilepsy are not abnormal in any other way. They usually know that fits can be triggered off by particular stimuli. Between epileptic attacks, their brain functions normally.

Causes

Epilepsy denotes electrical malfunctioning within the brain due to damage to brain cells or some inherited abnormality. There are many causes of epilepsy. Digestive disturbances, intestinal toxaemia and a strained nervous condition are very often the main cause of petit mal. Grand mal usually results from hereditary influences, serious shock or injury to the brain or nervous system. Meningitis, typhoid and other diseases, attendant with prolonged high temperature, can also lead to grand mal.

Epilepsy may be caused by several other factors. It may result from allergic reaction to certain food substances, especially some particular form of protein which is the main constitutent of meat. Circulatory disorders such as hardening of the arteries leading to the brain may also cause epileptic seizures. This type is rare and occurs only in very aged people.

Chronic alcoholism, lead poisoning, cocaine and other such habits can also lead to this disease. Other causes of epileptic seizure include mental conflict, deficient mineral assimilation, particularly of magnesium and calcium and wrong vitamin metabolism. According to some researchers, hypoglycemia or low blood sugar is also involved in most cases of epilepsy.

Dietetic Treatment

In the natural treatment, the sufferer from epilepsy has to follow a rigorous regimen consisting of a strict diet, complete relaxation and optimum exercise in the open air. He must adhere to a simple and correct natural life. He must assume a cheerful, optimistic attitude, refrain from mental and physical overwork and worry.

The most important aspect of the treatment is the diet. To begin with, the patient should be placed on an exclusive fruit diet for first few days. During this period, he should have three meals a day of fresh juicy fruits such as oranges, apples, grapes, grape-fruits, peaches, pears, pineapples and melons. Thereafter, he may gradually adopt a well-balanced diet of three basic food groups, namely seeds, nuts and grains; vegetables and fruits, with emphasis on sprouted seeds such as alfalfa seeds and mung beans, raw vegetables and fruits. The diet should include a moderate amount of raw milk, preferably raw goat's milk, and milk products such as raw butter and home-made cottage cheese.

The diet should eliminate completely all animal proteins, except milk, as they not only lack in magnesium but also rob the body of its own magnesium storage as well as of vitamin B6. Both these substances are needed in large amounts by the epileptics. Best food sources of magnesium are raw nuts, seeds, soyabeans, green leafy vegetables such as spinach, kale and beet tops. The patient should avoid all refined foods, fried and greasy foods, sugar and products made with it, strong tea, coffee, alcoholic beverages, condiments and pickles. He should avoid overeating and take frequent small meals rather than a few large ones.

If the patient has previously taken strong drugs for many years, he should not leave off engtirely, all at once. The dosage may be cut to half to begin with and then gradually reduced further until it can be left off completely.

Epileptics should strictly observe all the natural laws of good health and build and maintain the highest level of general health. They should remain active mentally but avoid all severe mental and physical stress. And above all, they should avoid excitement of all kinds.

TREATMENT CHART FOR EPILEPSY

A - DIET

I. An all-fruit diet for three to five days, taking three meals a day of fresh juicy fruits at five-hourly intervals.

II. Thereafter, adopt a well-balanced diet, on the following lines:-

1. *Upon arising:* A glass of lukewarm water with half a freshly-squeezed lime and a teaspoon of honey.
2. *Breakfast:* Fresh fruit, a glass of milk, preferably goat's milk, sweetened with honey and some nuts, preferably almonds.
3. *Lunch:* A bowl of freshly-prepared steamed vegetables, two or three whole wheat chappatis and a glass of butter milk.
4. *Mid-afternoon:* A glass of fresh fruit or vegetable juice.
5. *Dinner:* A bowl of raw vegetable salad and sprouts with lime juice dressing, followed by a hot course, if desired.

Brain: 1. cerebrum; 2. cerebellum; 3. spinal cord.

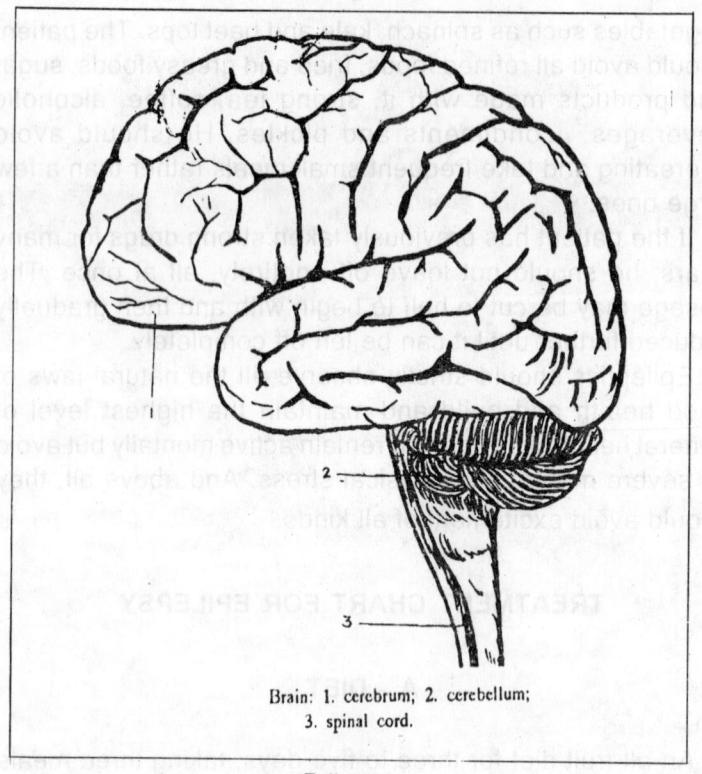

Epilepsy

6. *Bedtime Snack:* A glass of milk or one apple.

III. Always follow the undermentioned rules regarding eating:-

1. Do not take water with meals, but half an hour before and one hour afte a meal.
2. Eat very slowly and chew your food as thoroughly as possible.
3. Never eat to full stomach.

Home Remedies: Grape juice, vegetable juices, garlic, turnip, brahmi booti and Indian Spikenard (Jatamansi).

AVOID: Tea, coffee, sugar, white flour and products made

from them, refined foods, fried foods, flesh foods, tinned and preserved foods, condiments and pickles.

B - OTHER MEASURES

1. Fresh air, brisk walks, bycycling, swimming and shavasana.
2. Alternate hot and cold compresses to the back of the head at the base of the brain.

CHAPTER 29

Fatigue

Fatigue refers to a feeling of tiredness or weariness. It can be temporary or chronic. Almost every person has to work overtime on certain occasions, sacrificing rest and sleep, which may cause temporary fatigue. This condition can be remedied by adequate rest. Chronic or continuous fatigue is, however, a serious problem which requires a comprehensive plan of treatment.

Chronic fatigue can result from a variety of factors. A specific character trait, compulsiveness, can lead to continuous fatigue. Many persons constantly feel that they cannot take rest until they finish everything that needs to be done at one time. These persons are usually perfectionists, tense and cannot relax unless they complete the whole job, no matter how tired they may be.

Causes

The chief cause of fatigue is lowered vitality or lack of energy due to wrong feeding habits. Fatigue is an indication that the cells of the body are not getting sufficient live atoms in the food to furnish them with the constant flow of needed energy.

The habitual use of refined foods such as white sugar, refined cereals and white flour products as well as processed, tinned and preserved foods have a very bad effect on the system in general. Foods 'denatured' in this way are deprived, to a very great extent, of their invaluable vitamins and minerals. Such foods lead to nervousness, tiredness, obesity and a host of other complaints prevalent today.

Certain physical conditions can cause fatigue. Anaemia is a very common ailment leading to tiredness. It is known as 'tired blood' disturbance. In anaemia, very little oxygen reaches the tissues with the result that energy cannot be produced normally. This causes constant tiredness and mental depression. Anaemia usually results from deficiencies of iron and vitamin B12. Sometimes deficiencies of vitamin B6 and folic acid are also involved.

Insomnia or lack of sleep can be a cause of torturing fatigue. Sleep induced by sleeping pills and other drugs does not banish fatigue. In fact the longer sleeping pills are used, the more nagging and chronic the fatigue becomes. Besides causing fatigue, sleeping pills lead to nervous tension which increases fatigue still more. The harmful effects of wakefulness are indeed small compared with the effects of sleeping pills. Insomnia can be remedied by correcting diet and developing the will to relax.

Intestinal parasites can also lead to fatigue as they rob the body of good nourishment and gorge themselves on rich red blood. Other ailments which can cause fatigue are low blood pressure, low blood sugar, any kind of infection in the body, liver damage, a sluggish thyroid and allergy to certain foods and drugs caused by additives including artifical flavours, colours and preservatives.

Mental tension is one of the major causes of fatigue. The person who is tense and cannot relax has all the muscles of his body more or less contracted. This leads to needless waste of unusually large amounts of energy. Food is continuously burnt, lactic acid accumulates more rapidly than it can be carried to the liver for conversion to body starch. Persons who are high-strung, nervous and irritable usually suffer from this type of fatigue.

Unresolved emotional problems can also result in fatigue. Resentment to a situation, environment and even to a person can greatly contribute to the feeling of tiredness. It is better to express one's emotions rather than store them. Other emotional factors like worry, a feeling of boredom and a defeatist mentality can result in fatigue.

Dietary Treatment

Nutritional measures are most vital in the treatment of fatigue. Studies reveal that people who eat small midmeals suffer less from fatigue and nervousness, think more clearly and are more efficient than those who eat only three meals daily. These midmeals should consist of fresh or dried fruits, fresh fruit or vegetable juices, raw vegetables or a small sandwich of whole grain bread. The midmeal should be small and less food should be consumed at regular meals. They should be taken at specified times such as 11 a.m., 4 p.m. and before retiring.

The patient should eat healthy foods which supply energy to the body. Charles De Coti Marsh of London in his book 'Prescription for Energy' prescribes foods to relieve fatigue and gain energy. He says, "Regenerating must begin with foods.... They must be taken in their natural state. These cereals are corn seeds. They must be freshly milled. In uncooked cereals we do have one perfect food for perfect health which contains the essential vitamins and energy creators". In addition to cereal seeds, Marsh recommends fresh raw nuts taken directly from the shell and root vegetables. He says, "Any seed or root vegetable that will grow again will renew human vitality."

The patient should take an optimum diet made up of seeds, nuts and grains, vegetables and fruits. Roughly, each food group should supply the bulk of one of the three meals. Sprouting is an excellent way to eat seeds, beans and grains in raw form. Sprouting increases the nutritional value of foods and many new vitamins are created or multiplied in seeds during sprouting. The patient should supplement the three health-building food groups with special protective foods such as milk, high quality cold-pressed unrefined vegetable oils and honey.

The patient should also take natural vitamin and mineral supplements as an effective assurance against nutritional deficiencies as such deficiencies have been found to be a factor in fatigue. Lack of pantothenic acid, a B vitamin, in particular leads to extreme fatigue as deficiency of this vitamin is associated with exhaustion of the adrenal glands. It should, however, be remembered that while taking pantothenic acid separately, the entire B-complex should be added to avoid imbalance of other B vitamins. In fact the entire B-complex protects nerves and increases energy by helping to nourish and regulate glands. The vegetarian foods rich in vitamin B are wheat and other whole grain cereals, green leafy vegetables, unpolished rice, milk, nuts, banana, yeast, pulses and peas.

Other vitamins play specific roles in fatigue in connection with various ailments. The fatigue will disappear by correcting deficiencies. Minerals are also important. Potassium is especially needed for protection against fatigue. Raw green vegetables are rich in this mineral. Calcium is essential for relaxation and is beneficial in cases of insomnia and tension both of which can lead to fatigue. Sodium and zinc are also beneficial in the treatment of fatigue.

Raw vegetable juices, especially carrot juice, taken separately or in combination with juices of beets and cucumbers, is highly valuable in overcoming fatigue. The proportions considered helpful in the combination juice of sixteen ounces are carrot ten ounces, and beet and cucumber three ounces each.

The patient should avoid depending on crutches for energy lift such as taking aspirin, tranquilizers and other drugs, drinking coffee or alcohol, smoking, eating some sugar or sweets. They give only a temporary boost and this is soon followed by a downward plunge of energy, leaving a person worse than before. Such crutches are very harmful in the long run and may result in diseases such as hypoglycemia or low blood sugar and alcoholism.

TREATMENT CHART FOR FATIGUE

A - DIET

Take optimum diet, consisting of seeds, nuts and grains, vegetables and fruits supplemented by milk, high quality unrefined vegetable oils and honey, on the following lines:-

1. *Upon arising:* A glass of lukewarm water with half a freshly squeezed lime and a teaspoon of honey.
2. *Breakfast:* Fresh fruit, a glass of milk, sweetened with honey and some seeds or nuts.

The patient suffering from Fatigue should take optimum diet consisting of seeds, nuts and grains, vegetables and fruits.

3. *Mid-morning:* A small sandwitch of whole grain bread.
4. *Lunch:* A bowl of freshly-prepared steamed vegetables, two or three whole wheat chappatis and a glass of butter milk.
5. *Mid-afternoon:* A glass of fresh fruit or vegetable juice.
6. *Dinner:* A bowl of raw vegetable salad and sprouts such as alfalfa and mung beans, with lime juice and vegetable

oil dressing, followed by a hot course if desired.
7. *Bedtime Snack:* A glass of mil or one apple.

Important: Take frequent small meals rather than three large ones.

AVOID: Tea, coffee, sugar, white flour and products made from them, refined foods, fried foods, flesh foods, condiments, pickles, alcohol and smoking. Take salt in a very minute quantity.

Especially Beneficial: Whole grain cereals, fresh raw nuts, dates, grapefruit, sprouted seeds, raw green leafy vegetables, root vegetables, raw vegetables juices, natural vitamin and mineral supplements, especially B vitamins, potassium, calcium, sodium and zinc.

B - OTHER MEASURES

1. Fresh air, breathing and other light exercises.
2. Proper sleep and adequate rest.

CHAPTER 30

Fever

The term fever applies to a condition of the body in which the temperature goes above the normal. It is also characterised by disturbance in normal functioning of the system. It is a common ailment which affects persons of all age groups.

The normal temperature of the body in health ranges between 98.4° F and 99.5° or 36.9°C and 37.5°C. It is liable to marginal variations, depending on the intake of food, the amount of exercise and the temperature surounding the atmosphere. The lowest temperature of the body is between the hours 1.30 A.M. to 7 A.M. and the highest between 4 P.M. and 9 P.M.

The temperature can be taken by a clinical thermometer, which is basically a bulb of mercury connected to a narrow tube inside a glass case. There are marked degrees of temperature upon this thermometre. As the mercury is warmed, it rises up the cube and the body temperature is that at which the mercury stops. To get a true reading of the body temperature, it should not be measured after undue exertion, or after a hot drink either of which activities cause the temperature to rise and so give a false reading.

Symptoms

Fever usually begins by a slight shivering, headache, pain in other parts of the body, thirst and great lessitude. The urine is scanty. There may be constipation, nausea and vomiting. The pulse and respirations are speeded up. Then finally, there is profuse sweating, a copious flow of concentrated urine and general relief of symptoms.

A high temperature is often accomopanied by delirium. If the temperature of the body during an attack of fever reaches 106°F, the condition is known as hyper pyrexia (high fever). It is an indication of danger. If the temperature goes above 107°F, and remains so for any length of time, death may be inevitable.

Causes

Ther term fever has a very wide application. It is the symptom of a body's fight amongst infection. It is one of the most common features of several diseases. In many cases, it is a secondary symptoms of the disordered state of the body with which it is associated.

The real cause of all fevers, including common fever, however, is the accumulation of morbid matter in the system due to wrong feeding habits and unhygienic conditions of living. Fever is thus, a natural attempt on the part of the body to rid itself of toxic matter. It is not the result of germ infection, as is generally believed. If it was true, all persons exposed to an infection should get it.

Dietry Treatment

Fever being a natural healing crisis, it should be helped to run its normal course. Any interference with this natural process by administration of drugs will only enable the body to retain the morbid matter which caused this condition. If dealt with in natural way, the common fever, where there are no complications, will subside in two or three days.

To begin with, the patient should be put on a fast on orange juice and water. The procedure is to take the juice of an orange in a glass of warm water every two hours during the day. It will provide energy, increases urinary output and promote body resistance against infection, thereby hastening recovery. Warm-water enema should be given daily to cleanse the bowels during this period.

After the temperature has come down to normal and the

tongue has cleared, the patient may adopt an all-fruit diet for further two days. In this regimen, he should take three meals a day of fresh juicy fruits such as apple, pear, grapes, orange, pineapple, peach, melon or any othe juicy fruit in season. For drinks, unsweetened lemon water or plain water, either hot or cold may be taken. Thereafter, the patient may gradually embark upon a well-balanced diet, with emphasis on fresh fruits and raw or lightly-cooked vegetables.

Certain home remedies have been found beneficial in the treatment of common fever. The use of the leaves of holy basil (tulsi) is the most effective of these remedies. A decoction made by about 12 grams of these leaves, boiled with half a litre of water, should be administered with milk, sugar and powdered cardamon (chhoti elaichi). This will bring down the temperature.

A tea made from fenugreek (methi) seeds is equal in value to quinine in reducing fevers. It is particularly valuable as a cleansing and soothing drink. Fenugreek seeds, when moistened with water becomes slightly mucilagenous, and hence the tea made from them has the power to dissolve sticky substance like mucus.

Other Measures

Cold compresses may be applied to the head in case the temperature rises above 103°F. If this method does not succeed, cold pack may be applied to the whole body. The procedure is to bring out a sheet or large square piece of linen material in cold water, wrap it twice around the body and legs of the patient and then cover completely with a small blanket or similar warm material. This pack should be applied every three hours during the day while temperature is high and kept on for one hour or so each time. Hot water bottles may be applied to the feet and also against the sides of the body.

FEVER

TREATMENT CHART FOR FEVER

A - DIET

I. Fast on fruit juice till fever subsides. Take a glass of fresh fruit juice, diluted with water on 50:50 basis, every two hours. Use warm-water enema daily during the day.

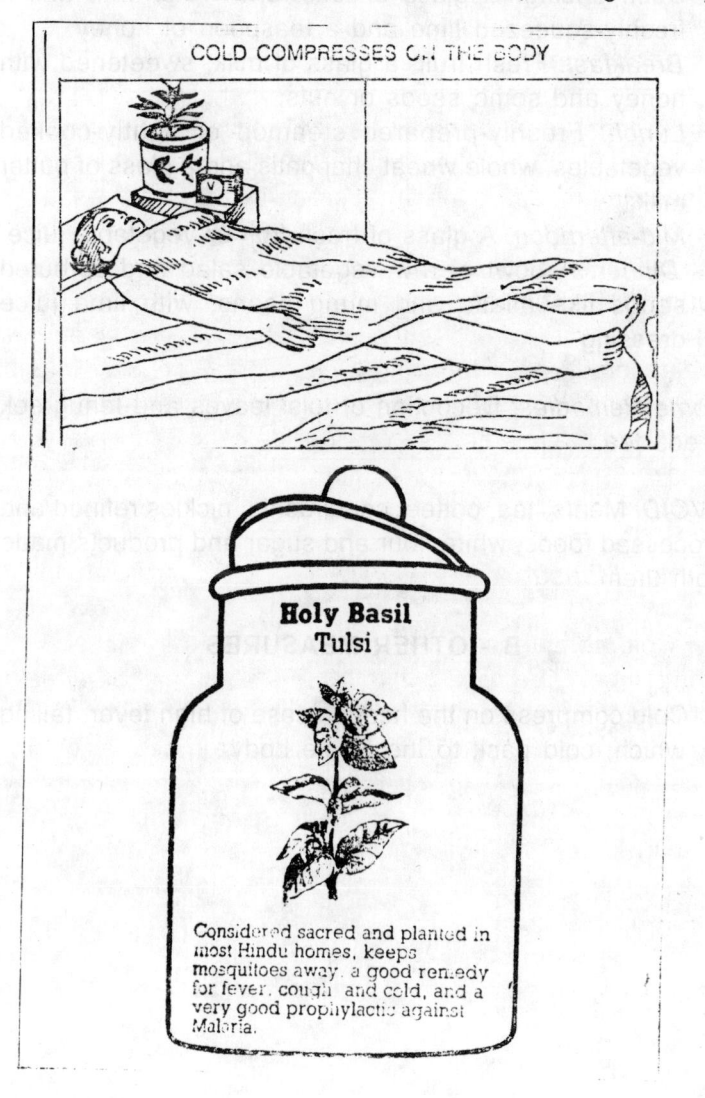

COLD COMPRESSES ON THE BODY

Holy Basil Tulsi

Considered sacred and planted in most Hindu homes, keeps mosquitoes away, a good remedy for fever, cough and cold, and a very good prophylactic against Malaria.

II. An all-fuit diet for further two days, taking three meals a day of fresh juicy fruits at five-hourly intervals.

III. Thereafter, gradually embark upon a well-balanced diet, on the following lines:-

1. *Upon arising:* A glass of lukewarm water with half a freshly-squeezed lime and a teaspoon of honey.
2. *Breakfast:* Fresh fruit, a glass of milk, sweetened with honey and some seeds or nuts.
3. *Lunch:* Freshly-prepared steamed or lightly-cooked vegetables, whole wheat chappatis and a glass of butter milk.
4. *Mid-afternoon:* A glass of fresh fruit or vegetable juice.
5. *Dinner:* A bowl of raw vegetable salad and sprouted seeds like alfalfa and mung beans, with lime juice dressing.

Home Remedies: Decoction of tulsi leaves and fenugreek seeds tea.

AVOID: Meats, tea, coffee, condiments, pickles refined and processed foods, white flour and sugar and products made from them.

B - OTHER MEASURES

1. Cold compress on the head in case of high fever, failing which, cold pack to the whole body.

CHAPTER 31

Gall Bladder Disorders

The main problems which afflict the gall-bladder are an inflammatory condition known as cholecystitis and gallstones. The inflammatory condition often leads to cholelithiasis or gall-stones which are usually caused by disturbances in the composition of the bile. A change in the ratio of cholesterol and bile salts may result in the formation of deposits.

The gall-bladder is a pear-shaped organ, ten cm. long and three to five cm. wide. It lies on the under-surface of the liver on the right side just under the lower margin of the ribs. The function of the gall-bladder is to store and concentrate the bile secreted by the liver and to deliver it into the duodenum at appropriate times to assist in the process of digestion. Bile is an excretion composed mainly of bile salts and acids, colour pigments and cholesterol. Bile assists in the digestion and absorption of fats and the absorption of fat-soluble vitamins A, D, E and K, minerals and calcium.

The gall-bladder is usually full and relaxed between meals. During the process of digestion, when food reaches the duodenum, a hormone called cholecystokinin begins to be produced in the internal mucosa. When this hormone reaches the gall-bladder through the blood stream, it causes the gall-bladder to contract, thereby releasing the bile concentrate into the duodenum via a common duct.

At the start, gall-stones may be in the form of fine gravel. But these fine particles constitute the nucleus for further deposits, utlimately leading to the formation of larger stones. The incidence of gall-stones is five times higher in females than in males, particularly in the obese and over 40 years of age.

Symptoms

The major symptom of gall-bladder disease is acute or intermittent epigastric pain. Indigestion, gas, a feeling of fullness after meals, constipation, nausea and disturbed vision are the other usual symptoms. Intolerance to fats, dizziness, jaundice, anaemia, acne and other lesions may also occur. Varicose veins, haemorrhoids and breakdown of capillaries are also disorders associated with gall-bladder troubles.

Causes

The association of gall-bladder disease with obesity together with their reported rarity in primitive people, living on simple diets, suggest that dietary factors play a major role in the development of this disease. The main causes of gall-bladder disorders is overnutrition caused by refined carbohydrates, especially sugar as the loss of fibre removes a natural barrier to energy intake. Overnutrition also leads to increased cholesterol secretion. Meals rich in fats may cause an attack of gall-bladder pain or gall-stone colic. Chronic constipation is a most important predispoing factor. Poor health, hereditary factors, stress, spinal displacements, bad posture and muscular tension may also cause gall-bladder disorders. The Chinese link the gall-bladder disorders with the emotion of anger.

Types of gall-stones

Ther are three types of gall-stones, depending on the cause of their formation. These are: cholesterol stones, caused by the change in the ratio of cholesterol to bile salts; pigment stones, composed of bile pigment and caused by the destruction of red blood cells due to certain blood diseases, and mixed stones consisting of layers of cholesterol, calcium and bile pigment resulting from stagnation of the bile flow. The third type is by far the most common.

Dietetic Cure

Surgery becomes necessary if the gall-stones are very large or in cases in which they have been present for long. Smaller gall-stones can, however, be cleared through dietetic cure. In cases of acute gall-bladder inflammation, the patient should fast for two or three days, until the acute condition is cleared. Nothing but water should be taken during the fast. After the fast, the patient should take fruit and vegetable juices for few days. The juice of carrots, beets, grape-fruits, pears, lemons or grapes may be used.

After the juices, the patient should adopt a well-balanced diet which should contain an adequate amount of all the essential nutrients. Ideally, the diet should be lacto-vegetarian, with emphasis on raw and cooked vegetables, fruit and vegetables juices, and a moderate amount of fruits and seeds. Pears should be eaten generously as they have a specific healing effect on gall-bladder. Yogurt, cottage cheese and a tablespoon of olive oil twice a day should also be included in the diet. Oil serves as a stimulant for the production of bile and lipase, the fat digesting enzymes. High quality vegetable oil in the diet also prevents gall-stone formation.

The patient should eat frequent small meals rather than three large meals. The following is the suggested menu for those suffering from gall-bladder disorders:

Upon arising: A glass of lukewarm water mixed with lemon juice and honey or fresh fruit juice.
Breakfast: Fresh fruit, one or two slices of whole meals toast and a cup of skimmed powder milk.
Mid-morning: Fresh fruit juice.
Lunch: Vegetable soup, a large salad consisting of vegetables in season with dressing of lemon or vegetable oil. Fresh fruit for dessert, if desired.
Dinner: Vegetable juice, one or two lightly cooked vegetables, baked potato, brown or unpolished rice or whole wheat chappatis and a glass of butter-milk.

Oil cure has been advocated by some nature cure practioners for the removal of gall-stones. Raw, natural, unrefined vegetable oils for egg, olive or sunflower oil are used. The procedure is to take one ounce of vegetable oil, preferably olive oil, first thing in the morning and follow it immediately with four ounces of grapefruit juice or lemon juice. This treatment should be taken each morning for several days, even weeks, if necessary.

The pain of gall-stone colic can be relieved by the application of hot packs or fomentation to the upper abdominal area. A warm water enema at body temperature will help eliminate faecal accumulations if the patient is constipated. Exercise is also essential.

TREATMENT CHART FOR GALL BLADDER DISORDERS

A - DIET

I. Fast on raw juices for five days. Take a glass of juice diluted with water every two hours during the day and use warm water enema to cleanse the bowels.

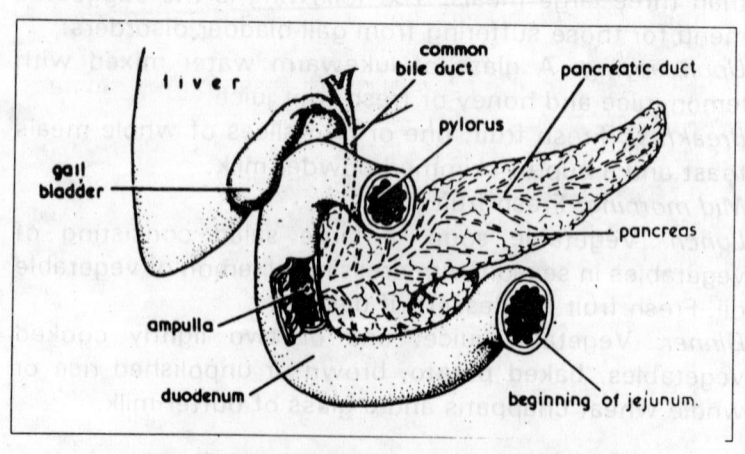

The Duodenum showing the Bile and Pancreatic Ducts

II. After the juice fast, adopt a lacto-vegetarian diet on the following lines:-
1. *Upon arising:* 30 ml. of olive oil and follow it immediately with 120 ml. of lemon juice or grapefruit juice.
2. *Breakfast:* Fresh fruit, one or two slices of whole meal toast and a cup of skimmed milk.
3. *Mid-morning:* Carrot juice or lemon juice.
4. *Lunch:* Vegetable soup, a large salad consisting of vegetables in season with dressing of lemon juice or vegetable oil. Fresh fruit for dessert, if desired.
5. *Mid-afternoon:* A glass of carrot or lemon juice.
6. *Dinner:* Vegetable soup or juice, one or two steamed vegetables, brown rice or whole wheat chappati and a glass of buttemilk.

AVOID: All meats, eggs, animal fats, sugar, white flour, all products made from them processed and denatured foods, fried and greasy foods, refined carbohydrates, alcohol, tea, coffee, spices, condiments, pickles and smoking.

B - OTHER MEASURES

1. Apply regularly hot and cold fomentation to the abdomen.
2. A cold hip bath for ten minutes on an empty stomach or three hours after meals.
3. Hot pack or fomentation to the upper abdominal region in case of pain of gall stone colic.
4. Brisk walks and yogic asanas like shalabhasana, bhujangasana and shavasana.

CHAPTER 32

Gastritis

Gastritis is an inflammation of the lining of the stomach. It is a troublesome condition which may lead to many complications, including ulcers if not treated in time. Constipation aggravates the condition more than any other disorder.

The inflammatory lesions may be either acute erosive gastritis or chronic atrophic gastritis. The latter type has been found to be present in half the patients suffering from severe iron deficiency anaemia.

Symptoms

The main symptoms of gastritis are loss of appetite, nausea, vomiting, headache and dizziness. There is also pain and a feeling of discomfort in the region of the stomach. In more chronic cases, there is a feeling of fullness in the abdomen especially after meals. The patients complains of heartburn. Prolonged illness often results in loss of weight, anaemia and occasional haemorrhage from the stomach. There may be an outpouring of mucus and a reduction in the secretion of hydrochloric acid during acute attacks and also in most cases of chronic gastritis.

Causes

The most frequent cause of gastritis is a dietetic indiscretion such as habitual overeating, eating of badly combined or improperly cooked foods, excessive intake of strong tea, coffee or alcoholic drinks, habitual use of large quantities of condiments, sauces, etc. It may sometimes follow certain diseases such as measles, diptheria influenza, virus pneumonia, etc. Frequently, it also results from worry, anxiety, grief and prolonged tension. Use of certain drugs, strong acids and caustic substances may also give rise to gastritis.

Dietetic Treatment

The patient should undertake a fast in both acute and chronic cases. In acute cases, the patient will usually recover after a short fast of two or three days. In chronic condition, the fast may have to be continued for a longer period of seven days or so. In the altnerative, short fasts may be repeated at an interval of one or two months, depending on the progress being made.

The fast may be conducted on fruit juices. By fasting, the intake of irritants is at once effectively stopped, the stomach is rested and the toxic condition, causing the inflammation, is allowed to subside. Elimination is increased by fasting and the excess of toxic matter accumulated in the system is thrown out.

After the acute symptoms subside, the patient should adopt an all-fruit diet for further three days. Juicy fruits such as apples, pears, grapes, grapefruits, oranges, pineapples, peaches and melons may be taken during this period at five-hourly intervals. The patient can, thereafter, gradually embark upon a well-balanced diet of three basic food groups, namely; seeds, nuts and grains, vegetables and fruits as outlined in Chapter 1 on Diet in Health and Disease.

The patient should avoid the use of alcohol, nicotine, spices and condiments, flesh foods, chillis, sour things, pickles, strong tea and coffee. He should also avoid sweets, pastries, rich cakes and aerated waters. Curds and cottage cheese may be taken freely.

Carrot juice in combination with the juice of spinach is considered highly beneficial in the treatment of gastritis. Six ounces of spinach juice should be mixed with ten ounces of carrot juice in this combination.

Too many different foods should not be mixed at the same meal. Meals should be taken at least two hours before going to bed at night. Eight to ten glasses of water should be taken daily but water should not be taken with meals as it dilutes the digestive juices and delays digestion. And above all, haste should be avoided while eating and meals should be served in a pleasing and relaxed atmosphere.

From the commencement of the treatment, a warm water enema should be usud daily for about a week to cleanse the bowels. If constipation is habitual, all steps should be taken for its eradication. The patient should be given daily dry friction and sponge. Application of heat, through hot compressor or hot water bottle twice a day either on an empty stomach or two hours after meals, will also be beneficial.

The patient should not undertake any hard physical and mental work. He should, however, undertake breathing exercises and other light exercises like walking, swimming and golf. He should avoid worries and mental tension.

TREATMENT CHART FOR GASTRITIS

A - DIET

I. An all-fruit diet for five days. Take three meals a day of fresh-juicy fruits at five-hourly intervals and use warm water enema during this period.

II. After an exclusive fresh fruit diet, gradually adopt a well-balanced diet on the following lines:-
1. *Upon arising:* 25 black raisins soaked overnight in water alongwith water kept overnight in a copper vessel.
2. *Breakfast:* Fresh fruit and a glass of milk, sweetened with honey.
3. *Lunch:* A bowl of freshly-prepared steamed vegetable, two or three whole wheat chappatis and a glass of buttermilk.
4. *Mid-afternoon:* A glass of carrot juice or coconut water.
5. *Dinner:* A large bowl of fresh green vegetable salad

with lemon juice dressing, mung bean sprouts, cottage cheese or a glass of buttermilk.
6. *Bedtime Snack:* A glass of milk or one apple.

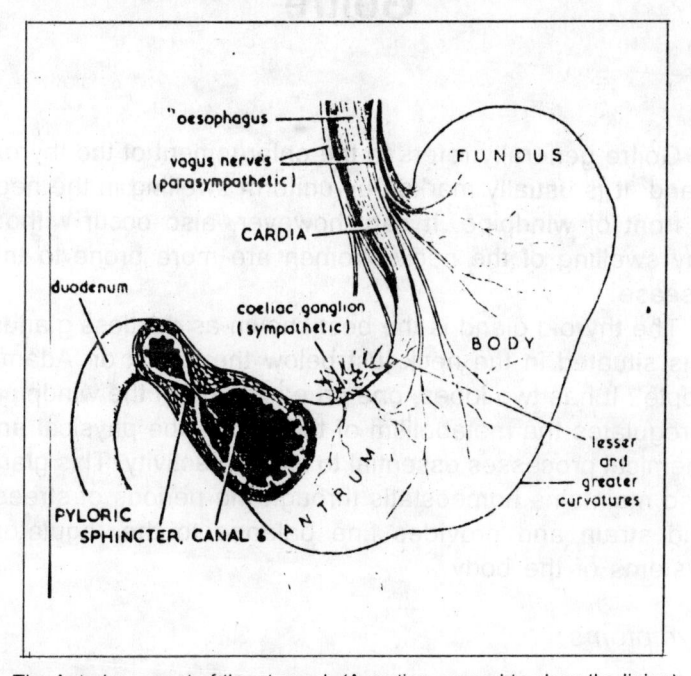

The Anterior aspect of the stomach (A portion opened to show the lining)

B - OTHER MEASURES

1. Do not take water with milk, but half an hour before and one hour after a meal.
2. Never hurry through a meal, never eat to full stomach and do not eat if appetite is lacking.
3. Wet girdle pack for one hour during night daily.
4. Cold hip bath for 10 minutes.
5. Yogic asanas such as uttanpadasana, pavanmuktasana, vajrasana, Yogamudra, bhujangasana, shalabhasana and shavasana.

CHAPTER 33

Goitre

Goitre generally refers to the enlargement of the thyroid gland. It is usually marked by uniform swelling in the neck in front of windpipe. It can, however, also occur without any swelling of the neck. Women are more prone to this disease.

The thyroid gland is the best known as ductless glands. It is situated in the neck just below the larynx or 'Adam's Apple'. It has two lobes, one on each side of the windpipe. It regulates the metabolism of the body - the physical and chemical processes essential to life and activity. This gland also maintains homeostatis through the periods of streess and strain and provides fine balance to the regulatory systems of the body.

Symptoms

The first symptoms of goitre usually appear as emotional upsets which are almost unnoticed. The spells of these upsets gradually increase in duration. Subsequently, other symptoms also appear. These include loss of power of concentration, depression and weeping. The patient appears to be very easily irritated. The approach of a nervous breakdown is often suspected.

The thyroid gland may swell but this has no relation to the severity of the diesease. There is a rapid, though regular, heart beat. In most cases, there may be a tremor of the hands and a feeling of extreme tiredness, together with a lack of power to make any real muscular effort. The eyes may incline to protrude. A most alarming symptom of goitre is the loss of weight which no treatment seems to check it.

Causes

Deficiency of iodine in the diet is the most common cause of goitre. The thyroid gland makes use of organic iodine in its secretion, and a diet deficient in organic iodine is a predisposing factor towards the appearance of this disease in certain cases, especially if other physical and emotional disturbances are present.

Dietary Treatment

The real treatment for goitre should be directed towards cleansing of the system and adoption of a rational dietary thereafter, combined with adequate rest and relaxation. To begin with, juices of fruits such as orange, apple, pineapple and grapes may be taken every two or three hours from 8 a.m. to 8 p.m. for five days. The bowels should be cleansed daily with lukewarm water.

After the juice fast, the patient may spend further three days on fruits and milk, taking three meals a day of juicy fruits such as apple, pineapple, grapes, papaya with a glass of milk, at five-hourly intervals. Thereafter, the patient may adopt a well-balanced diet consisting of seeds, nuts and grains, vegetables and fruits. The emphasis should be on fresh fruits and raw or lightly-cooked vegetables.

Certain foods and fluids are extremely injurious for goitre patients and should be avoided by them. These include white flour products, white sugar, flesh foods, fried or greasy foods, preserves, condiments, tea, coffee and alcohol.

Iodine is undoubtedly most helpful in many cases, but it should be introduced in organic form. All foods containing iodine should be taken liberally. These are asparagus, cabbage, carrots, garlic, onion, oats, pineapple, whole rice, tomatoes, watercress and strawberries.

Watercress (Jal-kumbji) has been discovered to be one of the best sources of the element iodine. It is valuable in correcting the functioning of the thyroid gland. Its regular use, therefore, is highly beneficial in the prevention and treatment of goitre. A paste made of this vegetable can also be applied beneficially over the affected parts. It will help reduce swelling.

Dandelion (kanphool) has also been found valuable in goitre. The leaves of this salad vegetable should be smeared with ghee, warmed and bandaged over the swollen parts for about two weeks. It will provide relief.

Half the daily intake of food should consists of fresh fruits and vegetables, and the starch element should be confined to whole wheat products and potatoes. The protein foods should be confined to cheese, peas, beans, lentils and nuts. All flesh proteins must be avoided.

Other Measures

Ice-bag should be applied to the throat for 20 to 30 minutes. It should then be applied over the heart for the same duration. The bag should be reapplied on the throat and the alternate application should be continued for one or two hours, and repeated two or three times a day.

The patient should take plenty of rest and spend a day in bed every week for the first two months of the treatment. Exercise should be resumed and gradually increase after the symptoms subside. Great care must be taken never to allow the body to become exhausted.

All efforts should be made to prevent emotional stress. There may be slight recurrence of this extremely nervous complaint for some times, but the attacks will become less severe and of shorter duration as the treatment progresses.

TREATMENT CHART FOR GOITRE

A - DIET

I. Fresh fruit juice for five days. During this period take a glass of juice of orange or other juicy fruit diluted with water every two hours from 8 a.m. to 8 p.m. and cleanse the bowels daily with warm water enema.

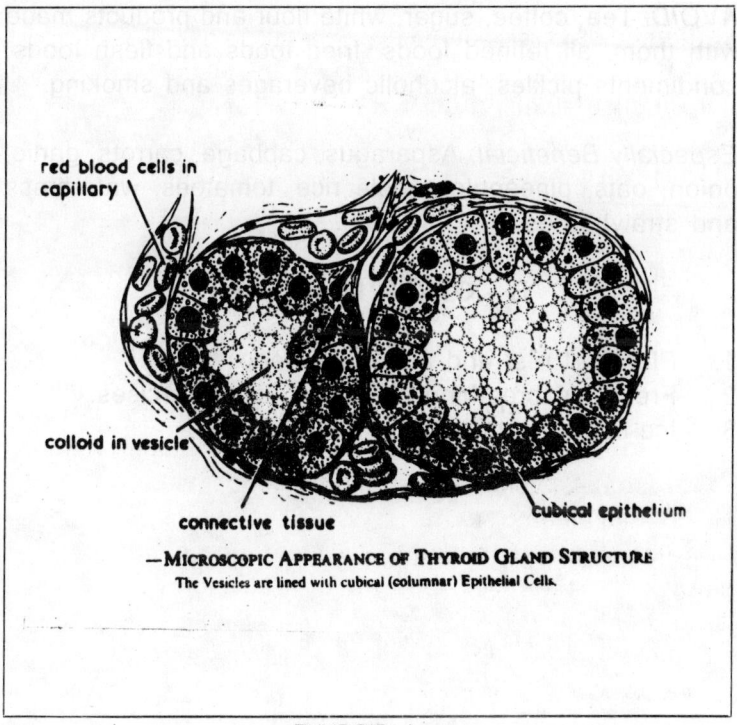

— Microscopic Appearance of Thyroid Gland Structure
The Vesicles are lined with cubical (columnar) Epithelial Cells.

THYROID

II. A diet of fresh juicy fruit for further five days, with three meals a day at five-hourly intervals.

III. Thereafter, adopt a well-balanced diet on the following lines:-
1. *Upon arising:* A glass of lukewarm water with a half a freshly-squeezed lime and a teaspoon of honey.
2. *Breakfast:* Fresh fruits, a glass of milk, sweetened with honey and some seeds or nuts.
3. *Lunch:* A bowl of freshly-prepared steamed vegetables, two or three whole wheat chappatis and a glass of buttermilk.
4. *Mid-afternoon:* A glass of fruit or vegetable juice.
5. *Dinner:* A large bowl of fresh green vegetable salad, with lime juice dressing and sprouted mung beans. Follow it with a hot course, if desired.

AVOID: Tea, coffee, sugar, white flour and products made with them, all refined foods, fried foods and flesh foods, condiments pickles, alcoholic beverages and smoking.

Especially Beneficial: Asparagus, cabbage, carrots, garlic, onion, oats, pineapple, whole rice, tomatoes, watercress and strawberries.

B - OTHER MEASURES

1. Plenty of rest and adequate sleep.
2. Fresh air, breathing and other light exercises.
3. Ice-bag over throat and heart region.

CHAPTER 34

Glaucoma

Glaucoma is a serious eye condition, characterised by an increase of pressure within the eye ball, called intraocular pressure. It is similar to high blood pressure in the body. The condition is therefore, also known as hypertension of the eye.

A certain amount of intraocular pressure is considered necessary, but too much can cause damage to the eye and may result in vision loss. Glaucoma is the major cause of blindness among adults today. One out of every eight blind persons is a victim of glaucoma. Far-sighted persons and more prone to develop this disease than near-sighted ones.

Symptoms

The first symptom of glaucoma is the appearance of halos or coloured rings round distant objects, when seen at night. In this condition, the iris is usually pushed forward, and the patient often complains of constant pain in the brow region, near the temples and the cheeks. Headaches are not uncommon. There is gradual impairment of vision as glaucoma develops, and this may ultimately result in blindness if proper steps are not taken to deal with the disease in the early stages.

Causes

Medical science regards severe eye-strain and prolonged working under bad lighting conditions as the chief cause of glaucoma. But, in reality, the root cause of glaucoma is a highly toxic condition of the system due to dietetic errors, a faulty life style and the prolonged use of suppressive drugs for the treatment of other diseases. Eye-strain is only a contributory factor.

Glaucoma is also caused by prolonged stress and is usually a reaction of adrenal exhaustion. The inability of the adrenal glands of produce aldosterone results in excessive loss of salt from the body and a consequent accumulation of fluid in the tissues. In the region of the eyes, the excess fluid causes the eye ball to harden, losing its softness and resilience. Glaucoma has also been associated with giddiness, sinus condition, allergies, diabetes, hypoglycemia, arteriosclerosis and an imbalance of the autonomic nervous system.

Dietetic Treatment

The orthodox medical treatment for glaucoma is through surgery which relieves the internal pressure in the eye due to excess fluid. This, lowever, does not remove the cause of the presence of the excess fluid. Consequently, even after the operation, there is no gaurantee whatsoever that the trouble will not recur, or that it will not effect the other eye. The natural treatment for glaucoma is the same as that for any other condition associated with high toxicity and is directed towards preserving whatever sight remains. If treated in the early stages, the results are encouraging. Though cases of advanced glaucoma may be beyond cure, even so, certain nutritional and other biological approaches can prove effective in controlling the condition and preserving the remaining sight.

Certain foodstuffs should be scrupulously avoided by patients suffering from glaucoma. Coffee in particular, should be completely avoided because of its high caffeine content. Caffeine causes stimulation of vasoconstrictors, elevating blood pressure and increasing blood flow to the eye. Beer and tobacco, which can cause constriction of blood vessels, should also be avoided. Tea should be taken only in moderation. The patient should not take excessive fluids, whether it is juice, milk or water at any time. He may drink small amounts, several times a day with a minimum of one hour intervals.

The diet of the patient suffering from glaucoma should be based on three basic food groups, namely seeds, nuts and grains, vegetables and fruits, with emphasis on raw vitamin C-rich foods, fresh fruits and vegetables. Valuable sources of vitamin C are citrus fruits such as oranges, lemons, grape-fruits and limes; green leafy vegetables like cabbages, beets and turnips; amla, sprouted Bengal and green grams. The same diet as that prescribed for cataract (Chapter 12) should be taken by those suffering from glaucoma. The various methods for relaxing and strengthening the eyes outlined in that chapter will also be beneficial in the treatment of glaucoma.

Certain nutrients have been found helpful in the treatment of glaucoma. It has been found that the glaucoma patients are usually deficient in vitamins A, B, C, protein, calcium and other minerals. Nutrients such as calcium and B-complex have proved beneficial in relieving the introcular condition. Many practitioners believe that introcular pressure in glaucoma can be lowered by vitamin C therapy. Dr. Michele Virno and his colleagues demonstrated recently in Rome, Italy that the average person weighing 150 pounds given 7000 mg. of ascorbic acid, five times daily, acquired acceptable introcular pressure within 45 days. Symptoms such as mild stomach discomfort and diarrhoea, resulting from the intake of large doses of vitamin C, were temporary and soon disappeared. It has been suggested that some calcium should always be taken with each dose of ascorbic acid to minimise any side-effects of the large dose.

The patient should avoid emotional stress and cultivate a tranquil and restful life style as glaucoma is considered to be a 'stress disease'. He should also avoid excessive watching of television and movies as also excessive reading as such habits can lead to prolonged straining of the eyes.

TREATMENT CHART FOR GLAUCOMA

A - DIET

I. An all-fruit diet for 5 days. In this regimen, take three meals a day of fresh juicy fruits such as orange, apple, pineapple, pear, peach, grapes and papaya at five-hourly intervals

The optic nerve in a case of advanced simple glaucoma. Note the cavernous atrophy towards the left of the figure (x 25) (Ashton).

II. Thereafter, adopt a well-balanced diet, based on seeds, nuts and whole grains, vegetables and fruits, on the following lines:-
1. *Upon arising:* 25 black raisins soaked overnight in water alongwith the water in which they are soaked and water kept overnight in a copper vessel.
2. *Breakfast:* Fresh fruit, a glass of milk, sweetened with honey, and some seeds or nuts.
3. *Lunch:* Freshly-prepared steamed vegetables, whole wheat chappatis and a glass of butter milk.
4. *Mid-afternoon:* A fresh fruit.
5. *Dinner:* Raw vegetable salad and sprouts such as alfaifa and mung beans, with lime juice dressing an cottage

cheese or butter milk.
6. *Bedtime Snack:* A glass of fresh milk with few dates.

Note: The menu for lunch and dinner are interchangable.

AVOID: Coffee, strong tea, soft drinks, alcohol and tobacco, excessive fluids, sugar, white flour and products made from them, refined foods, flesh foods, condiments and pickles.

Especially Beneficial: Raw vitamin C-rich foods like citrus fruits, green leafy vegetables, Indian goosebery (amla), sprouted Bengal and green grams, vitamin B-complex, and calcium.

B - OTHER MEASURES

1. Various methods of relaxing and strengthening the eyes.
2. Proper sleep and adequate rest.
3. Fresh air and outdoor exercises, especially brisk walks.

CHAPTER 35

Gout

Gout refers to a certain form of inflammation of the joints and swellings of a recurrent type. Although chronic in character, it breaks in acute attacks. It is a disease of the wealthy and chiefly affects the middle-aged men. Women, after menopause, are also sometimes affected by this disease.

Gout was known to the physicians of ancient Greece and Rome. The classical description was written in 1663 by Sydenham, himself a life-long sufferer, who clearly differentiated it from other joint disorders. It was recognised in the 18th century that large enjoyable meals and the consumption of alcoholic drinks were often the prelude to an attack of gout. This disease affected many famous men in history, including Alexander the Great, Luther, Newton, Milton, Dr. Johnson, Franklin and Louis XIV.

Symptoms

An attack of gout is usually accompanied by acute pain in the big toe, which becomes tender, hot and swollen in a few hours. Usually it is almost impossible to put any weight on the affected foot in the acute stage. It may also affect other joints such as the knees and wrists in a similar manner. Sometimes more than one joint may be affected at a time. The attack usually occurs at midnight or in the early hours of the morning, when the patient is suddeny awakened. The acute attack generally lasts for a week or so. During this period the patient may run a slight fever, and feel disinclined to eat. His general health usually remains unaffected.

The attack may occur **again** after several weeks or months. The interval becomes **shorter** if the disease is not treated properly. The joint gradually becomes damaged by arthritis. This is chronic gout, in which chalky lumps of uric acid crystals remain in the joint and also form under the skin.

Another serious complication of gout is kidney stones containing uric acid, causing severe colic pains in the stomach. In some cases the kidneys become damaged and do not function properly. This is a serious condition as the poisonous waste products which are normally removed by the kidneys accumulate in the blood.

Causes

The chief cause of gout is the formation of uric acid crystals in the joints, skin and kidneys. Uric acid is an end product of the body's chemical processes. Those affected by gout have a higher level of uric acid than the normal, due to either the formation of increased amounts of acid or to the reduced amounts of acid being passed out by kidneys in the urine. This uric acid usually remains dissolved in the blood. But when the blood becomes too full of it, the uric acid forms needle-shaped crystals in the joints which bring about attacks of gout.

Heredity is an important factor in causing this disease and certain races are prone to gout. Other causes include excessive intake of alcoholic drinks, regular eating of foods rich in protein and carbohydrate and lack of proper exercise. Stress is also regarded as an important cause of gout. During the alarm reaction, millions of body cells are destroyed and large quantities of uric acid freed from these cells enter the tissues after being neutralised by sodium.

Dietetic Treatment

For an acute attack, there is no better remedy than a fast. The patient should undertake a fast for five to seven days on orange juice and water. Sometimes, the condition may worsen in the early stages of fasting when uric acid, dissolved by juices, is thrown into the blood stream for elimination. This usually clears up if fasting is continued. In severe cases it is advisable to undertake a series of short fasts for three days or so rather than one long fast. A warm water enema should be used daily during the period of fasting to cleanse the bowels.

After the acute symptoms of gout have subsided, the patient may adopt an all-fruit diet for further three or four days. In this regime, he should have three meals a day of juicy fruits such as grapes, apples, pears, peaches, oranges and pineapples. After the all-fruit diet, the patient may gradually embark upon the following diet:

Breakfast: Fruits of any kind such as oranges, apples, figs, apricots, mangoes, etc., whole wheat bread or *dalia* and milk or butter-milk.

Lunch: Steamed vegetables such as lettuce, beets, celery, watercress, turnips, squash, carrots, tomatoes, cabbage and potatoes, chappatis of whole wheat flour, cottage cheese and butter-milk.

Dinner: Sprouts such as alfalfa and mung beans, a good-sized salad of raw vegetables such as carrots, cabbage, tomatoes, whole wheat bread and butter.

The patient should avoid all purine and uric acid producing foods such as all meats, eggs and fish. Glandular meats are especially harmful. He should also avoid all intoxicating liquors, tea, coffee, sugar, white flour and their products, and all canned and processed foods. Spices and salts should be used as little as possible. Foods high in potassium such as potatoes, bananas, leafy green vegetables, beans and raw vegetable juices are protective against gout. Carrot juice, in combination with juices of beet and cucumber is especially beneficial. Three ounces each of beet and cucumber juices should be mixed in ten ounces of carrot juice to make a pint or sixteen ounces of combined juice. Raw potato juice and fresh pineapple juice are also beneficial.

If the patient is overweight, he should bring his weight down by a general dietary regime, as explained in Chapter 37 on obesity. Because of the increased risk of stones in the urinary tract, patients should maintain a good intake of non-alcoholic fluids. They should drink at least eight glasses of cold or hot water daily.

The feet should be bathed in epsom salt foot baths twice daily. Half a pound to one pound of salt may be added to a foot bath of hot water. Full Epsom salt baths should also be taken three times a week. The baths may be reduced to two per week later. Cold packs at night applied to the affected joints will be beneficial. Fresh air and outdoor exercise are also essential. The patient should eliminate as much stress from his life as possible.

TREATMENT CHART FOR GOUT

A - DIET

I. Take the juice of an orange diluted with water every two hours from 8 a.m. to 8 p.m. and use warm water enema daily for five days.

II. An exclusive diet of fresh fruits for further five days, with three meals a day of fresh juicy fruits at five-hourly intervals.

III. Thereafter, gradually embark upon a well-balanced diet as under:-

1. *Upon arising:* A glass of lukewarm water mixed with the juice of half a lime and a teaspoon of honey.
2. *Breakfast:* Fresh juicy fruits, whole wheat bread or dalia and milk.
3. *Lunch:* Steamed vegetables, chappatis of whole wheat flour and buttermilk.
4. *Mid-afternoon:* A glass of fresh fruit or vegetable juice.
5. *Dinner:* Sprouts, a good-sized salad of raw green vegetables, whole wheat bread and butter.

AVOID: All purine and uric acid producing foods such as meats, eggs, and fish. Also avoid liquors, tea, coffee, sugar, white flour and their products, and all canned and processed foods.

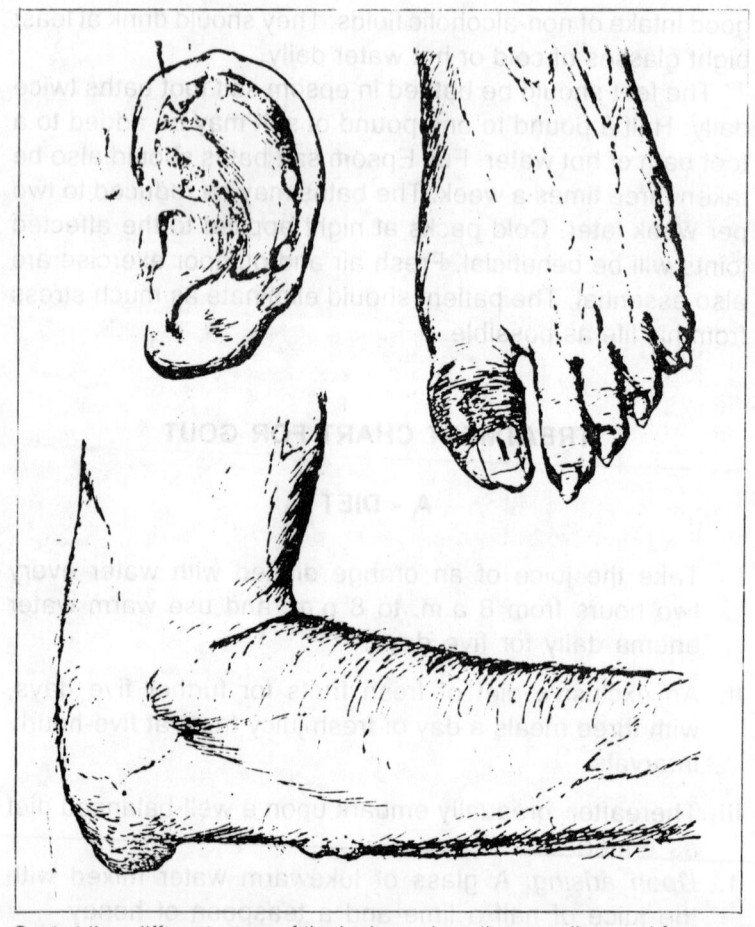

Gout strikes different areas of the body, such as the ear, elbow and forearm.

Restrict: Intake of spices and salt.

Take Liberally: Foods high in potassium such as potatoes, bananas, leafy green vegetables, beans and raw vegetable juices.

B - OTHER MEASURES

1. Drink at least eight glasses of water daily.
2. Bathe the feet in Epsom-salts bath twice daily.
3. Full epsom-salts bath twice a week.
4. Apply cold packs to the affected joints at night.

CHAPTER 36

Heart Disease

The term coronary heart disease covers a group of clinical syndromes arising particularly from failure of the coronary arteries to supply sufficient blood to the heart. They include angina pectoris, coronary thrombosis or heart attack and sudden death without infarction.

There has been a marked increase in the incidence of heart disease in recent years. Heart attacks have become the number one killer in western countries. They rank third in India, after tuberculosis and infections. The disease affects people of all ages and both sexes, although it is more common in men than in women, especially in those aged 40-60 years.

The heart, the most vital organ in the body, is a muscle about the size of a clenched fist. It starts working even before birth inside the womb. Weighing about 300 grams, it pumps about 4,300 gallons of blood every day through the body and supplies oxygen and nourishment to all the organs. It beats 1,00,000 times a day, continually pumping the blood through more than 60,000 miles of tiny blood vessels. The heart, in turn, needs blood for its nourishment, which is supplied by coronary arteries.

In the event of narrowing or hardening of the arteries on account of their getting plugged with fatty substances, the flow of blood is restricted. The heart then does not get sufficient oxygen. This condition is known as ischaemia of the heart or angina pectoris, which is a latin word meaning pain in the chest. It is actually a cry of the heart for more blood. In this condition, exercise or excitement provokes severe chest pain and so limits the patient's physical activity. It serves as a warning to slow down and prompt preventive measures will prevent a heart attack.

If the narrowed arteries get blocked due to a clot or thrombus inside them, causing death of that portion of the heart which depends upon the choked arteries, it is called a heart attack or coronary thrombosis. It may lead to death or heal, leaving a scar. Patients with healed lesions may be severely disabled or may be able to resume normal life with restrictions in their physical activities. A high proportion of cases of sudden death occur in persons who have had angina pectoris or coronary thrombosis.

The coronary arteries get narrowed due to various chemical deposits on their inner linings. These are caused by inherited or acquired defects in the metabolic processes of the body with regard to intake and absorption of various substances. A diet rich in fatty foods, especially animal fats, causes fatty substances to settle in the coronary arteries, thus blocking and narrowing them. The process of silting up of arteries is known as arterioscelrosis and is a major degenerative change affecting the circulatory system.

Symptoms

A common symptom of heart disease is shortness of breath, which is caused by the blood being deprived of the proper amount of oxygen. Another common symptom is chest pain or pain down either arm. Other symptoms are palpitation, fainting, emotional instability, cold hands and feet, frequent perspiration and fatigue. All these symptoms may be caused by many other disorders. Appropriate tests and studies are, therefore, essential to establish the true nature of these symptoms.

Causes

The basic causes of heart disease are wrong food habits, faulty style of living and various stresses. The famous Framingham Heart Study of the National Heart and Lung Institutes identified seven major risk factors in coronary heart disease. These are: (i) elevated blood levels of cholesterol, triglycerides and other fatty substances, (ii) elevated blood pressure, (iii) elevated blood uric acid levels (mainly caused by a high protein diet), (iv) certain metabolic disorders, notably diabetes, (v) obesity, (vi) smoking, and (vii) lack of physical exercise. Any one or a combination of these risk factors can contribute to heart disease. Most of them are of dietary origin. These risk factors can be controlled by changing one's life style and re-adjusting the diet. Constant worry and tension stimulates the adrenal glands to produce more adrenaline and cartisons. This also contributes to constricted arteries, high blood pressure and increased work for the heart.

Dietary Cure

The fundamental factor in all heart diseases is the diet. A corrective diet designed to alter body chemistry and improve the quality of general nutritional intake can, in many cases, reverse the degenerative changes which have occurred in the heart and blood vessels.

The diet should be lacto-vegetarian, low in sodium and calories. It should consist of high quality, natural organic foods, with emphasis on whole grains, seeds, fresh fruits and vegetables. Foods which should be eliminated are all white flour products, sweets, chocolates, canned foods in syrup, soft drinks, squashes, all hard fats of animal origin such as butter, cream and fatty meats. Salt and sugar should be reduced substantially.

Most flesh foods have a high sodium content and some meats are also very fatty. They are also highly acid-forming and create a high level of toxic matter in the system. They should be avoided by patients with a heart disease. The patient should also avoid tea, coffee, alcohol and tobacco. Tea and coffee contain caffeine which has a toxic effect on the heart and nervous system. Caffeine is a strong cardiac stimulant, which if taken regularly can cause palpitation or disturbances of heart rhythm.

Alcohol damages the liver and overstimulates the heart. It also alters the blood sugar level and depletes the body's vitamin B reserve. Nicotine has a toxic, irritant effect on the heart muscles and disturbs the blood sugar level.

The diet of the patient with heart disease should consist of nutrients as near to their whole natural state as possible so as to ensure an adequate intake of the essential vitamins, minerals and trace elements. Fruits and vegetables should form a large part of the diet and should be taken in their fresh raw state whenever possible. Grapes and apples are particularly beneficial. The essential fatty acids which reduce serum cholesterol levels and minimise the risk of arterioscelerosis can be obtained from sunflower seed oil, corn oil or safflower oil. Several studies have indicated that garlic can reduce the cholesterol level in persons whose body normally cannot regulate it. Another important cholesterol lowering herb is alfalfa. Lecithin helps prevent fatty deposits in arteries. Best food sources are unrefined, raw, crude vegetable oils, seeds and grains.

Patients with heart disease should increase their intake of foods rich in vitamin E, as this vitamin promotes heart functioning by improving oxygeneration of the cells. It also improves the circulation and muscle strength. Many whole meal products and green vegetables, particularly the outer leaves of cabbage, are good sources of vitamin E. The vitamin B group is important for heart and circulatory disorders. The best sources of vitamin B are whole grains.

Vitamin C is also essential as it protects against spontaneous breaks in capillary walls which can lead to heart attacks. It also guards against high blood cholesterol. The stress of anger, fear, disappointment and similar emotions can raise blood fat and cholesterol levels immediately but this reaction to stress can do little harm if the diet is adequate in vitamin C and panthothenic acid. The richest sources of vitamin C are citrus fruits.

The following is the suggested diet for persons suffering from some disorder of the heart:
Upon arising: Lukewarm water with lemon juice and honey.
Breakfast: Fresh fruits such as apples, grapes, pears, peaches, pineapples, oranges, melons, one or two slices of whole meal bread and skimmed milk.
Mid-morning: Fresh fruit juice or coconut water.
Lunch: Combination salad of vegetables such as lettuces, cabbage, endive, carrots, cucumber, beetroot, tomato, onion and garlic, one or two slices of whole meal bread or chappatis and curd.
Mid-afternoon: Fresh fruit juice.
Dinner: Fresh vegetable juice or soup, two steamed or lightly cooked vegetables, one or two whole wheat chappatis, and a glass fo butter-milk.

The patient should also pay attention to other laws of nature for health building such as taking moderate exercise, getting proper rest and sleep, adopting the right mental attitude and getting fresh air and drinking pure water.

TREATMENT CHART FOR HEART DISEASE

A - DIET

I. An all-fruit diet for three to five days, with three meals a day of fresh juicy fruits at five-hourly intervals and use warm water enema to cleanse the bowels.

II. Thereafter, adopt a well-balanced diet on the following lines:

1. *Upon arising:* A glass of lukewarm water with half a freshly squeezed lime and a teaspoon of honey.
2. *Breakfast:* Fresh fruits and skimmed milk, sweetened with honey.
3. *Lunch:* A bowl of freshly-prepared steamed vegetables, two or three whole wheat chappatis and a glass of buttermilk.
4. *Mid-afternoon:* Vegetable or fruit juice or coconut water.

5. *Dinner:* Fresh green vegetables salad and sprouts with lemon juice dressing. Follow it by a hot course, if desired.
6. *Bedtime Snack:* A glass of milk or one apple.

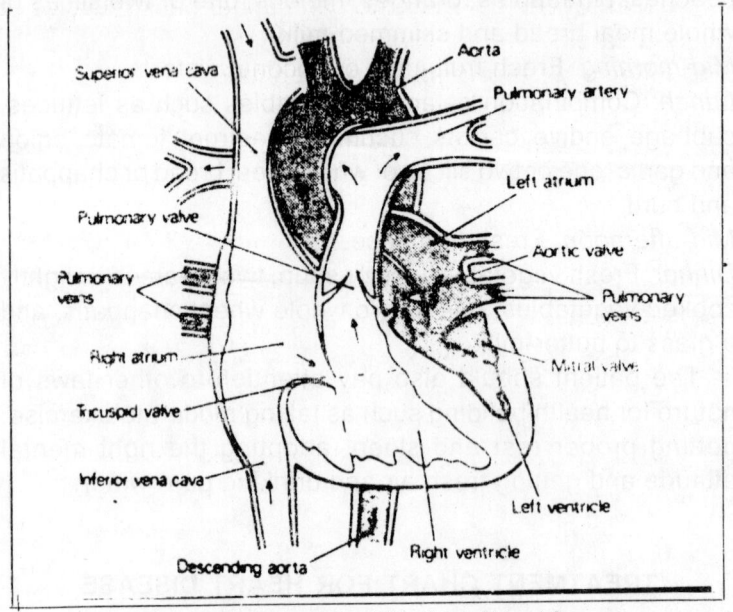

Anatomy of the heart and direction of blood flow

B - RULES FOR EATING

1. Do not take water with meals, but half an hour before or an hour after a meal.
2. Eat slowly, chew your food thoroughly and never eat to full stomach.
3. Restrict the intake of salt.
4. Take liberally foods rich in vitamin E.

C - OTHER MEASURES

1. Apply a hot compress on the left side of the neck for 30 minutes every alternate day and hot packs on the chest over the heart for one minute, followed by cold pack for

five minutes.
2. Practise yogic asanas like Shavasana, Vajrasana and gomekhasana.
3. Moderate exercise like walking.
4. Massage of the abdomen and upper back muscles once a week.
5. Fresh air and right mental attitude.

CHAPTER 37

Hiatus Hernia

Hiatus hernia refer to the displacement of a portion of the stomach through the opening in the diaphragm, through which the oesophagus passes from the chest to the abdominal cavity. In this disease, a part of the upper wall of the stomach protrudes through the diaphragm at the point where the gullet passes from the chest area to the abdominal area. The disease is common in all age groups, although it occurs more often after the middle age. In infants, the disease is usually associated with abnormally short oesophagus.

The diaphragm is a large dome-shaped muscle dividing the chest from the abdominal cavity. It is the muscle concerned with breathing and it is assisted by the muscles between the ribs during exertion. It has special openings in it to allow for the passage of important blood vessels and for the food channel, the oesophagus.

Symptoms

Hiatus hernia is characterised by pain in certain areas like behind the breast bone, on the left chest, the base of the throat, right lower ribs and behind the right shoulder blade. The pain increases on lying down or after heavy meals and on bending forward with effort. Other symptoms of this disease are heart-burn, especially after a meal, a feeling of fullness and bloatedness, flatulence and discomfort on swallowing. In infant, there may be vomiting which may be bloodstained.

Causes

The chief cause of the mechanical defect associated

with hiatus hernia is faulty diet. The consumption of white flour, refined sugar and products made from them such as cakes, pasteries, biscuits and white bread as well as preservatives and flavouring devitalise the system and weaken the muscle tone. As a consequence, the muscles become prone to decomposition and damage and ultimately leads to diseases like hiatus hernia.

Drinks like tea and coffee also effect the mucous lining of the stomach and irritate the digestive tract. These drinks, when taken with meals cause fermentation and produce gas. This increases the distension of the stomach and causes pressure against the diaphragm and the oesophageal opening, thereby increasing the risk of herniation. Other causes of hiatus hernia include overweight resulting from overeating, shallow breathing and mental tensions.

Dietary Cure

The patient should observe certain precautions in eating habits. The foremost amongst these is not to take water with meals, but half an hour before or an hour after a meal. This helps the digestive process considerably and reduces the incident of heart-burn. Other important factors in the treatment of this disease are to take frequent small meals instead of three large ones and thorough mastication of food so as to break up the food into small particles and to slow down the rate of intake.

The diet of the patient should consist of seeds, nuts and whole cereal grains, vegetables and fruits, with emphasis on fresh fruits, raw or lightly-cooked vegetables and sprouted seeds like alfalfa and mung beans. Atleast 50 per cent of the diet should consist of fruits and vegetables. The foods which should be avoided are over-processed foods, white bread, sugar, cakes, biscuits, rice puddings, over-cooked vegetables, condiments, pickles, strong tea and coffee.

Raw juices extracted from fresh fruits and vegetables are valuable in hiatus hernia. The patient should take three juices diluted with water, half an hour before each meal. Carrot juice is especially beneficial as it has a very restorative effect. It is an alkaline food, which soothese the stomach.

The hot drinks should always be allowed to cool a little before taking. Extremes in temperature, both in food and drink should be avoided. Drinks should not be taken hurriedly but sipped slowly.

Other Measures

In the beginning of the treatment, it will be advisable to raise the head end of the bed by placing bricks below the legs of the bed. This will prevent the regurgitation of food during the night. In case of the infant, all efforts should be made to keep the child upright day and night.

The next important step towards treating hiatus hernia is relaxation. An important measure in this direction is diaphragmatic breathing. The procedure is as follows:-

Lie down with both knees bent and feet close to buttocks. Feel relaxed, put both the hands lightly on the abdomen and concentrate the attention on this area. Now breathe in, gently pushing the abdomen up under the hands at the same time, until no more air can be inhaled. Then relax, breathing out through the mouth with an audible sighing sound and allow the abdominal wall to sink back. The shoulders and chest should remain at rest throughout.

TREATMENT CHART FOR HIATUS HERNIA

A - DIET

I. An all-fruit diet for 2 or 3 days, with three meals a day of fresh juicy fruits at five-hourly intervals.

II. Thereafter, adopt a well-balanced diet on the following lines:-

lines:-
1. *Upon arising:* A glass of lukewarm water with half a freshly-squeezed lime and a teaspoon of honey.
2. *Breakfast:* Fresh fruits and a glass of milk, sweetened with honey.
3. *Lunch:* Steamed vegetables as obtainable, 2 or 3 whole

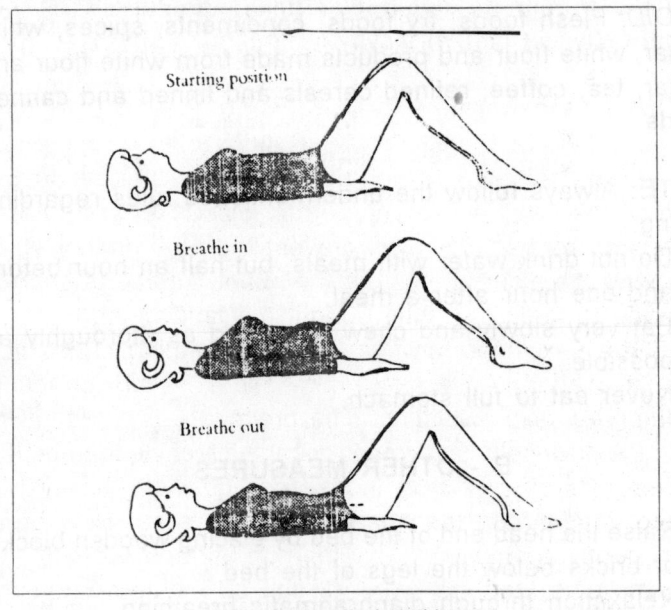

Diaphragmatic breathing

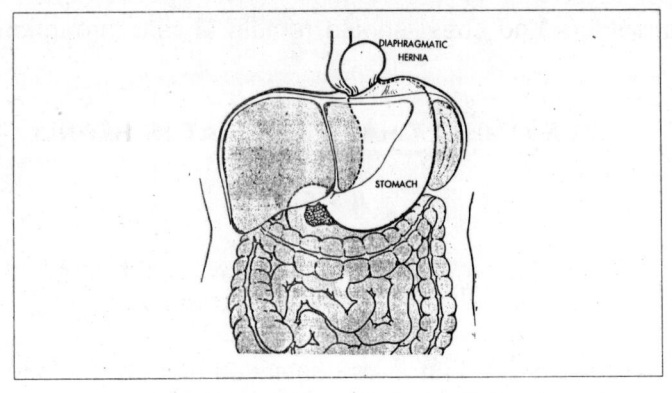

Drawing of a hiatus, or diaphragmatic hernia

wheat chappatis and a glass of buttermilk.
4. *Mid-afternoon:* A glass of fresh fruit or vegetable juice.
5. *Dinner:* A bowl of fresh green vegetable salad, with lime juice dressing, sprouted seeds and fresh home-made cottage cheese or a glass of buttermilk.
6. *Bedtime:* A glass of fresh milk or an apple.

AVOID: Flesh foods, fry foods, condiments, spices, white sugar, white flour and products made from white flour and sugar, tea, coffee, refined cereals and tinned and canned foods.

NOTE: Always follow the undermentioned rules regarding eating:-
1. Do not drink water with meals, but half an hour before and one hour after a meal.
2. Eat very slowly and chew your food as thoroughly as possible.
3. Never eat to full stomach.

B - OTHER MEASURES

1. Raise the head end of the bed by placing wooden blocks or bricks below the legs of the bed.
2. Relaxation through diaphragmatic breathing.

CHAPTER 38

High Blood Cholesterol

High blood cholesterol, known as hypercholesterolemia in medical parlance, refers to an increase in the cholestrol in blood above the normal level. It is mainly a digestive problem resulting from consumption of rich foods. It is a major factor in coronary artery disease. A person with high blood cholesterol is regarded as a potential candidate for heart attack, a stroke or high blood pressure.

Cholesterol is a yellow fatty substance and a principal ingredient in the digestive juice bile, in the fatty sheaths that insulate nerves and in sex hormones, namely estrogen and androgen. It performs several functions such as transportation of fat, providing defence mechanism, protecting red blood cells and muscular membrane of the body.

Most of the cholesterol found in the body is produced In the liver. However, about 20 to 30 per cent generally comes from the foods we eat. Some cholesterol is also secreted into the intestinal tract in bile and becomes mixed with the dietary cholesterol. The percentage of ingested cholesterol absorbed seems to average 40 to 50 percent of the intake.

The amount of cholesterol is measured in milligrams per 100 ml. of blood. Normal level of cholesterol varies between 150-250 mg. per 100 ml. Persons with atherosclerosis have uniformly high blood cholesterol, usually above 250 mg. per 100 ml.

In blood, cholesterol is bound to certain proteins-lipo proteins which have an affinity for blood fats, known as lipids. There are two main types of lipoproteins, a low density one (LDL) and a high density one (HDL). The low density lipoprotein is the one which is considered harmful and is associated with cholesterol deposits in blood vessels. The higher the ratio of LDL to the total cholesterol, the greater will be the risk of arterial damage and heart disease. The HDL on the other hand, plays a salutory role by helping remove cholesterol from circulation and thereby reduce the risk of heart disease.

Cholesterol has been the subject of extensive study by researchers since 1769, when French Chemist, Poluteir de La Salle purified the soapy-looking yellowish substance. The results of the most comprehensive research study, commissioned by the National Heart and Lung Institute of the U.S.A. were announced in 1985. The 10-year study, considered most elaborate and most expensive research project in medical history, indicates that heart disease is directly linked to the level of cholesterol in the blood and that lowering cholesterol in the blood significantly reduces the incidence of heart attacks. It has been estimated that for every one per cent reduction in cholesterol, there is decrease in the risk of heart attack by two per cent.

Causes

High blood cholesterol or increase in cholesterol is mainly a digestive problem caused by the consumption of rich foods such as fried foods, excessive intake of milk and its products like ghee, butter and cream, white flour, sugar, cakes, pasteries biscuits, cheese, ice-cream as well as non-vegetarian foods like meat, fish and eggs. Other causes of increase in cholesterol are irregularity in habits, smoking and drinking alcohol.

Stress has been found to be a major cause of increased level of cholesterol. Adernaline and cortison are both released in the body under stress. This, in turn, produces a fat metabolising reaction. Adernal glands of executive-type aggressive persons produce more adranaline than the easy going men. Consequently, they suffer six to eight times more heart attacks than the relaxed men.

Dietary Treatment

To reduce the risk of heart disease, it is essential to lower the level of LDL and increase the level of HDL. This can be achieved by improving the diet and changing the life style. Diet is the most important factor. As a first step, foods rich in cholesterol and saturated fats, which lead to increase in LDL level, should be reduced to the minimum. Cholesterol-rich foods are eggs, organ meats and most cheese. Butter, bacon, beef, whole milk, virtually all foods of animal origin as well as two vegetable oils, namely coconut and palm, are high in saturated fats and these should be replaced by polyunsaturated fats such as corn, safflower, soyabean and sesame oils, which tend to lower the level of LDL. There are monosaturated fats such as olive and peanut oils which have more or less neutral effect on the LDL level.

The American Heart Association recommends that men should restrict themselves to 300 mg. of cholesterol a day and women to 275 mg. It also prescribes that fat should not make up more than 30 percent of the diet and not more than one-third of this should be saturated. The Association, however, urges somewhat strict regimen for those who already have elevated levels of cholesterol.

The amount of fibre in the diet also influences the cholesterol levels and LDL cholesterol can be lowered by taking diets rich in fibres. The most significant sources of dietary fibre are unprocessed wheat bran, whole cereals such as wheat, rice, barley, rye, legumes such as potato, carrot, beet and turnips, fruits like mango and guava and leafy vegetables such as cabbage lady's finger, lettuce and celery. Oat bran is specially beneficial in lowering LDL cholesterol.

Lecithin, also a farry food substance and the most abundant of the phsopholipida, is beneficial in case of increase in cholestreol level. It has the ability to break up cholesterol into small particles which can be easily handled by the system. With sufficient intake of lecithin, cholesterol cannot build up against the walls of the arteries and veins. It also increases the production of bile acids made from cholesterol, thereby reducing its amount in the blood. Vegetable oils, whole grain cereals, soyabeans and unpasturised milk are rich sources of lecithin. The cells of the body are also capable of synthesizing it as needed, if several of the B vitamins are present.

Diets high in vitamin B6, cholin and inositol supplied by wheat germ, yeast, or B vitamins extracted from bean have been particularly effective in reducing blood cholesterol. Sometimes vitamin E elevates blood lecithin and reduces cholesterol, presumably by preventing the essential fatty acids from beign destroyed by oxygen.

Persons with high blood cholesterol level should drink atleast 8 to 10 glasses of water every day as copious drinking of water stimulates the excretory activity of the skin and kidneys. This is turn facilitates elimination of excessive cholesterol from the system. Regular drinking of corriander (dhania) water also helps lower blood cholesterol as it is a good diuretic and stimulates the kidneys. It is prepared by boiling dry seeds of coriander and straining the decoction after cooling.

Other Measures

Regular exercise also plays an important role in lowering LDL cholestrol and in raising the level of protective HDL. It also promotes circulation and helps maintain the blood flow to every part of the body. Jogging or brisk walking, swimming, bicycling and playing badminton are excellent forms of exercise.

Yogasanas are highly beneficial as they help increase perspiratory activity and stimulate sebaceous glands to effectively secrete accumulated or excess cholesterol from the muscular tissue. Asanas like ardhamatsyaendrasana, shalabhasana, padmasana and vajrasana are especially useful in lowering blood cholesterol by increasing systemic activity.

Hydrotherapy can be successfully employed in reducing excess cholesterol. Cold hip baths for 10 minutes, taken twice every day, have proved beneficial. Steam baths are also helpful except in patients suffering from hypertension and other circulatory disorders. Mud packs, applied over the abdomen improve digestion and assimilation. They improve the functioning of the liver and other digestive organs and activate kidneys and the intestines to promote better excretion.

TREATMENT CHART FOR
HIGH BLOOD CHOLESTEROL

A - DIET

I. Fast on raw juices for 3 days. During this period, take a glass of fruit or vegetable juice at two-hourly intervals from 8 a.m. to 8 p.m. and use warm water enema daily.

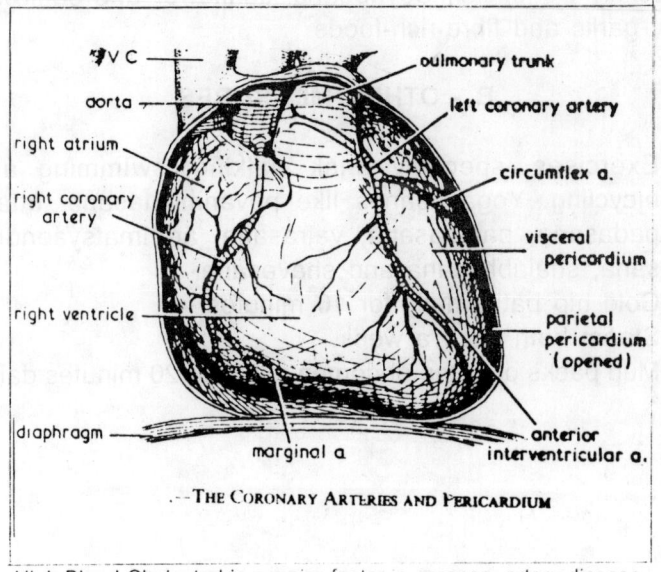

--THE CORONARY ARTERIES AND PERICARDIUM

High Blood Cholestrol is a major factor in coronary artery disease.

II. All-fruit diet for further 3 days, with three meals a day at five-hourly intervals.

III. Thereafter, the following diet may be adopted:-
1. *Upon arising:* A decoction of coriander seeds. This decoction is prepared by boiling the dry seeds and

straining it after cooling.
2. *Breakfast:* Fresh fruits, a handful of seeds, especially sunflower seeds and skimmed milk.
3. *Lunch:* Steamed vegetables, whole wheat chappatis or brown rice and a glass of buttermilk.
4. *Mid-afternoon:* A glass of carrot or orange juice.
5. *Dinner:* Salad of raw vegetables, mung sprouts and vegetable soup.

AVOID: Flesh foods, eggs, cheese, butter, whole milk, coconut and palm oils, sugar, white flour, tea, coffee, condiments, pickle, refined and processed foods and fried foods.

Specially Beneficial: Soyabeans, sunflower and safflower oils, garlic and fibre-rich-foods.

B - OTHER MEASURES

1. Exercises, specially brisk walking, swimming and bicycling. Yoga asanas like pavanmuktasana, uttanpadasana, padmasana, vajrasana, ardhmatsyaendrasana, shalabhasana and shavasana.
2. Cold hip baths daily for 10 minutes.
3. Steam bath once a week.
4. Mud packs over the abdomen for 15 to 20 minutes daily.

CHAPTER 39

Hypertension

Hypertension or high blood pressure, as it is more commonly known, is regarded as the silent killer. It is a disease of the modern age. The fast pace of life and the mental and physical pressures caused by the industrial and metropolitan environments give rise to pyschological tensions. Worry and mental tension increase the adrenaline in the blood stream and this, in turn, causes the pressure of the blood to rise.

Theblood which circulates through the arteries within the body supplies every cell with nourishment and oxygen. The force exerted by the heart as it pumps the blood into the large arteries creates a pressure within them and this is called blood pressure. A certain level of blood pressure is thus essential to keep the blood circulating in the body. But when the pressure becomes too high, it results in hypertension which is caused by spasms or the narrowing of the small blood vessels, known as capillaries, throughout the body. This narrowing puts more stress on the heart to pump blood through the blood vessels. Hence, the pressure of the blood to get through rises in proportion to the pressure on the heart.

The blood pressure is measured with an instrument called sphygmomanometer in millimeters of mercury. The highest pressure reached during each heartbeat is called systolic pressure and the lowest between two beats is known as diastolic pressure. The first gives the pressure of the contraction of the heart as it pushes the blood on its journey through the body and indicates the activity of the heart. The second represents the pressure present in the artery when the heart is relaxed and shows the condition of the blood vessels.

HYPERTENSION

The blood pressure level considered normal is 120/70, but may go up to 140/90 and still be normal. Within this range, the lower the reading, the better. Blood pressure between 140/90 and 160/95 is considered border line area. From 160/96 to 180/144, it is classed as moderate hypertension, while 180/115 upward is considered severe. A raised diastolic pressure is considered more serious than the raised systolic pressure as it has a serious long-term effect.

Symptoms

Mild and moderate hypertension may not produce any symptoms for years. The first symptom may appear in the form of pain in the back of the head and neck on waking in the morning, which soon disappears. Some of the other usual symptoms of hypertension are dizziness, aches and pains in the arms, shoulder region, leg and back, palpitations, pain in the heart region, frequent urination, nosebleeding, nervous tension and fatigue, crossness, emotional upsets, tiredness and wakefulness.

A person suffering from high blood pressure cannot do any serious work, feels tired and out of sorts all the time. He may experience difficulty in breathing and suffer from dyspepsia. Hypertension, if not eliminated, may cause heart attacks or strokes and other disabilities such as detachment of the retina.

Causes

The most important causes of hypertension are stress and a faulty style of living. People who are usually tense suffer from high blood pressure, especially when under stress. If the stress continues for a long period, the pressure may become permanently raised and may not come down even after removal of the stress. An irregular lifestyle, smoking and an excessive intake of intoxicants, tea, coffee, cola drinks and refined foods destroy the natural pace of life. The expulsion of waste and poisonous matter from the body is prevented and the arteries and the veins become slack. Hardening of the arteries, obesity, diabetes and severe constipation also lead to hypertension. Other causes of high blood pressure are excessive intake of pain-killers, table salt, food allergies and eating a high-fat, low-fibre diet and processed foods deficient in essential nutrients.

Dietary Cure

Drugs do not remove the cause, nor do they cure the condition. All drugs against hypertension without exception, are toxic and have distressing side-effects. The safest way to cure hypertension is to eliminate the poisons from the system which cause it. Persons with high blood pressure should always follow a well-balanced routine of proper diet, exercise and rest.

Diet is of primary importance. Meat and eggs cause blood pressure to rise more than any other food. The pressure is lowered and blood clotting diminished by partaking a diet with a higher fruit content, lower protein and non-flesh diet. A natural diet consisting of fresh fruits and vegetables, instead of a traditional diet, is helpful in getting rid of the poisons from the body. A hypertension patient should start the process of healing by living on an all-fruit diet for at least a week, and take fruits at five-hourly intervals, thrice a day. He should take juicy fruits such as oranges, apples, pears, mangoes, guavas, pineapples and grapes. Milk may be taken after a week of a diet of fruits only. The milk should be fresh and boiled only once. The patient can be permitted cereals in the diet after two weeks.

Vegetables are also good for a patient of hypertension. They should preferably be taken raw. If they are cooked, it could be ensured that their natural goodness is not destroyed in the process of cooking. Vegetables like cucumber, carrot, tomato, onion, raddish, cabbage and spinach are best taken in their raw form. They may be cut into small pieces and sprinkled with a little salt and the juice of a lemon added to them so as to make them more palatable. The intake of salt should be restricted; in any case it should not be taken more than four grams or half a teaspoon per day. Baking powder, containing sodium carbonate should also be avoided.

Garlic is regarded as one of the most effective remedies to lower blood pressure. The pressure and tension are reduced because it has the power to ease the spasm of the small arteries. Garlic also slows the pulse and modifies the heart rhythm besides relieving the symptoms of dizziness, numbness, shortness of breath and the formation of gas within the digestive tract. The average dosage should be two to three capsules a day to make a dent in the blood pressure.

Recent studies have revealed an important link between dietary calcium and potassium and hypertension. Researchers have found that people who take potassium-rich diets have a low incidence of hypertension even if they do not control their salt-intake. They have also found that people with hypertension do not seem to get much calcium in the form of dairy products. The two essential nutrients seem to help the body throw off excess sodium and are involved in important functions which control the working of the vascular system. Potassium is found in abundance in fruits and vegetables and calcium in dairy products.

The patient of hypertension should follow a plan of a well-balanced diet in which the constituents of food should be approximately in the following proportion: carbohydrate twenty per cent, protein ten to fifteen per cent, fat five per cent and fruits and vegetables sixty to sixty-five per cent. In this plan, one main meal should be based on raw foods while the second main meal may consist of cooked foods. Meals should be taken slowly and in a relaxed atmosphere. Food should be well masticated as the process of digestion begins in the mouth. The dinner should not normally be taken late.

TREATMENT CHART FOR HYPERTENSION

A - DIET

I. Juice diet for 5 days. Use warm water enema daily during this period.
II. All-fruit diet for further 5 days, with three meals a day at five-hourly intervals.
III. Thereafter, adopt the following diet:-
1. *Early Morning:* A glass of lukewarm water mixed with the juice of half a lime.
2. *Breakfast:* Fruits and skimmed milk.
3. *Mid-morning:* Coconut water.
4. *Lunch:* Steamed vegetables, whole wheat chappatis or brown rice and a glass of buttermilk.
5. *Mid-afternoon:* A glass of carrot juice or orange juice.
6. *Dinner:* Salad of raw vegetables, mung sprouts and vegetable soup.

AVOID: Meats, sugar, white flour, tea, coffee, condiments, pickles fried foods, and products made from sugar and white flour.

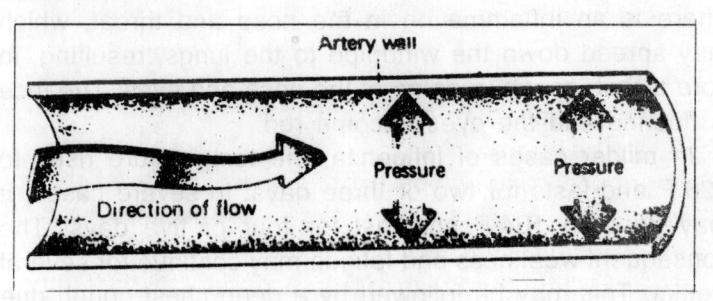

Pressure in an Artery

Important: Restrict the intake of salt and use liberally garlic and amla.

B - OTHER MEASURES

1. Exercise, specially brisk walking and yoga asanas like pavanmuktasana, uttanpadasana and shavasana.
2. Hot foot immersion in case of high blood pressure accompanied with headache.

CHAPTER 40

Influenza

Influenza; also known as flu, is the clinical condition that results from infection with influenza viruses. The main effects of the influenza viruses are on the upper respiratory tract, the nose and throat, with possible spread and involvement of the lungs and bronchi.

The disease is highly contagious and it has potential to cause widespread epidemics affecting sizeable portion of a population at anytime. Although it is more common during the cold months, it may strike at any time. It affects people of all ages.

Symptoms

Influenza strikes suddenly. It usually begins with chills, fever, headache, loss of appetite, vomiting and severe muscular pains. The patient feels miserable and weak. There is an inflammation in the nose and throat, which may spread down the windpipe to the lungs, resulting, in sore throat, cough, running of the nose and eyes. The face is flushed and the eyes become red.

In milder cases of influenza, the temperature rises to 120°F and lasts for two or three days. In severe cases, it may go upto 104°F and last for four or five days. The consequent weakness and fatigue may continue for several weeks. This may be followed by a deep chest cough due to irritation in the windpipe.

In children, the disease may start with a convulsion and a rapid rise in temperature to 105°F or 106°F. The patient feels extremely weak.

Causes

Influenza is what is known as ¬¬rm disease. It is,

however, not caused primarily by the action of the germs as is generally believed, but develops due to the toxic and run-down condition of the system of the affected person. This condition is brought about by the dietetic errors and a faulty style of living such as worry, overwork, lack of proper exercise, living in stuffy rooms and keeping awake late hours. No disease germs can find lodgement and become active in the system of a person who is perfectly healthy in the true sense of the term. Influenza is passed on with ease from the affected person to many others who are also in an equally low vital state. That is how an epidemic starts.

Treatment

Influenza, like all other acute diseases, is a natural attempt at self-cleaning and if rightly treated in a natural way, immense good can ensue so far as the future health of the patient is concerned. In acute stages of influenza, the patient should abstrin from all solid foods and only drink fruit and vegetable juices diluted with water on 50:50 basis for first three to five days, depending on the severity of the disease. The juice fast should be continued till the temperature comes down to normal. The warm water enema should be taken daily during this period to cleanse the bowels.

After fever subsides, the patient may adopt an all-fruit diet for two or three days. In this regimen, the patient should take three meals a day of fresh juicy fruits such as apples, pears, grapes, oranges, pineapple, peaches and melons at five-hourly intervals. Bananas or dried, stewed or tinned fruits, however, should not be taken. No other foodstuff should be added to the fruit meals, otherwise the value of the treatment will be lost. This may be followed by a further two or three days of fruits and milk diet. Thereafter, the patient may adopt a well-balanced diet consisting of seeds, nuts and grains, vegetables and fruits.

Spices and condiments and pickles, which make food more palatable and lead to overeating, must be avoided.

Lemon juice may be used in salad dressing. Alcohol, tobacco, strong tea and coffee, highly seasoned meats, over boiled milk, pulses, potatao, rice cheese, refined, processed, stale and tinned foods should all be avoided.

Certain home remedies have been found beneficial in the treatment of influenza. The most important of these is the use of long pepper. Half a teaspoon of the powder of long pepper with two spoons of honey and half a teaspoon of juice of ginger should be taken thrice a day. This will help greatly if taken in the initial stages of the disease. It is especially useful in avoiding complications which follow the onset of the disease, namely, the involvement of the larynx and the bronchial tube.

Another excellent remedy for influenza is the green leaves of basil or tulsi plant. About one gram of these leaves should be boiled alongwith some ginger in half a litre of water till about half the water is left. This decoction should be taken as tea. It gives immediate relief.

Garlic and turmeric are other effective food medicines for influenza. Garlic is useful as a general antiseptic and should be given as much as the patient can bear. Garlic juice may also be sucked up the nose. A teaspoon of turmeric powder should be mixed in a cup of warm milk and taken three times in a day. It will prevent complications arising from influenza and also activate the liver which becomes sluggish during the attack.

Ginger is an excellent remedy for influenza. A teaspoon of the fresh ginger juice mixed with a cup of fenugreek (methi) decoction and honey to taste is an excellent diaphoratic mixture which increases sweating to reduce fever in influenza.

Onion is another effective remedy for influenza. Equal amounts of onion juice and honey should be mixed and three or four teaspoons of this mixture should be taken daily in the treatment of this disease.

During the course of fever, the natural way of reducing temperature is by means of cold packs. It is advisable to apply a body pack several times a day, with one to the throat in case of a sore throat.

INFLUENZA

The pack is made by wringing out a sheet or other large square piece of linen material in cold water, wrapping it right round the body and legs of the patient and then covering completely with a blanket. In case of the throat pack, the linen may be covered with a piece of flannel. The packs can be kept for an hour or so. The body should be sponged with tepid water after removing the pack.

TREATMENT CHART FOR INFLUENZA

A - DIET

I. Fast on raw juices for three to five days. Take a glass of fresh fruit or vegetable juice, diluted with water on 50:50 basis, every two hours. Use warm-water enema daily during this period.

Garlic is beneficial in influenza

II. An all-fruit diet for three days after fever subsides. Take three meals a day of fresh juicy fruits at five-hourly intervals.

III. Fruit and milk diet for further three days.

IV. Thereafter, adopt a well-balanced diet, as follows:-
1. *Upon arising:* A glass of lukewarm water with half a freshy-squeezed lime and a teaspoon of honey.
2. *Breakfast:* Fresh fruit, a glass of milk, sweetened with honey and some seeds or nuts.
3. *Lunch:* A bowl of freshly-prepared steamed vegetables, two or three whole wheat chappatis and a glass of butter milk.
4. *Mid-afternoon:* A glass of fresh fruit or vegetable juice.
5. *Dinner:* A good-sized raw vegetable salad and sprouts, with lime juice dressing, followed by a hot course, if desired.

AVOID: Tea, coffee, alcohol, sugar, white flour and products made from them, refined foods, fried foods, flesh foods, condiments and pickles, tobacco and smoking.

Especially Beneficial: Garlic, turmeric, onion, ginger, grapefruit, carrot and spinach juices, finger millet and basil (tulsi) leaves.

B - OTHER MEASURES

1. Wet body pack several times a day during fever, sponging with the tepid water after the pack.
2. Bed rest till recovery.

CHAPTER 41

Insomnia

The term insomnia literally denotes a complete lack of sleep. It is, however, used to indicate a relative inability to sleep that consists of difficulty in falling asleep, difficulty in staying asleep, early awakening or a combination of any of these complaints. Insomnia deprives the person of mental rest and thereby interferes with his activities in the day time. It constitutes a severe health hazard when it becomes a habit.

Sleep is a periodic state of rest for the body which is absolutely essential for its efficient functioning. It is the indispensable condition to the recuperation of energy. It gives relief from tension, rests the brain and body and a person wakes up in the morning fresh and relaxed. Sleep has been aptly called the "balm of hurt minds and the most cheering restorative of tired bodies".

The amount of sleep varies within very wide limits from individual to individual. Normally, seven to eight hours of sleep every night is adequate for most people. Some, however, do well with four to five hours because their sleep is deeper and more refreshing.

Insomnia is common among the elderly for a variety of reasons. The sleep of the elderly is often punctuated by brief periods of wakefulness during the night. In such cases it is the quality rather than the quantity which is most affected. With age, there is a gradual reduction of periods of deep sleep. Sleep requirements also diminsh with ageing. From nine hours of sleep per night at the age of 12 the average sleep needs decrease to eight hours at the age of 20, seven hours at 40, 6½ hours at 60 and 6 hours at 80.

Symptoms

Although difficulty in staying asleep is the most common type of insomnia, the single symptom that most frequently marks the onset of insomnia is the difficulty in falling asleep. The signs of pathological insomnia are dramatic changes in the duration and quality of sleep, persistent changes in sleep patterns, lapses of memory and lack of concentration during the day. Other symptoms are emotional instability, loss of coordination, confusion and a lingering feeling of indifference.

Causes

The most common cause of sleeplessness is mental tension brought about by anxiety, worries, overwork and overexcitment. Suppressed feelings of resentment, anger and bitterness may also cause insomnia. Constipation, dyspepsia, overeating at night, excessive intake of starches, sweets, tea or coffee and going to bed hungry are among the other causes. Smoking is another unsuspected cause of insomnia as it irritates the nervous system, especially the nerves of the digestive system. Environment factors such as overcrowding, excessive noise and poor bedding or housing conditions may also lead to transient sleep difficulties. Often, worrying about falling asleep is enough to keep one awake.

Dietary Cure

Sleeping pills are no remedy for sleeplessness. They are habit-forming and become less effective when taken continuously. The side-effects of sleeping pills include indigestion, skin rashes, lowered resistance to infection, circulatory and respiratory problems, poor appetite, high blood pressure, kidney and liver problems and mental confusion.

Diet is an important factor in the treatment of insomnia. Research has shown that people with chronic insomnia almost have marked deficiencies of such key nutrients as B-complex vitamins and vitamin C and D as also calcium, magnesium, manganese, potassium and zinc. The sleep mechanism is unable to function efficiently unless each of these nutrients is present in adequate amounts in the diet.

Of the various food elements, thiamine or vitamin B1 is of special significance. It is vital for strong, healthy nerves. A body starved for thiamine over a long period will be unable to relax sufficiently to induce natural sleep. The valuable sources of this vitamin are whole grain cereals, pulses and nuts.

A balanced diet with simple modifications in the eating pattern will go a long way in the treatment of insomnia. Such diet should exclude white four products, sugar and its products, tea, coffee, chocolate, cola drinks, alcohol, fatty foods, fried foods, foods containing additives, preservatives, colouring and flavouring, excessive use of salt and strong condiments.

The patient may adopt an all-fruit diet for three or four days at the beginning of the treatment. In this regimen, he should have three meals a day of fresh juicy fruits such as oranges, grapes, apples, pears, peaches and pineapples. This will help cleanse the blood stream and relieve possible digestive and intestinal disturbances. The bowels should be cleansed daily with a warm water enema during this period.

After the all-fruit diet, the patient may follow a modified eating pattern in which breakfast should consist of fresh and dried fruits, seeds and yogurt. Of the two main meals, one should consist of a large mixed salad and the other should be protein based. A cup of milk sweetened with honey at bedtime is helpful as the amino acid tryptophan contained in the milk induces sleep. Celery is also considered beneficial in the treatment of insomnia. Its characteristic smell arising from the concentration of plant hormones and essential oils induce sleep.

Taking meals late in the night often leads to sleeplessness. The sufferer from insomnia should, therefore, eat his last meal at least three hours before going to bed. Food should never be taken when one is emotionally disturbed or suffering from fatigue or acute depression as it will result in gastric discomfort. Those suffering from insomnia should always take meals in a relaxed atmosphere. This is important at any time of the day, but more especially at night.

Alongwith dietary treatment, other effective measures should also be adopted to overcome the problem. These include application of hot fomentation to the spine, hot foot bath or an alternate hot and cold foot bath and prolonged neutral immersion bath (92° to 96°F) at bedtime.

All efforts should also be made to eliminate as many stress factors as possible. The steps in this direction should include regular practice of any relaxation method or meditation technique, cultivating the art of doing things slowly, particularly activities like eating, walking and talking, limiting the working day to nine or ten hours, and $5^{1/2}$ days weekly, cultivating a creative hobby and spending some time daily on this.

TREATMENT CHART FOR INSOMNIA

A - DIET

I. An all-fruit diet for three to five days, taking three meals a day of fresh juicy fruits at five-hourly intervals.
II. Thereafter, adopt a well-balanced diet as follows:-
1. *Upon arising:* A glass of lukewarm water with half a freshly squeezed lime and a teaspoon of honey.
2. *Breakfast:* Fresh fruit, a glass of milk, preferably goat's milk, sweetened with honey and some nuts, preferably almonds.
3. *Lunch:* A bowl of freshly-prepared steamed vegetables, two or three whole wheat chappatis and a glass of butter milk.
4. *Mid-afternoon:* A glass of fresh fruit or vegetable juice, preferably lettuce juice.
5. *Dinner:* A good-sized raw vegetable salad and sprouts with lime juice dressing, followed by a hot course if desired.
6. *Bedtime Snack:* A glass of milk sweetened with honey.

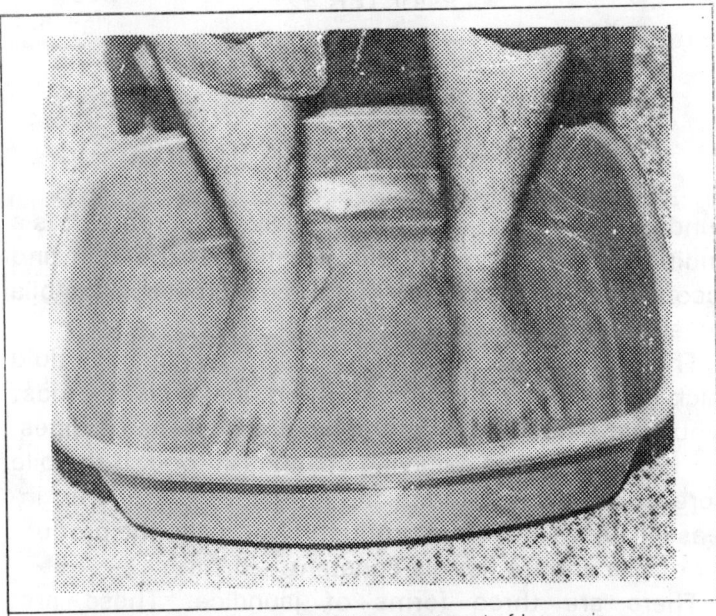

Hot foot bath is beneficialin the treatment of Insomnia.

III. Always follow the undermentioned rules regarding eating:-
1. Do not take water with meals, but half an hour before and one hour after a meal.
2. Eat very slowly and chew your food as thoroughly as possible.
3. Never eat to full stomach.

Home remedies: Thiamine, letuce, milk, curd, bottle gourd, aniseed, honey, and herb rauwolfia.

Avoid: Tea, coffee, sugar, white flour and products made from them, refined food, fried foods, flesh foods, tinned and preserved foods, condiments and pickles.

B - OTHER MEASURES

1. Fresh air, brisk walk, bicycling, swimming and shavashana.
2. Alternate hot and cold compresses to the back of the head at the base of the brian.

CHAPTER 42

Jaundice

Jaundice is the most common of all liver disorders. It is a condition in which yellow discoloration of the skin and mucous membranes occurs due to an increase in the bile pigment, bilirubin, in the blood.

The bile, produced by the liver, is a vital digestive fluid which is essential for proper nutrition. It exercises a most favourable influence on the general processes of digestion. It also prevents decaying changes in food. If the bile is prevented from entering the intestines there is an increase in gases and other products. Normally, the production of bile and its flow is constant.

There are three forms of jaundice. These are: haemolyptic jaundice due to excessive destruction of red blood cells resulting in increased bilirubin formation and anaemia; obstructive jaundice which occurs when there is a block to the pathway between the site of conjugation of bilirubin in the liver cells and the entry of bile into the duodenum; and hepatocellular jaundice resulting from damage to liver cells either by viral infection or by toxic drugs. All the three forms are marked by yellow discoloration of the skin and the whites of the eyes.

Symptoms

The symptoms of jaundice are extreme weakness, headache, fever, loss of appetite, undue fatigue, severe constipation, nausea and yellow coloration of the eyes, tongue, skin and urine. The patient may also feel a dull pain in the liver region. Obstructive jaundice may be associated with intense itching.

Causes

Jaundice is indicative of the malfunctioning of the

liver. It may be caused by an obstruction of the bile ducts which discharge bile salts and pigment into the intestines. The bile then gets mixed with blood and this gives a yellow pigmentation to the skin. The obstruction of the bile ducts could be due to gall-stones or inflammation of the liver, known as hepatitis, caused by a virus. In the latter case, the virus spreads and may lead to epidemics' owing to overcrowding, dirty surroundings, insanitary conditions and contamination of food and water. Other causes of jaundice are pernicious anaemia and certain diseases affecting the liver such as typhoid, malaria, yellow fever and tuberculosis.

Dietary Treatment

The simple form of jaundice can be cured rapidly by diet therapy and exercises. Recovery will, however, be slow in serious cases which have been caused by obstruction or pressure in the bile ducts. The patient should rest until the acute symptoms of the disease subside.

The patient should be put on a juice fast for a week. The juices of oranges, lemons, grapes, pears, carrots, beets and sugarcane can be taken. A hot water enema should be taken daily during this period to ensure regular bowel elimination, thereby preventing the absorption of decomposed, poisonous material into the blood stream. The juice fast may be continued till the acute symptoms subside.

After the juice fast, the patient may adopt an all-fruit diet for further three to five days. In this regimen, he should have three meals a day of fresh juicy fruits such as apples, pears, grapes, oranges and pineapples, but no bananas. Thereafter a simple diet may be resumed on the following lines:

Upon arising: A glass of warm water with juice of half a lemon.

Breakfast: One fresh juicy fruit such as apple, pear, mango, papaya, or some grapes, or berries. One cup wheat *dalia* or one slice of whole meal bread with a little butter.

Mid-morning: Orange or pear juice.

Lunch: Raw vegetable salad, two small chappatis of whole wheat flour, a steamed leafy vegetable such as spinach, *methi saag* or carrot and a glass of butter-milk.

Mid-afternoon: Coconut water or apple juice.

Dinner: One cup strained vegetable soup, two chappatis of whole meal, baked potato and one other leafy vegetable like *methi,* spinach, etc.

Before retiring: A glass of hot skimmed milk with honey if desired.

All fats like ghee, butter, cream and oils must be avoided for atleast two weeks, and after that butter and olive oil may be included in the diet but their consumption should be kept down to the minimum. A light carbohydrate diet, with exclusion of fats, best obtained from vegetables and fruits should be taken.

The patient should take plenty of fresh vegetables and fruit juices. Dandelion leaves, radishes with leaves, endive should be added to the daily raw vegetable salad. Raw apples and pears are especially beneficial. Barley water, drunk several times during the day, is considered a good remedy for jaundice. One cup of barley should be boiled in six pints of water and simmered for three hours.

Digestive disturbances must be avoided. No food with a tendency to ferment or putrefy in the lower intestines like pulses and legumes should be included in the diet. Drinking a lot of water with lemon juice will protect the damaged liver cells.

The jaundice patient can overcome the condition quite easily with the above regime and build up his sick liver until it functions normally once again. A recurrence of liver trouble can be prevented with reasonable care in the diet and life style, with regular, moderate exercise and frequent exposure to sunshine, fresh air and adequate rest.

Research has shown that the liver has an excellent capacity to regenerate itself provided all essential nutrients are adequately supplied. Diets high in complete proteins, vitamin C, and B vitamins, particularly choline, and vitamin E can hasten its regeneration. Even after recovery, it is essential to maintain the diet for a long period to prevent recurrence of the trouble.

TREATMENT CHART FOR JAUNDICE

A - DIET

I. Raw juice diet for 3 to 5 days. Oranges, lemons, sugarcane and carrots may be used for juices. During this period, the bowels should be cleaned daily with lukewarm water enema.

II. An all-fruit diet for further 3 to 5 days, with three meals a day at five-hourly intervals.

III. Thereafter, adopt the following diet :-
1. *Upon arising:* A glass of lukewarm water mixed with half a freshly-squeezed lime and a teaspoon of honey.
2. *Breakfast:* Fresh fruits and a cup of fresh toned or skimmed milk, sweetened with honey or jaggery.
3. *Mid-morning:* Lemon or Carrot juice.
4. *Lunch:* Raw vegetable salad, steamed vegetables, whole wheat chappatis and a glass of buttermilk.
5. *Mid-afternoon:* Coconut water or sugarcane juice.
6. *Dinner:* Vegetable soup, boiled vegetables with lime juice dressing and whole wheat chappatis.
7. *Before retiring:* A glass of skimmed or toned milk.

Food especially beneficial: Lime juice, pear, lemon, barley water, coconut water, sugarcane juice and radish leaves juice.

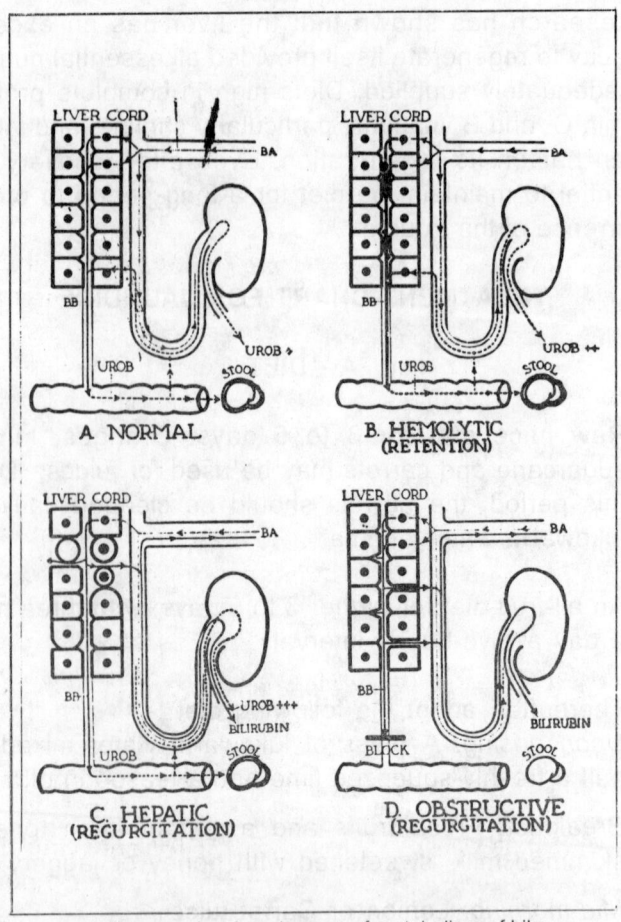

A diagram showing changes of metabolism of bile pigments in the various form of Jaundice.

Avoid: Fried and fatty foods, too much butter and ghee, sweets, meats, tea, coffee, pickles, condiments and pulses.

B - OTHER MEASURES

1. Drink plenty of water with lemon juice.
2. Adequate rest.
3. Avoid digestive disturbances.
4. Moderate exercise

CHAPTER 43

Kidney Stones

The formation of stones in the kidneys or urinary tract is a fairly common disorder. The stones are formed from the chemicals usually found in the urine such as uric acid, phosphorus, calcium and oxalic acid. They may vary in consistency from grit, sand and gravel-like obstructions to the size of bird's eggs.

Stones may form and grow because the concentration of a particular substance in the urine exceeds its solubility. This disorder occurs more frequently in middle age, with men being afflicted more often than women.

The kidneys are two bean-shaped organs, lying below the waist of either side of the spinal column on the back wall of the abdomen. They are soft, reddish brown in colour, and, on an average, measures 10 cm. in length, 6 cm. in width and is 2.5 cm. thick at its centre. They are each composed of approximately one million similar functional units called nepthrons.

Kidneys are the filtering plant for purifying the blood, removing water and salts from it which are passed into the bladder as urine. The kidneys are connected to the urinary bladder by two tubes called ureters in which the urine is stored. From here the urine is periodically emptied through another tube known as the urethra.

Symptoms

Kidney stones usually cause severe pain in their attempt to pass down the ureter on their way to the bladder. The pain is first felt in the side and thereafter in the groin and thighs. Other symptoms of kidney stones are a frequent desire to urinate, painful urination, scanty urination, nausea, vomiting, sweating, chills and shock. The patient may also pass blood with the urine. Sometimes large stones may remain in the kidneys without causing any trouble and these are known as 'silent' stones.

Causes

The formation of stones in the kidneys is the result of defects in the general metabolism. They usually occur when the urine becomes highly concentrated due to heavy perspiration or insufficient intake of fluids. They are aggravated by a sedentary life style. The other causes are wrong diet, excess intake of acid-forming foods, white flour and sugar products, meat, tea, coffee, condiments and spices, rich foods and overeating. Lack of vitamin A and an excessive intake of vitamin D may also lead to formation of stones.

Types of Stones

Chemically, urinary stones are of two categories, namely, primary stones and secondary stones. Primary stones are ordinarily not due to infection and are formed in acidic. urine. They usually result from alcoholism, sedentary life, constipation and excessive intake of nitrogenous or purine-rich foods. Secondary stones are due to local infection and are formed in alkaline urine.

Most kidney stones are composed either of calcium oxalate or phosphate, the latter being most common in the presence of infection. About ninety per cent of all stones contain clacium as the chief constituent. More than half of these are mixtures of calcium, ammonium and magnesium, phosphates and carbonates, while the remainder contain oxalate. Uric acid and cystine stones represent about four per cent and one per cent, respectively, of the total incidence of stones.

Dietary Treatment

A majority of patients suffering from kidney stones can be treated successfully by proper dietary regulations. These regulations will also prevent a recurrence of the symptoms. Only a few cases require surgery.

The general precaution in dietary treatment of kidney stones is to avoid foods which irritate the kidneys, to control acidity or alkalinity of the urine and to ensure adequate intake of fluids to prevent the urine from becoming concentrated. The foods which are considered as irritants to the kidneys are alcoholic beverages, condiments, pickles, certain vegetables like cucumbers, radishes, tomatoes, spinach, rhubarb, watercress and those with a strong aroma such as asparagus, onions, beans, cabbage and cauliflower, meat, gravies and carbonated waters.

In calcium phosphate stones, oversecretion of the parathyroid hormone causes loss of calcium from the bones resulting in a high blood level of calcium, with increased excretion of calcium in the urine. An abnormally high intake of milk, alkalis or vitamin D may also result in the formation of calcium phosphate stones.

For controlling the formation of calcium phosphate stones, a moderately low calcium and phosphorus diet should be taken. The intake of calcium and phosphates should be restricted to minimal levels consistent with maintaining nutritional adequacy. The maintance level of calcium is 680 mg. and of phosphorus 1,000 mg. In this diet, milk should constitute the main source of calcium and curd or cottage cheese, lentils and groundnuts should form the main sources of phosphorus. Foods which should be avoided are whole wheat flour, Bengal gram, pea soyabean, beet, spinach, cauliflower, turnips, carrots, almonds and coconuts.

When stones are composed of calcium and magnesium phosphates and carbonates, the diet should be so regulated as to maintain an acidic urine. In such a diet, only one pint of milk, two servings of fruits and two servings of vegetables (200 grams) should be taken. The vegetables may consist of asparagus, fresh green peas, squash, pumpkins, turnips, cauliflower, cabbage and tomatoes. For fruits, watermelons, grapes, peaches, pears, pineapples, papayas and guavas may be taken.

On the other hand, the urine should be kept alkaline if oxalate and uric acid stones are bein formed. In this diet, fruits and vegetables should be liberally used and acid-forming foods should be kept to the minimum necessary for satisfactory nutrition. When the stones contain oxalate, foods with high oxalic acid content should be avoided. These foods include almonds, beets, brinjals, brown bread, cabbages, cheeries, chocolates, french beans, potatoes, radishes and soyabeans.

Uric stones occur in patients who have an increased uric acid in the blood and increased uric acid excretion in the urine. Since uric acid is an end product of purine metabolism, foods with a high purine content such as sweet breads, liver, and kidney should be avoided. The patient should take a low-protein diet, restricting protein to one gram per kg. of food. A liberal intake of fluid upto 3,000 ml. or more daily is essential to prevent the production of urine at the concen-tration level where the salts precipitate out.

The patient should be given a large hot enema, followed by a hot bath with a temperature of 100°F., gradually increased to 112°F. The head should be kept cold with cold application. Hot fomentation applied across the back in teh region of the kidneys will relieve the pain. Certain yogasanas such as pavanmuktasana, uttampadasana, bhujangasana, dhannura-sana, ardhmatsyendrasana and halasana are highly beneficial as they stimulate the kidneys.

TREATMENT CHART FOR KIDNEY STONES

A - DIET

I. Take carrot or orange juice diluted with water on 50:50 basis every two hours for three days, and use warm water enema daily during this period.

II. An all-fruit diet for further three days, with three meals a day at five-hourly intervals.

III. Fruit and milk diet for further five days. In this regimen, add fresh milk to each fruit meal.

IV. Thereafter, gradually adopt a well-balanced low-protein diet on the following lines:-

1. *Upon arising:* 25 black raisins soaked overnight in water along with water in which they are soaked.

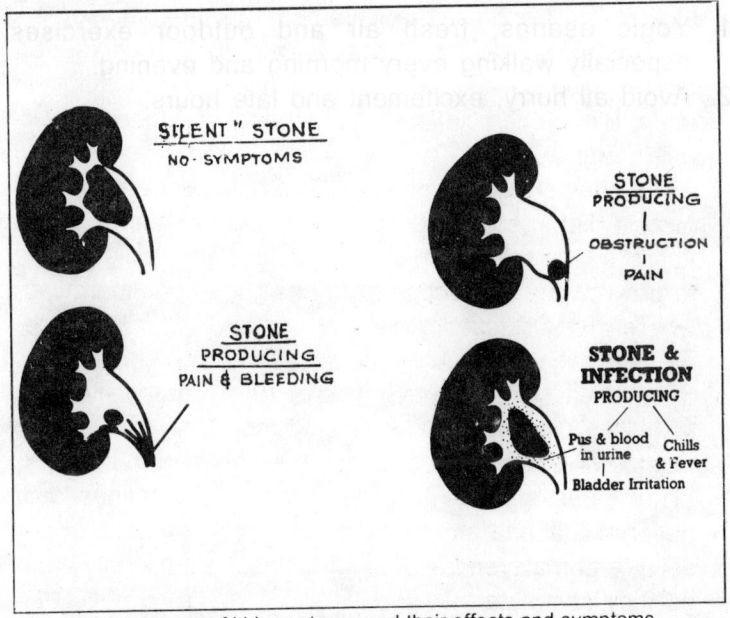

Various types of kidney stones and their effects and symptoms

2. *Breakfast:* Milk sweetened with honey and fresh fruits.
3. *Lunch:* Freshly-prepared steamed vegetables, whole wheat chappatis, unsalted butter and buttermilk.
4. *Mid-afternoon:* Carrot juice or coconut water.
5. *Dinner:* Fresh green vegetable salad, with lemon juice dressing and mung beans sprouts.
6. *Bed time snack:* A glass of milk sweetened with honey.

Avoid: Tea, coffee, alcoholics beverages, flesh foods, salt, condiments, sugar, denatures, cereals, and foods containing oxalic acid.

Specially beneficial: Garlic, cucumber, french beans, carrot, bananas, papaya, watermelon, and pineapple juice.

Note: Short juice fast followed by all-fruit diet and fruit and milk diet should be repeated every two months.

B - OTHER MEASURES

1. Yogic asanas, fresh air and outdoor exercises, especially walking every morning and evening.
2. Avoid all hurry, excitement and late hours.

CHAPTER 44

Low Blood Pressure

Low Blood Pressure or hypotension, as it is known in medical parlance, refers to the fall in blood pressure below the normal.

It is a condition in which the action of the heart in forcing the blood through the arteries is weak. This is a direct outcome of a weakened and devitalised condition of the system.

The blood pressure is measured with an instrument called Sphygmomanometer in millimeters of mercury. The highest pressure reached during each heart beat is called systolic pressure and the lowest between two beats is known as diastolic pressure.

The normal systolic pressure ranges between 100-140 and diastolic pressure ranges between 60-90. This varies from person to person, according to the age, sex and emotional status. A person is said to suffer from low blood pressure if there is difference of 40 mm or more between the present blood pressure and his usual blood pressure. Thus for instance, if the usual reading is 160/90 and it comes down to 120/70 or less, it can be taken as low blood pressure.

Symptoms

The patient with chronic low blood pressure may complain of lethargy, weakness, fatigue and dizziness. He may faint, especially if arterial pressure is lowered further when he assumes an erect position. Other symptoms of low blood pressure are darkness before the eyes and cold sweating. These symptoms are presumably due to a decrease in prefusion of the brain, heart, skeleton muscle and other organs.

Causes

The most important cause of low blood pressure is faulty nutrition. It makes the tissues forming the walls of blood vessels to become overrelaxed and oxygen and nutrients to the tissues. Malnutrition can result from diet deficient in calories, proteins, vitamin C or almost any one of the B Vitamins.

Sometimes, the blood pressure falls rapidly because of haemmorrhage or loss of blood. Low blood pressure may also develop gradually because of slow bleeding in the gastrointestinal tract, or through the kidneys or bladder. Emotional problems are a far more frequent cause of low blood pressure. To a lesser degree, prolonged disappointment and frustration may result in a subnormal blood pressure. Sometimes in young women with no abnormal disease, blood pressure tends to be on the low side, say, 90/60 or less. Heredity also plays a role and low blood pressure runs in certain families. Their blood pressure continues to be low, irrespective of what they eat and how they live.

Dietary Treatment

The treatment for low blood pressure should aim at regeneration of the whole system. To begin with, the patient should adopt an exclusive fresh fruit-diet for about five days, taking three meals a day of fresh juicy fruits such as orange, apple, pineapple, grapes, pear, peach and papaya at five-hourly intervals. Thereafter, he may adopt fruit and milk diet for two or three weeks. After the fruit and milk diet, the patient may gradually embark upon a well-balanced diet consisting of seeds, nuts and grains, with emphasis on fresh fruits and raw vegetables. Further periods on an all-fruit diet, followed by milk and fruit diet may be necessary at two or three-monthly intervals in some cases, depending on the progress being made.

The warm-water enema should be used daily to cleanse the bowels during the first few days of the treatment, and afterwards, if necessary. Those who are habitually constipated should take all possible steps for its eradication in a natural way.

Protein, vitamin C and all vitamins of B groups have been found beneficial in the prevention and treatment of low blood pressure. Of these, pantothenic acid is of particular importance. Liberal use of this vitamin also often helps in raising the blood pressure. A diet which contains adequate quantities of complete proteins, the B-vitamins and particularly the nutrients that stimulate adrenal production, normalize low blood pressure.

The juice of raw beet root(chukandar) has been found to be one of the most effective remedies for low blood pressure. The patient should drink a cup of this juice twice daily for treating this condition. Considerable improvement will be noticeable within a week.

The use of salt is valuable in low blood pressure. Until the blood pressure reaches normal levels through proper dietary and other remedies, it is essential that the patient should take salty foods and half a teaspoon of salt in water daily.

Other Measures

Daily dry fiction and sponge should be undertaken by those suffering from low blood pressure. They should also undertake breathing and other light exercise like walking, swimming and bicycling. The patient should take sun and air bath and spend as much as possible in open air.

The hot Epsom-salt bath is one of the simplest remedy for low blood pressure. The bath is prepared by dissolving one to one and a half kg. of commercial Epsom-salts in an ordinary bath of hot water. The patient should remain immersed in the bath from 10 to 20 minutes. This bath should be taken just before retiring to bed, and care should be exercised not to get chilled afterwards.

All habits of living tending to set up enervation of the system, such as overwork, excess of all kinds, needless worry, wrong thinking, must eliminated as far as lies within tea power of the sufferer.

TREATMENT CHART FOR LOW BLOOD PRESSURE

A - DIET

I. An all-fruit diet for 5 days, with three meals a day of fresh juicy fruits at five-hourly intervals. Use warm water enema daily during this period.

Beet juice is beneficial in Low Blood Pressure

II. Fruit and milk for further two weeks, adding milk to each fruit meal.

III. Thereafter, adopt the following diet:-
1. *Upon arising:* 25 black raisins soaked overnight in water along with water in which they are soaked and the water kept overnight in a copper vessel.
2. *Breakfast:* Fresh fruit, a glass of milk sweetened with honey and some nuts, especially almonds.

3. *Lunch:* A bowl of freshly-prepared steamed vegetables, two or three whole wheat chappatis, butter and a glass of buttermilk.
4. *Mid-afternoon:* A glass of carrot or orange juice.
5. *Dinner:* A large bowl of fresh green vegetable salad, alfalfa or mung bean sprouts and cottage cheese.

Note: Repeat an all diet for 3 days, followed by fruit and milk diet for 5 days at regular intervals.

Avoid: Meats, sugar, white flour, tea, coffee, refined and processed food, fried foods, condiments and pickles.

B - OTHER MEASURES

1. Daily dry friction and sponge.
2. Breathing and other light exercises.
3. Sun and air baths.
4. Hot Epsom-salts bath just before retiring twice weekly.
5. Avoid over work, excess of all kinds and heedless worry.

CHAPTER 45

Low Blood Sugar

Low blood sugar, or hypoglycemia, to give it a proper medical term, is a disorder of blood sugar metabolism. It is a condition in which the pancreas produce excessive insulin, causing the blood sugar to drop. This may result in diabetes in later life.

Hypoglycemia sometimes occurs in healthy people some hours after a meal rich in carbohydrates, especially following muscular exertion. It is frequently found in the first few days of life, especially in premature infants.

Hypoglycemia is a serious disorder as the brain cannot function properly when the blood sugar level is too low. Like all other organs of the body, the brain receives its fuel from the diet. But it can use only the sugar produced by the body from carbohydrates. Unlike many other body tissues, it cannot store its fuel. Therefore, it must get a constant supply of sugar through the blood stream. Mental disturbances caused by low blood sugar levels can seriously affect a person's life and repeated attacks of hypoglycemia may lead to permanent mental changes.

Symptoms

A craving for sweets and starches in excessive amounts between meals is the first sign of a low blood sugar level. When the blood sugar level falls much below normal, symptoms such as palpitations, excessive sweating, nervousness, irritability, fatigue, depression, disturbed vision and headache appear. Other symptoms are trembling, numbnes, absent-mindedness, dizziness, and some sexual disturbances. Most patients feel hungry and eat frequently to get over the feeling of weakness and emotional irritability. They feel tense if they have to go without food for several hours. The onset is sudden and the patient may quickly become confused and clumsy. If the condition is not treated promptly, he may become unconscious or very sleepy.

Causes

Low blood sugar is usually caused by an excessive intake of refined foods, sugar and sugary foods as well as soft drinks, cola drinks and coffee. These substances cause the pancreas, the adrenal glands and the liver to lose their ability to handle the sugar properly. An attack of hypoglycemia may be precipitated by administration of insulin or similar drugs without adequate carbohydrate coverage during the treatment of diabetes mellitus.

Other causes of low blood sugar are tumours of the islet cells of pancreas which secrete insulin, disturbed functioning of the liver, pituitary gland or adrenal glands. Stress intensifies this condition as it weakens the adrenal glands and starts a faulty pattern of glucose intolerance.

Dietetic Cure

The high animal protein diet generally prescribed for hypoglycemia is not suitable for this disorder. It may help control the condition temporarily, but it is harmful in many other respects. Continuous intake of high protein diet may lead to other diseases like heart trouble, arthritis, kidney problems and cancer.

The ideal diet for hypoglycemia should be based on three basic food groups, namely grains, seeds and nuts, vegetables and fruits, supplemented by milk, milk products and vegetable oils. Seeds, nuts and grains should be the main constituents of this diet. Seeds and nuts should be taken in their raw form. Grains, in the form of cereals, should be cooked. Cooked grains are digested slowly and they release the nutrients and sugar into the blood stream gradually, six to eight hours after meals. This will keep the blood sugar level normal and constant for a long period.

Persons suffering from low blood sugar should take six to eight small meals a day instead of two or three large ones. Eating raw nuts and seeds such as pumpkin or sunflower seeds or drinking milk, butter-milk or fruit juices between meals will be highly beneficial. All refined and processed foods, white sugar, white flour and their by-products should be completely eliminated from the diet. Coffee, alcohol and soft drinks should also be avoided. The consumption of salt should be reduced as an excessive intake of salt causes loss of blood potassium, which causes blood sugar to drop.

The following is the menu suggested for low blood sugar:-

Upon arising: A glass of fresh fruit juice. Sweet juices should be diluted with water.

Breakfast: Nuts, seeds, fruits, cottage cheese and butter-milk.

Mid-morning: Fruit, fruit juice or tomato juice.

Lunch: Cooked cereals with oil and milk or vegetable salad with yogurt and two whole wheat chappatis and butter.

Mid-afternoon: A glass of fruit or vegetable juice or a snack consisting of nuts.

Dinner: Raw vegetable salad with a cooked vegetable from among those allowed, one or two slices of whole grain bread, cottage cheese and butter-milk.

Before retiring: A glass of milk or butter-milk.

Vegetables which can be taken in hypoglycemia are asparagus, beets, carrots, cucumbers, egg plants, peas, radishes, tomatoes, spinach, kale, lettuce, beans, baked potatoes. Fruits which can be taken are apples, apricots berries, peaches and pineapples. Consumption of citrus fruits should be limited.

Foods rich in vitamin C, E and B-complex will be highly beneficial in the treatment of low blood sugar. Vitamins C and B increase tolerance to sugar and carbohydrates and help normalise sugar metabolism. Pantothenic acid, B6 and B-complex help to build up adrenals which are generally exhausted in persons with hypoglycemia. Vitamin E improves glycogen storage in the muscles and tissues.

Proper rest is essential for those suffering from low blood sugar. A tranquil mind is of utmost importance in this condition. Nervous strain and anxiety should be relieved by simple methods of meditation and relaxation. Yogasans like vakrasan, bhujangasan, halasan, sarvangasan and shavasan will be beneficial. A prolonged neutral immersion bath will also be helpful in relieving mental tension.

TREATMENT CHART FOR LOW BLOOD SUGAR

A - DIET

Adopt a well-balanced optimum diet on the following lines:-
1. *Upon arising:* Fresh fruit juice. Dilute sweet juices with water.
2. *Breakfast:* Cooked cereals like coarsely broken wheat (dalia), milk sweetened with honey, and few almonds.
3. *Mid morning:* One fresh fruit.
4. *Lunch:* Steamed or lightly cooked vegetables, whole wheat chappatis with butter and a glass of buttermilk.
5. *Mid afternoon:* Fresh fruit or vegetable juice or few nuts.
6. *Dinner:* Raw vegetable salad, with lime juice and vegetable oil dressing , cooked vegetable from among those allowed, one or two whole wheat chappatis, cottage cheese and buttermilk.
7. *Before retiring:* A glass of milk sweetened with honey.

Important: Take frequent small meals rather than three large ones.

Especially Beneficial: Vitamin C, E, and B-complex, potassium, apple and molasses(sheera).

Avoid: Tea, coffee, sugar, white flour and products made from them, refined foods, fried foods, flesh foods,

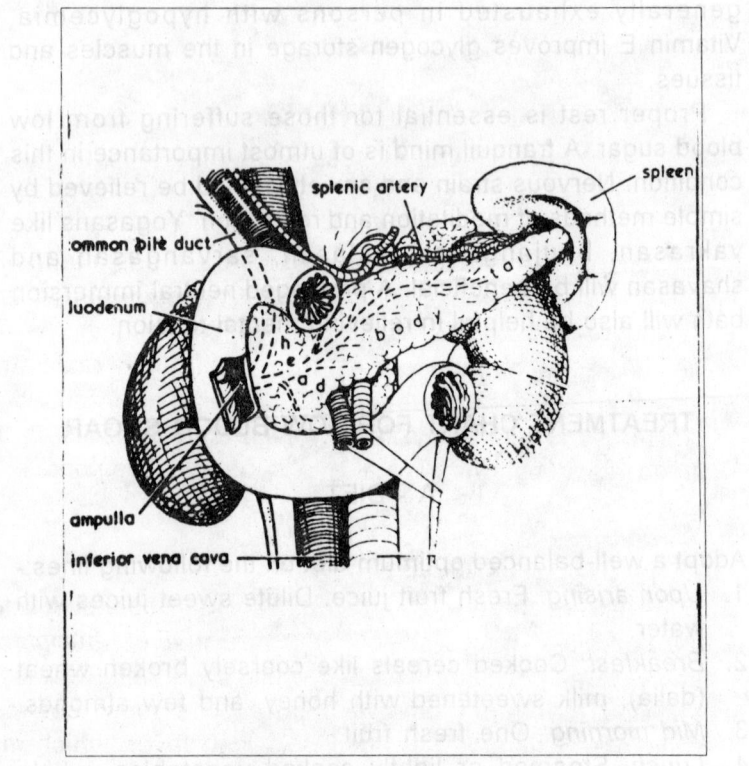

The Pancreas and its relations

condiments, pickles, alcohol and smoking. Restrict consumption of salt.

B - OTHER MEASURES

1. Fresh air, breathing and other exercises, including yogasanas.
2. Adequate rest, proper sleep, relaxation and meditation.
3. A prolonged neutral immersion bath.

CHAPTER 46

Malaria

Malaria is one of the intermittet fevers. It has a tendency to return again and again to haunt the sufferers. It is a serious infections disease.

The world malaria comes from the Italian ma'a aria, meaning bad air. It was once supposed to be caused by bad air. It is one of the most widespread diseases in the world, especially in tropical and subtropical regions.

Symptoms

There are three main types of malaria, depending upon the parasites which cause it. These are vivax, falciparum and malaria commonly called tertian fever, quarten fever and the malignant tertian malaria. The most common symptom of all types of malaria is high fever, which may come every day, on alternate days or every fourth day. The fever is accompanied by chill, headache, shivering and pain in the limbs. The temperature comes down after some time with profuse sweating. One of the main effects of malaria is anaemia. Other complications of the disease are kidney failure and dysentery.

Causes

Malaria is caused by a tiny parasite called plasmodium. The parasites grow in the liver of a person for a few days and then enter the bloodstream where they invade the red blood cells. The disease spreads from a sick person to a healthy one by the female anopheles mosquito. She draws a small quantity of blood containing the parasites, when she bites a person who has malaria. These parasites then pass through several stages of developmet within the mosquito's body, and finally find their way to its salivary glands. There they lie in wait for an opportunity to enter the bloodstream of the next person and mosquito bites. The malaria-carrying mosquito breads in stagnant water.

The real cause of malaria, however, as in case of other infectious diseases, is wrong feeding and faulty style of living. This results in the system being clogged with accumulated systemic refuse and morbid matter. It is on this soil that the malaria germs breed.

The habitual use of denatured foods of today, such as white sugar, white flour and products made from them, as well as tinned foods, strong tea, coffee and alcoholic beverages, lower the vitality of the system and paves the way for the developmet of malaria.

Dietary Treatment

Diet is of utmost importance in the treatment fo malaria. To begin with, the patient should fast on orange juice and water for 5 gto 10 days, depending on the severity of the fever. The warm-water enema should be administered daily during this period to cleanse the bowels.

After the fever has subsided, the patient should be placed on an exclusive fruit diet for further three days in this regimen, he should take three meals a day, at five-hourly intervals of fresh, juicy fruits like orange, grapes, grape-fruit, apple, pineapple, mango and papaya. Milk may be added to the fruit-diet after this period and this dietary may be continued for further few days. Thereafter, the patient may gradually embark upon a well-balanced diet of natural foods, consisting of seeds, nuts and grains, vegetables and fruits, with emphasis on fresh fruits and raw vegetables.

The patient should avoid strong tea, coffee, refined and processed foods, fried foods, condiments, sauces, pickles, white sugar, white flour, and all products made from them. He should also avoid all meats alcoholic drinks and smoking.

Certain home remedies have been found beneficial in the treatment of malaria. One such remedy is the use of grapefruit (chakotra). This fruit contains a natural quinine. This substance can be extracted from the fruits by boiling a quarter of the grapefruit and straining its pulp.

Lime and lemon are beneficial in the treatment of quarten type of malaria fever. About three grams of lime should be dissolved in about 60 ml. of water and juice of one lemon added to it. This water should be taken before the onset of the fever.

Cinnamon (Dalchini) is regarded as an effective cure for all types of colds, including malaria. It should be coarsely powdered and boiled in a glass of water with a pinch of pepper powder and honey. This can be used beneficially as a medicine in malaria.

Other Measures

The best way to reduce temperature naturally, during the course of the fever, is by means of the cold pack, which can be applied to the whole body. This pack is made by wringing out a sheet or other large square piece of linen material in cold water, wrapping it right round the body and legs of the patient and then covering completely with a small blanket or similar warm material. This pack should be applied every three hours during the day while temperature is high and kept on for an hour or so. Hot-water bottles may be applied to the feet and also against the sides of the body. A cold pack may also be applied to the throat.

Prevention

The preventive aspect in malaria is as important as the curative one. The best way to protect against malaria is to adopt all measures necessary for preventing mosquito bites. For this purpose, it is essential to maintain cleanliness of surroundings, environmental hygiene and to eradicate stretches of stagnant water. As the mosquito generally perches itself on the walls of the house after biting a person, it would be advisable to spray the walls with insecticides.

The leaves of holy basil (tulsi) are considered beneficial in the prevention of malaria. An infusion of some leaves can be taken daily for this purpose. The juice of about 11 grams of tulsi leaves, mixed with three grams of powder of black pepper, can be taken beneficially in the cold stage of the malaria fever. This will check the severity of the disease.

TREATMENT CHART FOR MALARIA

A - DIET

I. A fast on orange juice for 5 to 10 days. During this period, take orange juice diluted with water every two hours during the day and cleans the bowels daily with warm water enema.

II. All-fruit diet for further three days, with three meals a day of fresh juicy fruits at five-hourly intervals.

III. Thereafter, adopt the following diet:-
1. *Upon arising:* A glass of lukewarm water mixed with half a freshly-squeezed lime and a teaspoon of honey.
2. *Breakfast:* Fresh fruits and a cup of milk sweetened with honey.
3. *Lunch:* A bowl of steamed vegetables, whole wheat chappatis and buttermilk.
4. *Mid afternoon:* A glass of fresh fruit or vegetable juice.
5. *Dinner:* A bowl of fresh green vegetable salad, with lime juice dressing, sprouted seeds and home-made cottage cheese.

Avoid: Flesh foods, sugar, white flour, products made from them, tea, coffee, condiments and pickles.

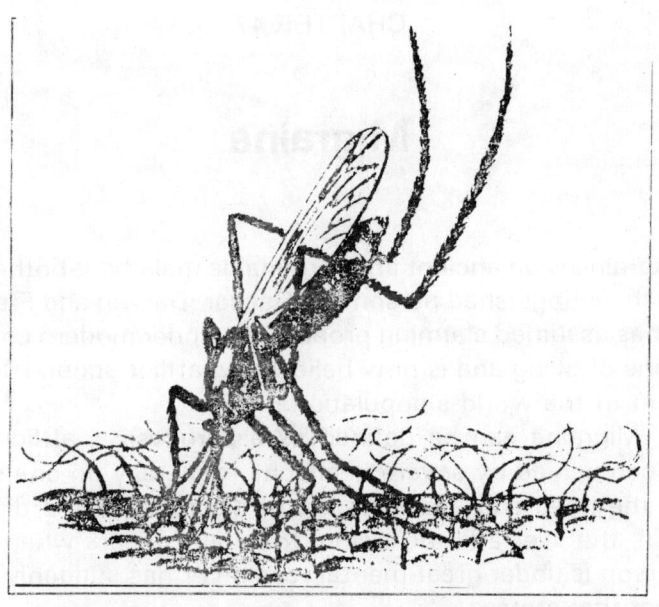

The malaria germ is carried by the anopheles mosquito. When biting, this mosquito assumes the position shown in the drawing.

B - OTHER MEASURES

1. Application of cold pack to the whole body to reduce temperature. Cold pack may also be applied to the throat.
2. Maintenance of cleaniness of surroundings, environmental hygiene and eradication of stretches of stagnant water to prevent mosquitoes.

CHAPTER 47

Migraine

Migraine is an ancient and formidable malady. It bothered such distinguished persons as Caesar, Darwin and Freud. It has assumed alarming proportions under modern conditions of living and is now believed to afflict about 10 per cent of the world's population.

Migraine can be defined as a paroxysmal affliction, accompanied by severe headache, generally on one side of the head and associated with disorders of the digestion, the liver and the vision. It usually occurs when the person is under great mental tension or has suddenly got over that state.

Persons who suffer from this disease have a migrainous personality. They are intelligent, sensitive, rigid, methodical and tend to be perfectionists. For them, everything has to be done right away and when they finish, they come down suddenly from a state of utmost mental tension to a feeling of great relief. Then all of a sudden, comes the migraine which is a purely psychological process. The head and neck muscles, reacting from continuous stress become overworked. The tight muscles squeeze the arteries and reduce blood flow. Then, when the person relaxes suddenly, the constricted muscles expand, stretching the blood-vessel wall. With each heartbeat, the blood pushes through these vessels and expands them further, causing intense pain.

Migraine headaches are believed to be related to the daily cycle of adrenal hormone secretion. Adrenal hormone levels are at their peak during the morning and taper off during the evening, reaching a low level around 3 a.m. An important function of these hormones is to regulate vascular muscle tone and to prevent vascodilation. When adrenal hormones production is low, blood vessels are more prone to dilation. Thus migraine headaches are generally triggered in the evening and rarely in the morning.

Symptoms

There is a definite pattern for migraine. The pain rages on only one side of the head and often radiates from the eye. The right side of the head may be affected in one attack and in the next it may be the left side. Migraine attacks are usually preceded by a short period of depression, irritability and loss of appetite. Some persons get attacks daily, others every month or every two or three months and still others only once or twice in several years.

Migraine is also known as sick headache. The main symptoms are a pounding pain, nausea and vomiting. The blood vessels on the affected side of the head will be prominent and pulsating. Migraine gives fair warning before striking. The patient sees flashes of light or black spots or only parts of the objects in front of him. He may also feel numbness or weakness in an arm or leg, or on one side of the face. Sometimes the numbness may affect both sides of the face and tongue and whole mouth, making speech slurred and difficult. As the headache develops, disturbed digestion becomes a marked feature.

A severe attack of migraine is very tiring and the patient may have to rest in bed so as to exclude light and noise as far as possible, because both cause painful irritations. The whole of the head becomes hypersensitive and even the slightest movement adds to the intense pain.

The duration of the attack varies with each individual. Some may get over the acute symptoms in a matter of hours. Others may require a day's rest to come to a normal state. Still others, who are less fortunate, may drag on for two, three, or even four days.

Causes

Migraine may result from a variety of causes such as

low blood sugar, allergy, infection, excessive intake of certain drugs like vitamin A, weak constitution, low energy, nutritional deficiency, overwork, improper sleep and rest, excessive smoking, drinking and sex. Menstruation in women may also be one of the important causes of migraine due to the effect of chemical hormone changes occuring during this period. This form of migraine is usually eliminated with menopause.

There are various factors which trigger off migraine. The most important is consuming food which the patient may be allergic to. Such foods include certain chocolates, cheese and other dairy products, fried foods in general, onions, tomatoes, citrus fruits as well as coffee, tea, nicotine and alcoholic drinks which stimulate or depress the nerves and alter the size of blood vessels. Other triggers include excessive bright light, eye-strain, excitement, fright, hurry, anger, resentment and depression after hard work.

Dietary Treatment

Painkilling drugs may give temporary relief but they do not remove the cause. The patient soon gets addicted to strong drugs which also lose their effectiveness in course of time. The best treatment for migraine is to prevent it.

A lowered energy level, however, is the chief factor which contributes towards migraine. Any successful treatment for this ailment should, therefore, aim at a complete toning up and revitalisation of the whole organism. To achieve this, it will be essential to undertake a thorough cleansing of the system and adopt vitality-building measures.

To begin with, the patient should resort to fasting on orange juice and water for two or three days. The procedure is to take the juice of an orange in a glass of a warm water every two hours from 8 a.m. to 8 p.m. Alternatively, juices of vegetables such as carrot, cucumber and celery may be taken. A warm water enema may be taken each day while fasting to cleanse the bowels. After the short juice fast, the patient may adopt an all-fruit diet for about five days, taking three meals a day of fresh juicy fruits such as apples, pears, grapes, grapefruits, oranges, pineapples, peaches and melons. No other food stuff should be taken during this period, otherwise the value of the whole treatment will be lost.

After the all-fruit diet, the sufferer should follow a well-balanced diet of three basic food groups, namely seeds, nuts and grains, vegetables and fruits. This diet should be supplemented with milk, yogurt, butter-milk, vegetable oils and honey. Further short fasts or periods on the all-fruit diet may be necessary at intervals of a month or two, according to the needs of the case. If constipation is habitual, all steps should be taken towards its eradication.

The foods which should be avoided in future are white flour products, sugar, confectionary, rich cakes, pastries, sweets, refined cereals, flesh foods, rich, heavy and greasy foods, tinned or preserved foods, pickles, condiments and sauces. Too much cereals should also be avoided. The patient should eat six small meals rather than a few large ones. Overeating should be avoided.

Niacin especially, has proved helpful in the treatment of migraine. It is, however, necessary that when taking any of the separate B vitamin factors, the entire B-complex should be taken in some form as too much of one factor can throw the other factors into imbalance. This may result in other undersirable problems. In fact, the entire B-complex range is beneficial in the prevention of migraine.

Drinking lots of water, hot foot baths, fomentations over the stomach and spine, cold compress (40°F to 60°F) to the head and towels wrung out of very hot water and frequently applied to the neck will go a long way in relieving migraine headaches. The patient should also undertake plenty of exercise and walking in fresh air.

TREATMENT CHART FOR MIGRAINE

A - DIET

I. Take carrot and orange juice diluted with water on 50:50 for three days and cleanse the bowels daily with warm water enema this period.

II. An all-fruit diet for further three days, with three meals a day at five hourly intervals.

III. Thereafter, gradually adopt a well-balanced diet on the following lines:-

1. *Upon arising:* 25 black raisins soaked overnight in water alongwith water in which they are soaked and water kept overnight in a copper vessel.

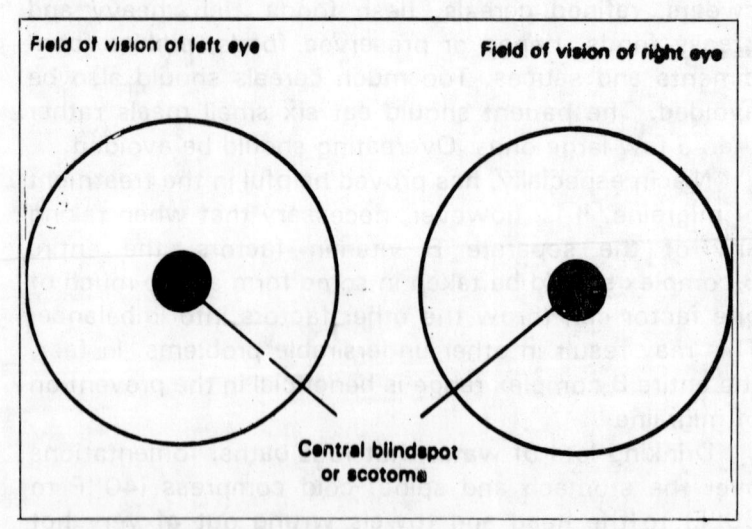

Field of vision of left eye	Field of vision of right eye
●	●
Central blindspot or scotoma	

One type of visual disturbance in migraine, where a blindsport may occur in the centres of the fields of vision of both eyes.

2. *Breakfast:* Seven almonds kernels, after removal of the skin, milk sweetened with honey and fresh fruits.
3. *Lunch:* A bowl of freshly-prepared steamed vegetables.
4. *Mid afternoon:* A glass of carrot juice or coconut water.

5. *Dinner:* A large bowl of fresh green vegetable salad with lemon juice dressing, mung bean sprouts and cottage cheese or nuts.
6. *Bed time snacks:* A glass of milk sweetened with honey or one apple.

Avoid: Tea, coffee, alcoholic beverages, flesh foods, condiments, highly flavoured dishes, sugar and white flour products.

B - OTHER MEASURES

1. Drink atleast eight glasses of water daily, but do not take water with meals.
2. Apply frequently fomentations over the stomach and spine, cold compress to the head and hot towels to the neck.
3. Take foot bath at the time of severe headache.
4. Yogic asanas, plenty of rest, and fresh air and deep breathing.

CHAPTER 48

Nephritis

Nephritis refers to an inflammation of the kidneys. It is a serious condition and may be either acute or chronic. A synonym for nephritis is Bright's disease, for Bright (1789-1858) described examples of many different diseases which can be included under the term.

This disease most often strikes in childhood or adolescence. It can become progressively worse and result in death, if not treated properly in the initial stages. In the alternative, it may subside into a chronic stage where the patient gets better but not well.

Symptoms

The main symptoms of acute nephritis are a pain in the kidneys, extending down to the ureters, fever, dull pain the back and scanty and highly coloured urine. Often the urine, may contain blood, albumin and casts consisting of clumps of red and white cells which come from the damaged kidneys. The patient suffers from puf-finess in the face and swelling of the feet and ankles.

In the chronic stage of nephritis, which may drag on for many years, the patient passes large amounts of albumin in the urine. Later, there may be a rise in the blood pressure and the patient may develop uraemia. There may be frequent urination, especially during night.

Causes

Nephritis usually follows some streptococcus infec- tion of the throat or an attack of scarlet fever or rheumatic fever. The underlying causes of nephritis are the same as for diseases of the kidneys in general, namely wrong food habits, excessive drinking, suppressive medical treatment of some former diseases, the habitual use of chemical agents of all kinds for the treatment of indigestion and other stomach disorders and frequent use of aspirin and other painkillers.

Nutritional deficiencies can also lead to nephritis. The disease has been produced in many species of animals by diets deficient in the B vitamin choline. Animals lacking in essential fatty acids and magnesium also develop nephritis. When vitamin B6 and magnesium by sharp crystals of oxalic acid combined with calcium. Nephritis also occurs if vitamin E is deficit.

Dietary Treatment

The safest treatment for acute nephritis is fasting. By means of the fast, the toxins and systemic impurities responsible for setting up of the inflammatory kidney conditions are removed rapidly. The patient should resort to juice fasting for seven to ten days till the acute symptoms subside. Mostly, vegetable juices such as carrot, celery and cucumber should be used during this period. A warm water enema should be taken each day while fasting to cleanse the bowels of the toxic matter being thrown off by the self-cleansing process resulting from the fast.

After the juice fast, the patient may adopt an all-fruit diet for four or five days. Juicy fruits such as apples, grapes, oranges, pears, peaches and pineapples should be taken during this period at five-hourly intervals.

After the all-fruit diet, the patient may adopt a fruit and milk diet. In this regimen, milk, preferably raw goat's milk, may be added to the fruit diet mentioned above for further seven days. The patient may, thereafter, gradually embark upon a well-balanced low-protein vegetarian diet, with emphasis on fresh fruits and raw and cooked vegetables.

In case of chronic nephritis a short juice fast for three days may be undertaken. Thereafter, a week or ten days may be spent on a restricted diet. In this regimen, oranges or orange juice may be taken for breakfast. Lunch may consist of a salad of raw vegetables in season, with olive oil and lemon juice dressing and dinner may consist of one or two vegetables steamed in their own juices and a few nuts. Thereafter, the patient may gradually adopt a well-balanced low-protein vegetarian diet.

Further short juice fasts followed by a week on the restricted diet should be undertaken at intervals of two or three months until the kidney condition has shown signs of normalisation.

The patient should avoid vegetables containing large quantities of oxalic acid such as spinach and rhubarb. Chocolate and cocoa also contain oxalic acid and must not be taken. Garlic, asparagus, parsley, watercress, cucumber and celery are excellent vegetables. Best fruits are papaya and bananas. Both have a healing effect on the kidneys. A small amount of soured milk and home-made cottage cheese can be included in the diet. All salt should be eliminated from the diet. Five or six small meals should be taken in preference to a few large ones.

The diet should be adequate in all essential nutrients. Supplements should be given to furnish the nutrients not obtained from food. The supplements may include one tablespoon of lecithin, 30 mg. of vitamin B6, 25,000 IUs of vitamin A, and 300 to 600 IUs of vitamin E.

Smoking and drinking, where habitual, must be completely given up. Studies have shown that smoking impairs kidney function. The patient should avoid white bread, sugar, cakes, pastries, puddings, refined cereals, greasy, and fried foods. He should also avoid tea, coffee, all flesh foods, condiments, pickles and sauces.

All measures should be adopted to relieve the kidneys of work by increasing elimination through other channels. A hot Epsom salt bath should be taken every alternate day to induce elimination through the skin as much as possible.

Fresh air and outdoor exercises will be of great benefit in all cases of nephritis and where possible, the patient should walk for at least three kilometres once or twice daily. The sufferer from chronic nephritis should never exert himself when doing anything. He should avoid all hurry and excitement. He should also avoid late hours.

If the above treatment is faithfully carried out, the patient of acute nephritis will soon be on the way to recovery. Even in advanced cases of chronic nephritis a great deal can be done to improve the sufferer's condition by perseverance, with the treatment outlined above.

TREATMENT CHART FOR NEPHRITIS

A - DIET

I. A fast on carrot or orange juice and water for three days. Use warm water enema this period.

II. An all-fruit diet for further three days, with three meals a day at five-hourly intervals.

III. Fruit and milk diet for further five days. In this regimen fresh milk may be added to each fruit meal.

IV. Thereafter, gradually adopt a well-balanced low-protein diet on the following lines:-

1. *Upon arising:* 25 black raisins soaked overnight in water alongwith water in which they are soaked.
2. *Breakfast:* Milk sweetended with honey and fresh fruits such as papaya, banana, apples, grapes, pear, peaches, pineapple.
3. *Lunch:* A bowl of freshly-prepared steamed vegetables such as carrot, cabbage, cauliflower, beans, two or three whole wheat chappatis, unsalted butter and a glass of buttermilk.
4. *Mid afternoon:* A glass of carrot juice or coconut water.
5. *Dinner:* A large bowl of fresh green vegetable salad, with lemon juice dressing and mung beans sprouts.
6. *Bed time snack:* A glass of milk sweetened with honey.

Avoid: Tea, coffee, flesh foods, salt, condiments, sugar, white flour products, refined cereals, and foods containing oxalic acid such as spinach, chocolate and cocoa.

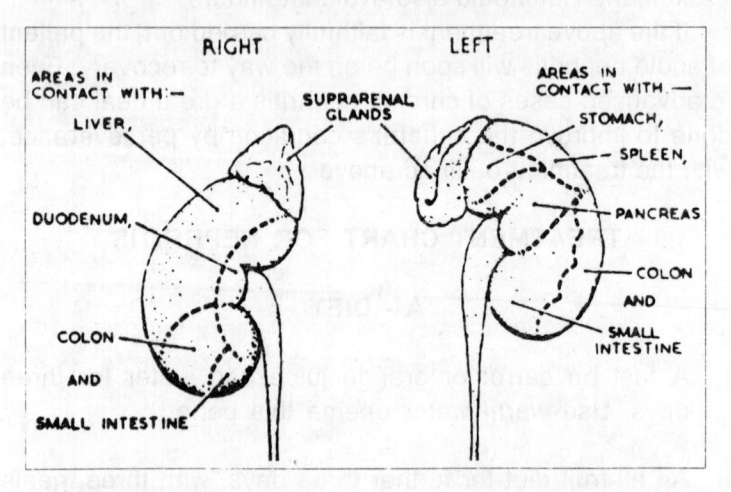

Anterior surface of the kidneys, showing the position of Adrenal glands and the relations of the Kidney.

Take liberally: Garlic, cucumber, french bean, carrot, bananas, papaya, watermelon and pineapple juice.

Note: Repeat short juice fast followed by all-fruit diet and fruit and milk diet at intervals of two months.

B - OTHER MEASURES

1. Fresh air, brisk walks, and yogasanas.
2. Avoid all hurry, excitement and late hours.

CHAPTER 49

Neuritis

Neuritis is one of the most serious nervous disorders. It refers to an inflammation of the nerves, involving a single nerve or a series of nerves. At times, several different groups of nerves in various parts of the body may be involved. This condition is known as polyneuritis. It is also known as polyneuropathy, for strictly speaking, the condition is not an inflammation, but a change in the state of the nerves resulting in weakness, loss of the reflexes and changes of sensation.

Symptoms

The main symptoms of neuritis are tingling and burning and stabbing pains in the affected nerves. In severe cases, there may be numbness and loss of sensation and paralysis of the nearby muscles. Thus, temporary paralysis of the face may result from changes in the facial nerves on the affected side. During the acute stage of this condition, the patient may not be able to close the eyes due to loss of normal tone and strength in the muscles on the affected side of the face. Neuritis may also be caused by pernicious anaemia, involving the nerves of the spine. The patient with this condition may find it very difficult to walk in the darkness.

Causes

The chief cause of neuritis is chronic acidosis, that is, an excessive acidic condition of the blood and other body fluids. All the body fluids should be alkaline in their reaction, but when the acid waste matter is continuously formed in the tissues over a long period due to a faulty diet, it results in acidosis. Wrong habits of living, overwork, etc., lower the tone of the nervous system and contribute towards neuritis. The disease can also result from a variety of nutritional deficiencies and metabolic disturbances such as faulty calcium metabolism, deficiencies of several B vitamins like B12, B6, B1, pantothenic acid and B2 and general toxaemia.

Other causes of neuritis include a blow, a penetrating injury, a bad bruise or heavy pressure over a nerve trunk and dislocation or fracture of the bones. Any violent muscular activity or overextension of the joint as in sprains may injure the nerves and cause neuritis. The condition may also result from certain infections such as tuberculosis, diptheria, tetanus, leprosy and diabetes mellitus, poisoning with insecticides, mercury, lead, arsenic and alcohol.

Dietetic Treatment

Treatment of neuritis by painkilling drugs may give temporary relief but it does not remove the trouble effectively. The pain is relieved for the time being at the cost of the health of other parts of the body, especially the heart and kidneys, and the neuritis remains.

The best treatment for neuritis is to ensure that the patient gets optimum nutrition, well assimilated with all the vitamins and other nutrients. The diet should be made up of three basic food groups, namely seeds, nuts and grains, vegetables and fruits, with special emphasis on whole grains, particularly whole wheat, brown rice, raw and sprouted seeds, raw milk, especially in the soured form and home-made cheese.

In this regimen, the breakfast may consist of fresh fruits, handful of raw nuts or a couple of tablespoons of sunflower and pumpkin seeds. Steamed vegetables, whole wheat chappatis and a glass of butter-milk may be taken for lunch. The dinner may comprise a large bowl of fresh, green, vegetable salad, fresh home-made cottage cheese, fresh butter and a glass of butter-milk.

In severe cases, the patient should be put on a short juice fast for four or five days before being given the optimum diet. Carrots, beets, citrus fruits, apples and pineapples may be used for juices.

All vitamins of the B group have proved highly beneficial in the prevention and treatment of neuritis. The disease has been helped when vitamins B1, B2, B6, B12 and pantothenic acid have been given together and extreme pain, weakness and numbness in some cases have been relieved within an hour.

The patient should avoid white bread, white sugar, refined cereals, meat, fish, tinned foods, tea, coffee and condiments which form the root of the trouble by continuously flooding the tissues with acid impurities.

The patient should be given two or three hot Epsom salt baths weekly, remaining in the bath for 25 to 30 minutes. The affected parts should also be bathed several times daily in hot water containing Epsom salt - a tablespoon of salt to a cupful of hot water. The patient should undertake a walking and other moderate exercises.

TREATMENT CHART FOR NEURITIS

A - DIET

I. Take raw fruit or vegetable juices for 4 or 5 days with a glass of juice every 2 or 3 hours diluted with warm water. Use warm water enema during this period.

II. Thereafter, adopt the strict lacto-vegetarian diet on the following lines:-
1. *Upon arising:* A glass of fresh fruit or vegetable juice.
2. *Breakfast:* Fresh fruits and milk sweetened with honey and a handful of raw seeds or nuts.
3. *Lunch:* A bowl of steamed vegetables, one or two whole wheat chappatis, unsalted fresh butter and a glass of buttermilk.
4. *Mid afternoon:* A glass of fruit or vegetable juice.
5. *Dinner:* Fresh green vegetable salad with lime juice dressing and homemade cottage cheese.

Avoid: Tea, coffee, salt, chocolate, spices (mustard, pepper and vinegar), sugar, white flour and its products and refined foods.

Specially beneficial: All fruits an berries, vegetables such as carrots, cabbage, radishes, cucumber, red beets and tomatoes.

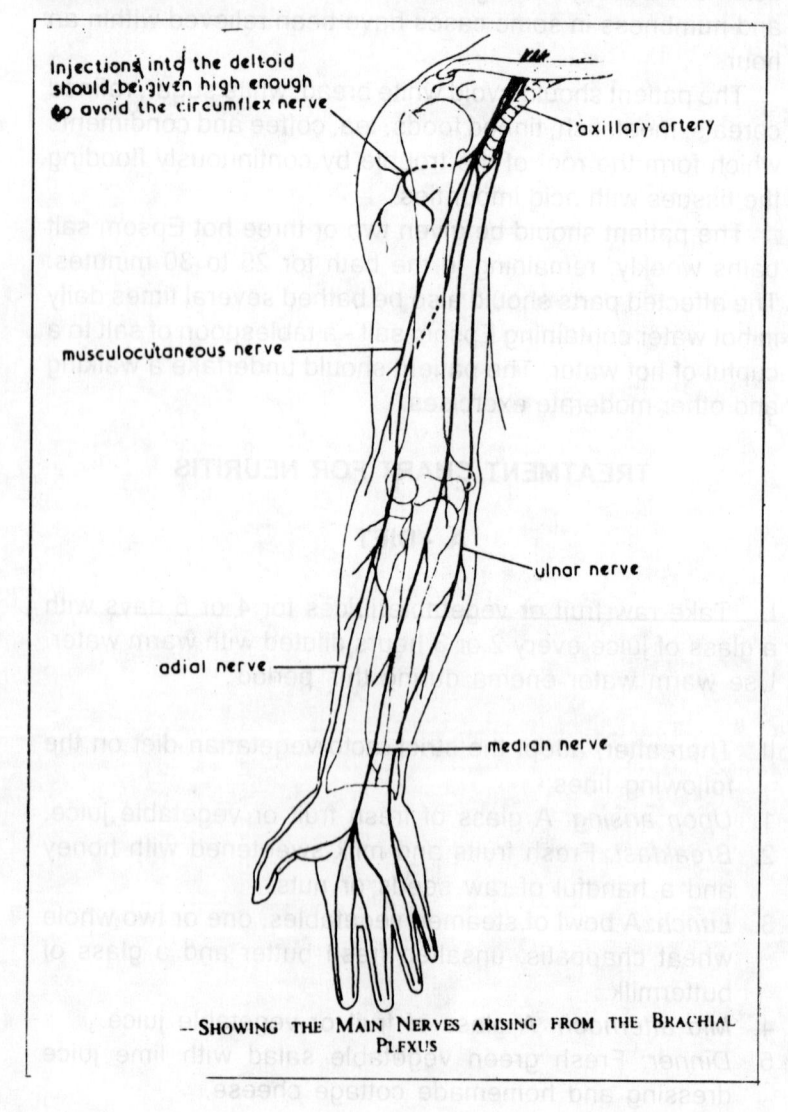

SHOWING THE MAIN NERVES ARISING FROM THE BRACHIAL PLEXUS

B - OTHER MEASURES

1. Hot epsom-salt bath twice a week.
2. Neutral immersion bath (92° to 95° F.) one hour daily at bed time.
3. Massage once a week.
4. Walking and moderate exercise including yogic asanas like ekpadatsana, varasana and shavashana.

CHAPTER 50

Obesity

Obesity may be described as a bodily condition characterised by excessive storage of fat in the adipose tissues. It usually results from consumption of food in excess of physiological needs. Obesity is common among people in Western countries and among the higher income groups in India and other developing countries.

Obesity can occur at any age in either sex. Its incidence is higher in persons who consume more food and lead sedentary lives. In women, obesity is liable to occur after pregnancy and at menopause. A woman usually gains about 12 kg. weight during pregnancy. Part of this is an increase in the adipose tissue which serves as a store against the demands of lactation. Many women gain more and retain a part of this weight. They become progressively obese with each succeeding child.

Assessment

Obesity is generally assessed by relating the patients' weight to charts of standard weight according to age, sex and height and then categorise them as 10, 20, or 30 per cent overweight. However, normal weight depends on body build and some people, who inherit a large frame and bulky muscles, may weigh more than the standard weight, without being obese. A more scientific assessment of obesity would, therefore, be by the proportion of fat in the total body weight. Mean values of body fat for the normal young men are about 12 per cent and for young women about 26 per cent. A man whose body fat amounts to more than 20 per cent of his total weight may be regarded obese and for a woman a figure of more than 30 per cent represents obesity.

Obesity is a serious health hazard as the extra fat puts a strain on the heart, kidneys and liver as well as the large weight-bearing joints such as the hips, knees and ankles, which ultimately shortens the life span. It has been truly said, 'the longer the belt, the shorter the life'. Overweight persons are susceptible to several diseases like coronary thrombosis, heart failure, high blood pressure, diabetes, arthritis, gout and liver and gall-bladder disorders.

Causes

The chief cause of obesity, most often, is overeating — that is, the intake of calories beyond the body's energy requirement. Some people have a habit of eating too much while others may be in the habit of consuming high-calorie foods. These people gain weight continuously as they fail to adjust their appetite to reduced energy requirements. There has, in recent times, been an increasing awareness of the psychological aspects of obesity. Persons who are generally bored, unhappy, lonely or unloved, those who are discontented with their families, or social or financial standing usually tend to overeat as eating is a pleasure and solace to them.

Obesity is sometimes also the result of disturbances of the thyroid or pituitary glands. But glandular disorders account for only about two per cent of the total incidence of obesity. In such persons the basal metabolic rate is low and they keep gaining weight unless they take a low-calorie diet.

Dietary Cure

A suitably planned course of dietetic treatment, in conjunction with suitable exercise and other measures for promoting elimination, is the only scientific way of dealing with obesity. The chief consideration in this treatment should be the balanced selection of foods which provide the maximum essential nutrients with the least number of calories.

To begin with, the patient should undertake a juice fast for seven to ten days. Juices of lemon, grapefruit, orange, pineapple, cabbage, celery may be taken during this period. Long juice fast upto forty days can also be undertaken, but only under expert guidance and supervision. In the alternative, short juice fasts should be repeated at regular intervals of two months or so till the desired reduction in weight is achieved. During the first few days of the treatment and afterwards if necessary, the bowels should be cleansed daily with a warm water enema.

After the juice fast, the patient should spend a further four to five days on an all-fruit diet. In this regimen he should have three meals a day of fresh juicy fruits such as oranges, grape-fruit, pineapples and papayas. Thereafter, he may gradually embark upon a low-calorie well-balanced diet of three basic food groups, namely seeds, nuts and grains, vegetables and fruits, with emphasis on raw fruits, vegetables and fresh juices.

The foods which should be drastically curtailed or altogether avoided are high-fat foods such as butter, cheese, chocolate, cream, ice cream, fat meats, fried foods, foods high in carbohydrates like breads, candy, cake, cookies, cereal products, legumes, potatoes, honey, sugar, syrup and rich puddings; beverages such as all cold drinks and alcoholic drinks.

To overcome the hunger pangs brought on by a lowered consumption of food, the patient should sip water gradually or take low-calorie and high-water foods like vegetables and certain fruits. Skimmed milk, buttermilk, barley water, fruit juices, green steamed vegetables and raw salads are good for reducing weight. Six to eight glasses of water should be taken every day but never with meals.

Other precautions which should be taken in regard to foods are: meals should be taken at fixed hours and snacks should be avoided in between; all foods should be taken in small quantities; salt should be restricted in the diet as excessive intake produces water retention.

Fletcherism

One sure method of reducing weight is by practising what is known as "Fletcherism". It was discovered in 1898 by Horace Fletcher of the U.S.A. Fletcher, who at 40, considered himself an old man. He was 50 pounds overweight, contracted flu every six months and constantly complained of indigestion and a tired feeling. After a deep study, he made some important discoveries and prescribed the rules for "Fletcherism" which are as follows:

1. Chew your food to a pulp or milky liquid until it practically swallows itself.
2. Never eat until hungry.
3. Enjoy every bite or morsel, savouring the flavour until it is swallowed.
4. Do not eat when tired, angry, worried, and at mealtimes refuse to think or talk about unpleasent subjects.

Fletcher considered complete mastication the most important rule of all. He tried fixing an ideal number at first but found that chewing less than thirty times per mouthful was insufficient. Consequently, he decided that chewing food to a pulp or liquid should become the standard. Horace Fletcher followed these rules for five months. As a result he lost more than 60 pounds and felt better than he had for 20 years. A weight reducing programme built on Fletcherism works wonders and is worth a trial.

Suggested Menu

It is important that the overweight person should so devise his diet as to lose weight gradually — a pound in a week or ten days. This will enable him to get used to the new eating habits. The following menu is suggested as a guideline:

Early morning: A glass of warm water mixed with the juice of half a lemon.

Breakfast: Wheat, mung or Bengal gram sprouts and one cup skimmed milk.

Mid-morning: A glass of orange, pineapple or carrot juice.

Lunch: Salad or raw vegetables such as carrot, beat, cucumber, cabbage, cauliflower, tomato and onion, wholewheat dry chappatis and a glassof butter-milk.

Mid-afternoon: Coconut water or any fruit juice (except apple juice) or lemon tea or vegetable soup.

Dinner: Whole wheat dry chappatis, steamed vegetables and any seasonal fruit, except banana and apple.

Along with dietetic treatment, the patient should adopt all other natural methods of reducing weight. Exercise is an importat part of weight reduction plan. It helps to use up calories stored in body fat and relieves tension, besides toning up the muscles of the body. Certain yogic asanas such as sarvangasana, bhujangasana, dhanurasana, chakrasana, vajrasana and yogamudra are also highly beneficial. They help slimming by breaking up or redistributing fatty deposits and strengthen the flabby areas. The patient should adopt measures which bring on excessive perspiration such as sauna baths, steam bath and heavy massage. They help to reduce weight. And above all, the obese persons should make every effort to avoid negative emotions such as anxiety, fear, hostillity and insecurity and develop a positive outlook on life.

TREATMENT CHART FOR OBESITY

A - DIET

I. Raw juice diet for five to seven days. Take a glass of fresh fruit or vegetable juice, diluted with water on 50:50 basis , every two hours during the day. Use warm water enema to cleanse the bowls.

II. An all-fruit diet for further five to seven days, taking three meals a day of fresh juicy fruits at five hourly intervals.

III. Thereafter, adopt a low-calorie diet on the following lines:-

1. *Upon arising:* Luke warm water with half a freshly-

squeezed lime.

Foods with high sugar content like sweets have high calorie content and there consumption can lead to obesity

2. *Breakfast:* Fresh fruits and a glass of skimmed milk.
3. *Lunch:* Freshly-prepared steamed vegetables, whole wheat chappatis and a glass of butter milk.
4. *Mid afternoon:* Vegetable or fruit juice or coconut water.
5. *Dinner:* Fresh green vegetable salad and sprouts with lime juice dressing, followed by hot course, like vegetable soup, if desired.

Home Remedies: Lime and lemon juices, leaves of jujube or Indian plum(ber), cabbage, tomato and finger millet(ragi)

Avoid: Tea, coffee, sugar, white flour, all products made with white flour, and white flour, refined foods, high-fat foods, fried foods and flesh foods, condiments, pickles, alcohol and smoking.

B - OTHER MEASURES

1. Brisk walk for 45 minutes morning and evening, other exercises like swimming, jogging, cycling and yogasanas.

2. Steam bath and heavy massage one a week.

CHAPTER 51

Peptic Ulcer

Peptic ulcer is one of the most common diseases today. It refers to an eroded lesion in the gastric intestinal mucosa. An ulcer may form in any part of the digestive tract which is exposed to acid gastric juice, but is usually found in the stomach and the duodenum. The ulcer located in the stomach is known as gastric ulcer and that located in the duodenum is called a duodenal ulcer. Usually both are grouped together and termed peptic ulcer. An ulcer is, usually one-fourth to one inch in diameter, and it is either round or oval shaped.

Duodenal ulcers are about ten times more frequent than gastric ulcers. They are more common in sedentary workers than manual workers. The incidence of peptic ulcers is four times higher in men than women. Men are more affected by duodenal ulcers whereas women usually get ulcers in the stomach. Both kinds affect young to middle-aged persons and are most common in the 35-40 age group.

Symptoms

The most common symptoms of peptic ulcer are sharp and severe pain and discomfort in the upper central abdomen. The pain is commonly described as burning or gnawing in character. Gastric ulcer pain usually occurs an hour after meals and rarely at night. Duodenal ulcer pain usually occurs between meals when the stomacy is empty and is relieved by food, especially milk. It is often described as hunger pain and gets the sufferer out of bed between 2 and 4 a.m. As the disease progresses there is distension of the stomach due to excessive flatulence, besides mental tension, insomnia and gradual weakening of the body. It may also cause constipation with occasional blood in the stools. If an ulcer bleeds slowly, there is anaemia.

A really severe peptic ulcer can lead to serious complications like haemorrhage, perforation or obstruction of the orifice through which the food passes from the stomach to the intestine. Unless treated in time, it can lead to massive bleeding and shock, or even death.

Causes

Peptic ulcers result from hyperacidity which is a condition caused by an increase in hydrochloric acid in the stomach. This strong acid secreted by the cells lining the stomach affects much of the break-down of food. It can be potentially dangerous and, under certain circumstances, it may eat its way through the lining of the stomach or duodenum producing, first, irritation of the stomach wall and eventually an ulcer.

Dietetic indiscretion, like overeating, taking of heavy meals or highly spiced foods, coffee, alcohol and smoking are the main factors contributing to this condition. Alcohol is a very powerful acid producer and has a burning effect on the stomach lining. Coffee also increases the production of acid especially when it is taken black The ingestion of certain drugs, particularly asprin, food poisoning, infections like influenza and septicaemia and gout may also cause ulcers.

Emotional stress or nervous tension also plays a major role in the formation of ulcers. The stomach is a highly sensitive organ and nervous activity can slow down or speed up digestion. Those given to excessive worry, anger, tension, jealousy and hurry are thus more prone to suffer from ulcers than those who are easy-going and relaxed. Ulcer patients are usually highly strung, irritable and ambitious people who live very active lives. They generally take on many things at one time and worry about the results of their various projects.

Certain occupations appear to predispose individuals to peptic ulcers. Doctors and those in responsible positions in industry such as business executives are particularly prone to it. Presumably stress and strain, hurried and irregular meals, and inadequate mastication are important contributory factors in their cases.

Dietetic Cure

Persons who treat themselves with antacids may do themselves more harm than good. Though they may get initial relief because the tablet neutralises the acid, the stomach responds by producing even more acid because the basic cause of the hyperacidity has not been dealt with. Ulcers can be best treated by natural methods.

Milk, cream, butter, fruits and fresh, raw and boiled vegetables, natural foods and natural vitamin supplements are the best diet for an ulcer patient. The fruits recommended are bananas, mangoes, musk melon and dates. Such a diet will progressively reduce the acidity in the stomach. A low-salt diet can greatly help in curing hyperacidity and ulcers. Those in an advanced state of the disease should avoid whole grains, nuts and whole grain bread and cereals in the beginning and should take only milk and bananas. Milk should be taken in moderate quantities — about 250 to 300 millilitres — every hour. Bananas are highly beneficial. They are said to contain an unidentified compound called, perhaps jokingly, vitamin U (against ulcers). Well-cooked millet and cooked white rice with milk can be added later.

Diet is of utmost importance in the treatment of ulcer. The diet should be so arranged as to provide adequate nutrition to afford rest to the disturbed organs, to maintain continuous neutralisation of the gastric acid, to inhibit the production of acid and to reduce mechanical and chemical irritation.

Almond milk made from balanced almonds in a blender is very beneficial as it binds the excess of acids in the stomach and supplies high quality protein. Raw goat's milk is also highly beneficial. It actually helps to heal the peptic ulcer.

Raw fruits and vegetables should be avoided for a few weeks, as many of these are especially irritating. Potatoes, squashes, yams and raw bananas are, however, well tolerated. All sour fruits should be avoided, especially citrus fruits.

Certain foods definitely do not agree in cases of gastric complaints and should be completely eliminated. These include fried and greasy foods which are always difficult to digest and require very efficient stomach and liver action; flesh foods which require a high amount of acid in the stomach for their digestion and acid causes more pain and flatulence in the sensitive stomach; condiments, preserves and sugar which are stomach irritants; and tea, coffee, tobacco and alcohol which create an acidic reaction in the stomach. The healing capacity and vitality of the body will increase if these harmful and unsuitable foods are avoided.

How rapidly the ulcer heals will largely depend on the correct assortment of essential amino acids and sufficient ascorbic acid. Iron absorption depends on an acid medium and is facilitated by the presence of ascorbic acid. The neutralisation of stomach acid, therefore, interferes with iron absorption. Several studies have shown that vitamin E and A, especially taken together, have not only a protective effect against development of ulcers caused by stress, but also a curative effect on existing ulcers.

The observance of certain rules by an ulcer patient with regard to eating habits are essential. He should never eat when tired or emotionally upset, nor when he is not hungry even if it is mealtime, nor when his mouth is dry. He should chew every morsel thoroughly. He should eat only natural foods and take food in as dry form as possible. Meals must be small and frequent. All foods and drinks which are either too hot or too cold should be avoided.

The patient should drink eight to ten glasses of water every day. However, he should not drink water during or with meals, but only half an hour before or one hour after he has eaten. In case of haemorrhage in the stomach, a rectal enema should be administered four times daily with water temperature at 110° to 115°F. In case of abdominal or stomach pain, hot packs should be placed on the abdomen with water temperature at 120°F. Hot pack should also be placed between the shoulder blades.

Daily massage and deep breathing exercises also help. Above all, the patient must try to rid himself of his worries and stay cheerful. He should also cultivate regularity in his habits — be it work, exercise or rest.

TREATMENT CHART FOR PEPTIC ULCER

A - DIET

I. Milk and banana diet for three to five days.
II. Thereafter, the following diet may be adopted:-
1. *Upon arising:* 25 black raisins soaked overnight in water alongwith the water in which they are soaked and also water kept overnight in copper vessel.
2. *Breakfast:* Fruits such as bananas, mangoes, musk melon, custard apple, papaya and figs and a glass of milk. Avoid sour fruits.
3. *Mid-morning:* Carrot juice or coconute water.
4. *Lunch:* Steamed vegetables, whole wheat chappatis or rice.
5. *Mid-afternoon:* Few dates and milk.
6. *Dinner:* Lightly cooked vegetables, whole wheat chappatis and fruits.
NOTE: Introduce grdually raw vegetables and sprouted mung.
7. *Before retiring:* A glass of milk.

AVOID: Tobacco, alcohol, flesh foods, coffee, tea, condiments, all chillies, white sugar, white flour and their products, fried and greasy foods.

IMPORTANT: Take low-salt diet, smal and frequent meals, avoid too hot or too cold foods and drink eight glasses of water everyday.

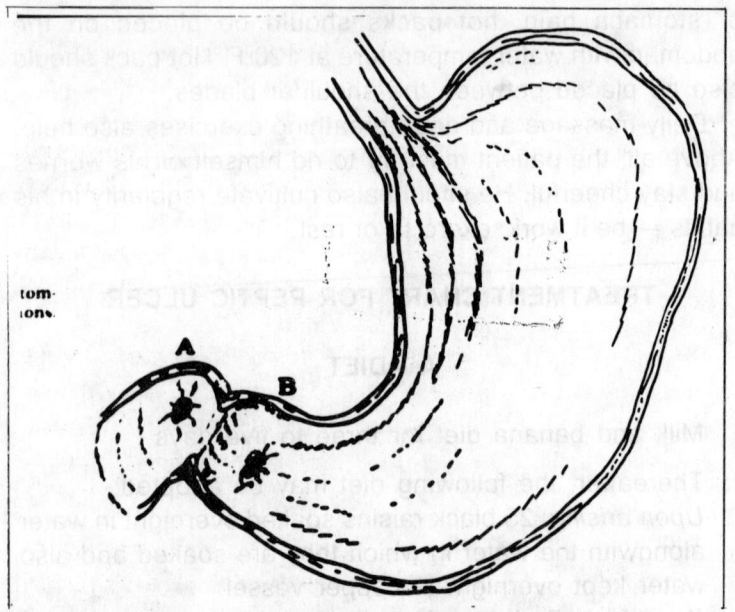

Diagram showing stomach and duodenum with crooked lesions.
A. Duodenal ulcer B. Gastric ulcer.

B - OTHER MEASURES

1. We packs for one hour in the morning and evening on an empty stomach, hot packs in case of abdominal pain.
2. Yogasanas like uttanpadasan, pavanmuktasan, bhujangasan and shavasan.
3. Avoid stress, nervous strain, and worries.
4. Adequate rest and relaxation.

CHAPTER 52

Piles

Piles or Haemorrhoids are among the most common ailments today, especially in the Western World. They are a varicose and often inflamed condition of the veins inside or just outside the rectum. In external piles, there is a lot of pain but not much bleeding. In the case of internal piles, there is discharge of dark blood.

Haemorrhoids are classified from mild to severe depending on the degree of prolapse, that is, how much they protrude from the anus. In some cases the veins burst and this results in what is known as bleeding piles.

Symptoms

Pain at passing stools, slight bleeding in the case of internal trouble, and a feeling of soreness and irritation after passing a stool are the usual symptoms of piles. The patient cannot sit comfortably due to itching, discomfort, and pain in the rectal region.

Causes

The primary cause of piles is chronic constipation and other bowel disorders. The pressure applied to pass a stool to evacuate constipated bowels and the congestion caused by constipation ultimately lead to piles. The use of purgatives to relieve constipation, by their irritating and weakening effect on the lining of the rectum, also result in enlargement and inflammation of veins and bleeding of the mucus lining. Piles are more common during pregnancy and in conditions affecting the liver and upper bowel. Prolonged periods of standing or sitting, strenuous work, obesity and general weakness of the tissues of the body are the other contributory causes of piles.

Mental tension is also one of the main causes of haemorrhoids. Persons who are always in a hurry often strain while passing stools. They rush through defecation instead of making it a relaxed affair. The pressure thus exerted by the anal muscles affect the surrounding tissues. The extra rectal pressure and resultant congestion of veins ultimately lead to haemorrhoids. Hereditary factors also probably, involved in the development of piles.

Dietetic Treatment

There is no local treatment to cure piles. The treatment of the basic cause — namely, chronic constipation — is the only way to get rid of the trouble. To begin the dietetic treatment, the whole digestive tract must be given a complete rest for a few days and the intestines thoroughly cleansed. For this purpose the patient should adopt an all-fruit diet for at least seven days. He should have three meals a day of fresh juicy fruits such as grapes, apples, pears, peaches, oranges, pineapples and melons. For drinks, unsweetened lemon water or plain water either hot or cold may be taken.

In long-standing and stubborn cases, it will be advisable to have a short fast for four or five days before adopting an all-fruit diet. When on a short fast, the patient may have the juice of an orange in a glass of warm water, if desired. An enema with lukewarm water should be taken daily in the morning while fasting. This will cleanse the bowels and give much needed rest to the rectal tissues.

After the all-fruit diet, the patient may adopt a diet of natural foods aimed at securing soft stools. The diet should be low in fat, it should not contain more than 50 grams of fat. Foods which contain less fat are skimmed milk, butter-milk, curd and cottage cheese made from skimmed milk; all vegetables except cabbage, onions, dried beans and peas; cooked and dried cereals, whole wheat chappatis and fruits and fruit juices.

The ideal diet for the patient with piles should consist of fruits like papaya, musk melon, apple and pear; green vegetables particularly spinach, cabbage and radish; wheat, porridge, whole meal cereals and milk. Lentils and *daals* should be avoided, as they constipate the bowels. The patient should also abstain from meat, fish, eggs, cheese, white sugar, sweets, rice, all fried foods and all white flour products. Tea and coffee should be avoided. Dry fruits such as figs and raisins and coconuts should form part of the diet which could be on the following lines:

Breakfast: Papaya, figs or prunes and milk.

Lunch: Raw vegetable salad, whole meal bread with a small quantity of butter and butter-milk.

Dinner: Two or three non-starchy steamed vegetables, nuts, curd, raisins and a fresh fruit.

Foods rich in vitamin C, bioflavonoids and vitamin E are essential in the treatment of haemorrhoids. Such foods include fresh raw vegetables and fruits, especially cabbage, citrus fruits, whole grains, seeds and nuts. Vitamin B6 is also considered highly beneficial in the treatment of this disease. Piles have been produced in volunteers deficient in vitamin B6 and corrected when this vitamin was given. The patient with piles should supplement his diet with 10 mg. of B6 after each meal.

The patient should drink at least six to eight glasses of water a day. He should avoid straining to pass stool. Cold water treatment helps the veins to shrink and tones up their walls. The treatment is done by sitting in a tub filled with cold water for two minutes with knees drawn up to your chin. The water level should cover the hips. This should be done twice a day. Cold compress applied to the rectal area for an hour before bedtime is also very helpful.

The patient with piles must make an all-out effort to tone up the entire system. Exercise plays an important corrective role in this condition. Movements which exercise the abdominal muscles will improve circulation in the rectal region and relieve congestion.

TREATMENT CHART FOR PILES

A - DIET

I. An all-fruit diet for 5 days, with three meals a day of fresh juicy fruits at five-hourly intervals.

II. Thereafter, gradually adopt a well-balanced diet on the following lines:-

1. *Upon arising:* 25 black raisins soaked overnight in water alongwith water in which they are soaked and water kept overnight in copper vessel.

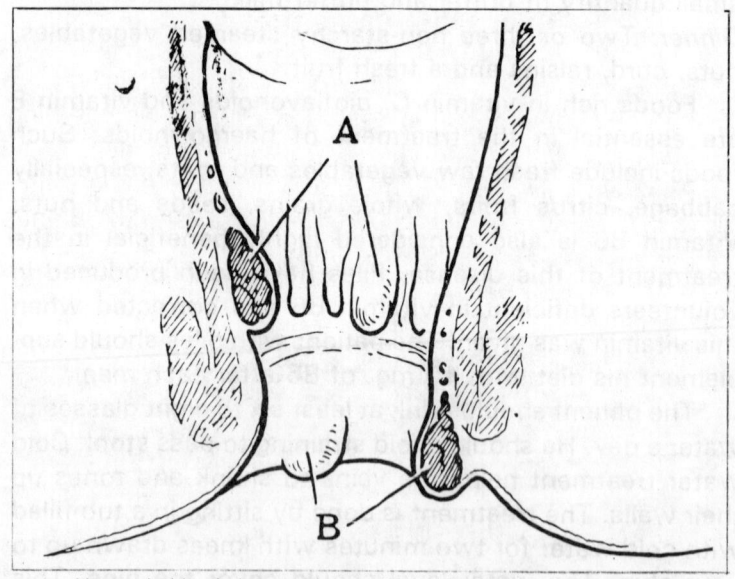

Hemorrhoids. A, internal hemorrhoids; B, external hemorrhoids.

2. *Breakfast:* Fresh fruits and a glass of milk, sweetened with honey.
3. *Lunch:* A bowl of freshly-prepared steamed vegetables two or three whole wheat chappatis and a glass of buttermilk.
4. *Mid-afternoon:* A glass of carrot juice or coconut water.
5. *Dinner:* A large bowl of fresh green vegetable salad with lemon juice dressing, mung bean sprouts, and

cottage cheese or a glass of buttermilk.
6. *Bedtime Snack:* A glass of milk or one apple.

B - RULES FOR EATING

1. Do not take water with meal, but half an hour before and one hour after meals.
2. Never hurry through a meal. Eat very slowly and chew your food as throughly as possible.
3. Never eat to full stomach.

AVOID: Tea, coffee, sugar, white flour, and all products made from them, all refined cereals, fried foods, flesh foods, condiments and pickles.

C - OTHER MEASURES

1. Drink at least six to eight glasses of water daily.
2. Cold hip bath for 10 minutes daily and wet heating compress for one hour daily on empty stomach.
3. Brisk walk for 45 minutes morning and evening daily.
4. Yogasanas like Uttanapadasana, pavanmuktasana, vajrasana and shavasana.

CHAPTER 53

Prostate Disorders

Nearly one-third of all men over 50 years suffer from prostate troubles of one form or another. The percentage rises with age and reaches 75 after the age of 80 years. Prostate and bladder disorders can lead to numerous other ailments such as arthritis, kidney disorders and uremia. It is, therefore, of utmost importance to detect the disease in its early stages and commence treatment.

The prostate gland is a male gland, comparable in shape and size to a large chestnut. It is reddish brown in appearance. It measures approximately one and a half inches in width and about an inch in length and weighs approximately 25 grams. It is situated at the base of the urinary bladder and around the commencement of the urethra, the membranous tube for the passage of the urine. It is thus vital in relation to the emptying of the bladder and bears a close relationship to the rectum.

The prostate gland is composed of both muscular and glandular tissues. It is firmly attached to the pelvis by a dense fascial sheath. Like all muscular and glandular tissues in the body, it is adequately supplied with blood vessels, arteries, veins and nerves. The gland plays an important role in normal sexual life and its function is to secrete a fluid which is added to semen during sexual intercourse.

Various Disorders

There are various types of prostate disorders. Of these, the most important are prostatitis or inflammation in the prostate gland and hypertrophy or enlargement of the prostate gland. Prostatitis may be acute or chronic. It is a painful and distressing disorder, but can be cured with proper treatment, without any adverse effects.

Enlargement of the prostate gland or hypertrophy is the most common complaint affecting the gland. This occurs mostly in men of middle or advanced age. The enlargement develops so gradually over a long period that it often assumes serious proportions before it is detected.

Symptoms

There are two warning signals to indicate the possibility of prostate disorders. The first is the interference with the passage of urine and the second is the need to void the urine frequently during the night's sleep. Both these symptoms are very definite. Other symptoms are a dull aching pain in the lower back and pain in the hips, legs and feet.

Prostate enlargement affects the glandular system as a whole. The patient experiences all the symptoms of disturbed health such as lack of energy and physical, mental and nervous disturbances. Proper treatment of the disorder is, therefore, of utmost importance.

Causes

The position of the prostate gland makes it liable to congestion and other disorders. In an erect position, pressure falls on the pelvic region just where the prostate gland is situated. With ageing, the body gets heavier and loses its flexibility which makes the pressure on the pelvis even greater and increases the vulnerability of the prostate gland. Prolonged periods of sitting down, as in certain occupations, also increases the pressure on the pelvic region resulting on congestion of the tissues in and around the prostate gland. With the passage of time, changes such as inflammation or enlargement occur in the gland. Acute prostatitis may also result from exposure to cold and chill and from an infectious disease. Chronic prostatitis is an after-effect of the acute condition. It may also result from continual irritation of the gland due to excessive sexual treatment.

Another important cause of prostate disorders is constipation. In constipation, the faeces becomes hardened and the rectum or lower bowel overloaded. This causes undue pressure on the prostate gland. It also entails a great deal of straining to pass stools and this adversely affects the prostate gland due to its proximity to the rectum.

Dietary Treatment

The dietetic treatment for prostate enlargement consists of detoxicating the system by proper fasting and diet. To begin with, the patient should forgo all solid foods and subsist on water only for two or three days. The intake of water should be as plentiful as possible. Nothing should be added to the water except a little lemon juice, if desired. The water may be taken cold or hot and it should be taken every hour or so when awake. This will greatly increase the flow of the urine.

An enema may be taken once a day during fasting to clear the lower bowel of accumulations. After thorough cleansing of the bowels, hot and cold applications may be used directly on the prostate gland and its surrounding parts. The heat relieves the tissues and a brief cold immersion tones them up. The patient should take alternate hot and cold baths. These are of great value in relieving pain and reducing congestion. While taking hip baths, it should be ensured that the buttocks and pelvis are well covered with water. The hot bath should be taken first for ten minutes, followed by cold bath for one minute only.

After the short fast, the patient should adopt an all-fruit diet for three days. The fruits should include apples, pears, oranges, grape-fruits, grapes, sweet limes, mangoes, melons and all other juicy fruits. This will help to clear toxins from the body and will also enable excess fat to be reduced to some extent.

The exclusive fruit diet should be followed by a diet, consisting of two meals of fruits and one of cooked vegetables for further seven days. The vegetable meal should be taken in the evening and could consist of all kinds of cooked vegetables, preferably steamed. Thereafter, the following general diet may be adopted:

Breakfast: This should consist of fresh fruits in season such as grapes, oranges, apples, bananas, pears, peaches and grape-fruits. A handful of raw seeds and nuts may be added to the fruit meal which has a cleansing and stimulating effect.

Lunch: This meal should be largely a raw salad which should consist of tender vegetables such as lettuce, tomatoes, endive, watercress and cucumber. Carbohydrates, in the form of whole wheat chappatis or rice may be added to this meal. Fresh lemon juice should be used in salad dressing as it is both rich in vitamins and minerals. In addition to citric acid, it contains the B-complex vitamins and vitamin C together with calcuim, magnesium, potassium, sodium, phosphorus, choline and sulphur. With lemon juice, vegetable oil and a little sea salt, an excellent dressing can be made that adds taste as well as food value to the salad.

Dinner: This meal should consist mainly of cooked vegetables like green beans, carrots, peas and potatoes which should be combined with protein foods like cottage cheese, legumes such as dried beans, lentils, peanuts and sweet fruit, fresh or dried.

The short lemon juice fast, followed by all-fruit diet and a further period on fruits and vegetables may be repeated after two or three months if necessary, depending on the progress being made.

The patient should use, liberally, raw seeds and nuts, especially pumpkin and squash seeds, sunflower seeds and almond. All these foods are rich in high quality protein. Unsaturated fatty acids and zinc are essential to the health of the prostate. The patient should also use liberally vitamin E — rich foods as vitamin E is an important factor for prostate health.

Heavy starches, sweet stimulants and highly seasoned foods are entirely forbidden, as they cause direct irritation on the prostate gland and bladder. The diet should also exclude spices, condiments, salt in excess, sauces, red meats, cheese, asparagus, water cress, greasy or fried foods, alcohol, tobacco and too much tea or coffee. The patient should avoid hurried meals and must chew his food thoroughly and slowly. Water should be taken between meals and not at mealtimes.

The patient should avoid sexual excesses, irregularities in eating and drinking, long periods of sitting and vigorous exercise. He should guard against constipation by taking plenty of fruits, bran and nuts. All efforts should be made to tone up the general condition of the body. With a general improvemet in health, the condition will be greatly relieved. Surgery should be resorted to only if the condition does not improve even after the dietary treatment and other measures outlined here.

TREATMENT CHART FOR PROSTATE DISORDERS

A - DIET

I. Fast on water mixed with lemon juice for three days. Take plenty of water and use warm water enema daily during this period. Use hot and cold applications directly on the prostate gland and its surrounding parts.

II. An all-fruit diet for further three days, with three meals a day at five-hourly intervals.

III. Thereafter, adopt a restricted diet, consisting of two meals of fruits and one of steamed vegetables for seven days.

IV. After the restricted diet, adopt the following diet:-

1. *Upon arising:* A glass of lukewarm water with half a freshly-squeezed lime and a teaspoon of honey.
2. *Breakfast:* Fresh fruits, a cup of fresh milk, sweetened with honey and nuts.
3. *Lunch:* A bowl of steamed vegetables, whole wheat chappatis with butter and a glass of buttermilk.

4. *Mid-afternoon:* Fresh fruit or vegetable juice or sugar cane juice.

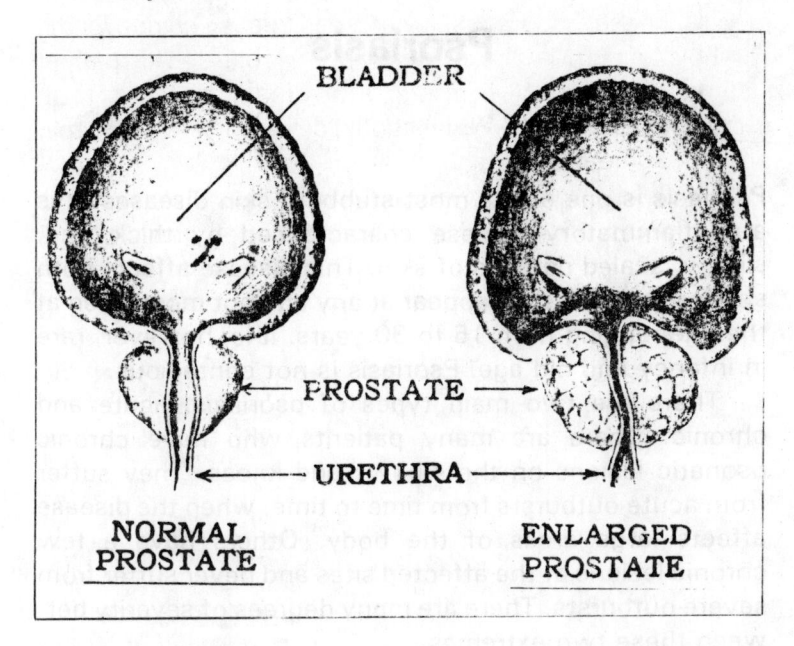

BLADDER

PROSTATE

URETHRA

NORMAL PROSTATE

ENLARGED PROSTATE

5. *Dinner:* Fresh green vegetable salad, with lime juice dressing, sprouted mung beans and fresh home-made cottage cheese.

Note: Repeat a short fast on water and lemon juice, followed by an all fruit diet and restricted diet after every two or three months.

AVOID: Meat, sugar, tea, coffee, condiments, pickles, refined and processed foods, fried, heavy, or greasy foods and products made from sugar and white flour.

B - OTHER MEASURES

1. Hot and cold applications and hot and cold hip bath.
2. Wet girdle pack.
3. Avoid sexual excesses.
4. Avoid irregularities in eating and drinking, long period of sitting, vigorous exercise and constipation.

Psoriasis

Psoriasis is one of the most stubborn skin diseases. It is an inflammatory disease characterised by thick, red, silvery, scaled patches of skin. This disease affects both sexes equally. It may appear at any age but most often at the age ranging from 15 to 30 years. It is, however, rare in infancy and old age. Psoriasis is not contagious.

There are two main types of psoriasis, acute and chronic. There are many patients who have chronic psoriatic lesions on the elbows and knees. They suffer from acute outbursts from time to time, when the disease affects large areas of the body. Others have a few chronic lesions at the affected sites and never suffer from severe outbursts. There are many degrees of severity between these two extremes.

It is estimated that between one and four per cent of the world's population may have visible psoriasis at any one time. There is a higher incidence of this disease among the inhabitants of cold damp countries like Iceland than those of dry warm climate. The most commonly affected areas are usually those shaded from the sun by hair or clothing. It would thus appear that a psoriatic skin requires an abnormal amount of exposure to sunlight.

Symptoms

Generally, the skin of the person suffering from psoriasis appears red and irritated and may be covered with bright silvery scales. The scales are composed of thin layers of dead abnormal skin cells. Sometimes there is itching. Areas usually involved are elbows, knees, the skin behind the ears, trunk and scalp. It mostly appears first at the back of the elbows and the front of the knees.

The disease may also affect the underarm and genital areas. In some cases, it may be restricted to the scalp, where it is often confused with dandruff. The lesions vary from one or two small localised patches to an extensive spread over the body. Quite often, they are discs from half an inch to several inches in size. In severe cases, it may disfigure almost the whole body, which can adversely affect the skin's ability to control the body's temperature and thereby prove greatly hazardous. The lesions of psoriasis are always dry and rarely become infected.

Causes

The modern medical system has not been able to establish the exact cause of psoriasis. The main cause of the disease appears to be the faulty utilisation of fats. It has been noted that persons with this abnormality have excessive amounts of cholesterol in their skin and blood. Recent studies have shown that psoriasis involves an abnormality in the mechanism in which the skin grows and replaces itself. This abnormality is related to the metabolism of amino acids, the protein chemicals which are nature's basic building blocks for the reproduction of cell tissues.

Heredity also plays a role in the development of psoriasis as it tends to occur in families. About 30 per cent of the patients have a family history of the disease. Occasionally it misses a generation and then appears in some members of the next one.

The factors that aggravate or precipitate the outbreak of psoriasis are injury to skin in the form of cuts, burns, minor abrasions, changes in the seasons, defective kidney elimination, infections and the use of certain medicines for the treatment of other disease. Chronic psoriasis is occasionally linked with deep repressed emotional factors and severity and chronicity of the erruptions depend on the psychological state of the patient.

Dietary Treatment

Since psoriasis is a metabolic disease, a cleansing juice fast for about two weeks is always desirable in the beginning of treatment. Carrots, beets, cucumbers and grapes may be used for juices. Juices of citrus fruits should be avoided. A warm water enema should be used daily to cleanse the bowels during the fast.

After the juice fast, the patient should adopt the diet of three basic food groups, namely seeds, nuts and grains, vegetables and fruits, with emphasis on raw seeds and nuts especially sesame seeds, pumpkin seeds, sunflower seeds and plenty of organically grown raw vegetables and fruits. In this regimen, the breakfast may consist of fresh fruits such as apples, grapes, pears, peaches, pineapples and a handful of raw nuts or a couple of tablespoons of raw seeds. A large bowl of fresh green vegetable salad and sprouts may be taken for lunch and dinner may consist of steamed vegetables and whole wheat chappatis.

After noticeable improvement, goat's milk, yogurt and home-made cottage cheese may be added to the diet. Juice fast may be repeated after four weeks on the diet. All animal fats, including milk, butter and eggs should be avoided. Refined or processed foods and foods containing hydrogenated fats or white sugar, all condiments, tea, coffee, alcohol and tobacco should also be avoided.

Lecithin has proved effective in the treatment of psoriasis. The disease has also been helped by vitamins A and B6. The patient should take three tablespoons of granular lecithin daily along with all nutrients needed to help the liver produce its own lecithin. He should also take generous amounts of vitamins C, E and B-complex.

The hot Epsom salt bath is highly beneficial in the treatment of psoriasis. Three full baths should be taken weekly until the trouble begins to subside. The number of baths thereafter may be reduced to two weekly and finally to one. Regular sea water baths and application of sea water externally over the affected parts once a day are also beneficial.

In many cases, psoriasis responds well to sunlight. The affected parts should be frequently exposed to the sun. The patient should undertake plenty of regular exercise in fresh air, especially exposing the affected parts and deep breathing exercises. He should avoid all nervous tensions and should have adequate rest.

TREATMENT CHART FOR PSORIASIS

A - DIET

I. Fast on fruit or vegetable juices for 5 to 7 days. Use warm water enema daily during this period.

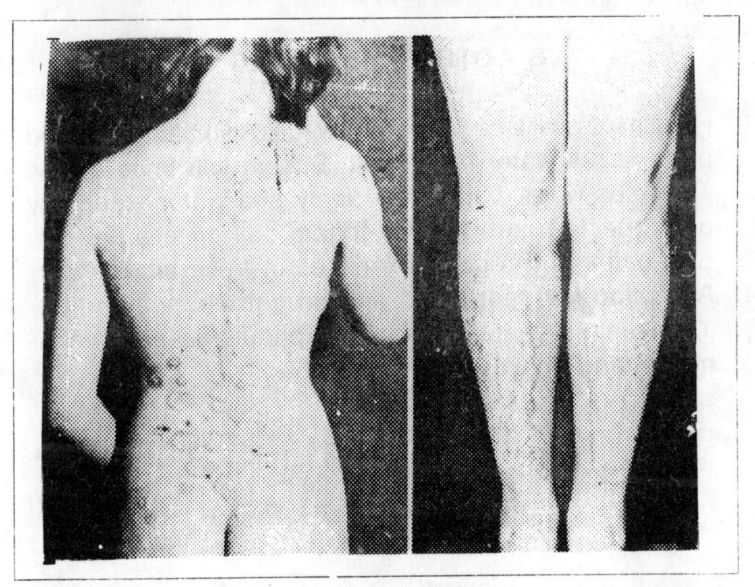

Psoriasis on back and legs.

II. Thereafter, the following diet may be adopteD:-
1. *Upon arising:* 25 black raisins soaked overnight in water alongwith water in which they are soaked as well as water kept overnight in a copper vessel.

2. *Breakfast:* Fresh fruits and a glass of buttermilk.
3. *Lunch:* A bowl of freshly-prepared steamed vegetables, two or three whole wheat chappatis and a glass of buttermilk.
4. *Mid-afternoon:* Coconut water.
5. *Dinner:* Fresh green vegetable salad, and mung bean sprouts with lime juice dressing.

Note: After noticeable improvement, add milk and home-made cottage cheese to the diet. Repeat juice fast for shorter periods, at monthly intervals.

AVOID: Animal fats, refined or processed foods and foods containing hydrogenated fats or white sugar, condiments, tea, coffee, alcohol and tobacoo.

B - OTHER MEASURES

1. Hot Epsom-salts baths twice a week. Also bathe affected parts in hot water mixed with Epsom salt once a day.
2. Take sea-water bath. Also apply sea water externally over affected parts with a cottom ball once a day.
3. Sun baths and regular exercises in fresh air.
4. Avoid too frequent baths and do not use soap.
5. Yogasanas like padmasana, ekpaduttanasana, yoga-mudra and shavasana.

CHAPTER 55

Rheumatism

The word rheumatism is derived from the Greek word "rheuma", which means a swelling. It refers to an acute or chronic illness which is characterised by pain and swelling of the muscles, ligaments and tendons or of the joints. It is a crippling disease which causes widespread invalidism, but seldom kills.

This disease affects men and women, both young and old. Quite often, it extends to the heart and the valves and the lining of this vital organ becomes inflamed. It is the most common cause in 80 per cent of the cases of valvular organic diseases of the heart.

Rheumatism, perhaps, more than any other disease, although readily diagnosed, is never the same in any two individuals. There are too many variations in the development of this disease. Broadly speaking, however, rheumatism, which may be acute or chronic, can be roughly grouped into two classes. These are muscular rheumatism which affects the muscles and articular rheumatism which affects the joints. The muscular variety is, however, far less common than that affecting the joints. In the acute form, it is found among children and young people, but in the chronic form, it is generally confined to the adults.

Symptoms

The onset of acute types of rheumatism is characterised by fever and rapid pulse with intense soreness and pain. In the acute muscular type, the tissues become so sensitive that even the weight of bed clothing aggravates the pain. The liver is found to be swollen. Acute rheumatism is extremely painful but it leaves no permanent defects, if treated properly. It may settle into a chornic state under a wrong mode of treatment.

The symptoms of chronic muscular rheumatism are pain and stiffness of the affected muscles. The pain increases when an effort is made to move these muscles. In case of chronic articular rheumatism, pain and stiffness are felt in one or more joints of the body, with swelling in most cases. It is not usually fatal but there is a danger of permanent deformities.

Causes

The chief cause of rheumatism is the poisoning of the blood with acid wastes, which results from imperfect elimination and lowered vitality. Meat, white bread, sugar and refined cereals, to which modern man is most addicted, leave a large residue of acid toxic wastes in the system. These acid wastes are not neutralised due to absence of sufficient quantities of alkaline mineral salts in the foods eaten. This upsets the acid-alkaline balance in the body and produces the condition described as acidosis.

When there is abundant vitality, excess acids are ejected almost before they reach any appreciable concentration in one or the other of the acute cleansing efforts such as colds and fevers. When vitality is low, the acid wastes are concentrated around the joints and bony structure, where they form the basis of rheumatism. The reason why large quantities of acid wastes piling up in the system are attracted towards body structure for storage is that lime, which is the most prominent constituent of the bony structure, is an alkaline substance. In certain cases, infection from the teeth, tonsils and gall-bladder may produce rheumatism. The disease is aggravated by exposure to cold water.

Dietary Treatment

In the case of acute rheumatism, the patient should be put on a short fast of orange juice and water for three or four days. The procedure is to take the juice of an orange diluted in warm water, if desired, every two hours from 8 a.m. to 8 p.m. Nothing else, whatsoever, should be taken, otherwise the purpose of the fast will be entirely lost. While fasting, the bowels should be cleansed through a warm water enema.

After the juice fast, the patient should be placed on a restricted diet for 14 days. In this regimen, orange or grape fruit may be taken for breakfast; lunch may consist of raw salad of any vegetables in season, with raisins, prunes, fig or dates; and for dinner, one or two steamed vegetables such as spinach, cabbage, carrots, turnips and cauliflower and a few nuts or some sweet fruit may be taken. No bread or potatoes or other starchy food should be taken, otherwise the effect of the diet will be lost. Thereafter, the patient may gradually commence a well-balanced diet of three basic food groups, namely seeds, nuts and grains, vegetables and fruits.

In case of chronic rheumatism, the patient may be placed on an all-fruit diet for four or five days. In this regimen, he should have three meals a day of fresh, juicy fruits such as apples, grapes, peaches, pears, oranges, pineapples and grapefruits. He may, thereafter, gradually adopt a well-balanced diet of three basic food groups.

The short juice fast followed by a restricted diet in case of acute rheumatism and the all-fruit diet in chronic cases may be repeated at intervals of two or three months, depending on the progress being made.

The patient should take ripe fruits and fresh vegetables in abundance. Lemons are valuable and the juice of two or three lemons may be taken each day. Lots of butter-milk should be taken. The foods which should be avoided are meat, fish, white bread, sugar, refined cereals, rich, indigestible and highly seasoned foods, tea, coffee, alcohol, sauces, pickles and condiments.

Rheumatism is particularly responsive to raw vegetable juice. The alkaline action of raw juices dissolve the accumulation of deposits around the joints and in other tissues. The carrot juice combined with juices of red beet and cucumber is especially valuable. Three ounces each of beet and cucumber juices may be mixed in ten ounces of carrot juice in this combination.

Other helpful methods in the treatment of rheumatism are application of radiat heat and hot packs to the affected parts, a hot tub bath, cabinet steam bath, dry friction and sponge. The hot Epsom salt bath is also beneficial and should be taken twice a wek for three months in case of chronic rheumatism and once weekly thereafter. The affected parts should also be bathed twice daily in hot water containing Epsom salt (¼ lb. of salt to a bowlful of hot water) after which some olive oil should be applied. Fresh air, deep breathing and light outdoor exercises are also beneficial. Dampness and cold should be avoided.

TREATMENT CHART FOR RHEUMATISM

A - DIET

I. Fast on orange juice and water for three to five days. Take warm water enema daily during this period.

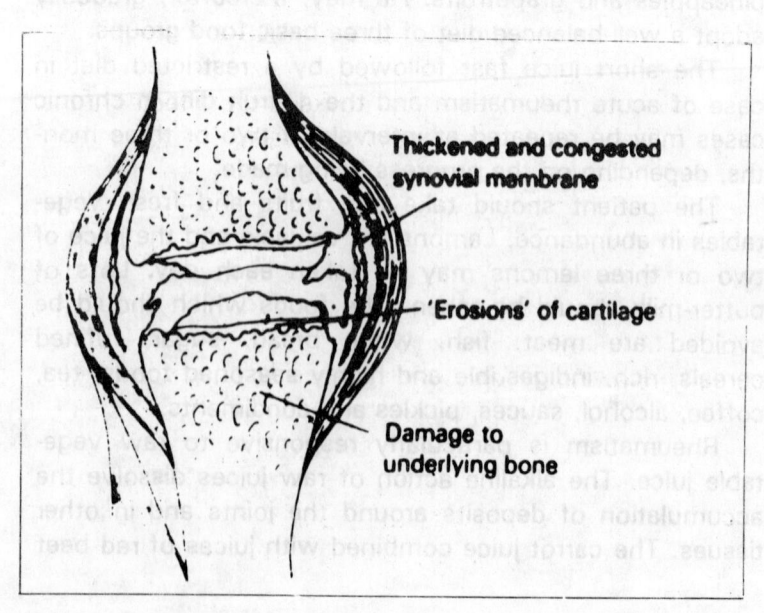

II. An all-fruit diet for further three to five days, taking three meals a day of fresh juicy fruits at five-hourly intervals.

III. Thereafter, adopt a well-balanced diet as follows:-
1. *Upon arising:* A glass of lukewarm water with half a freshly-squeezed lime and a teaspoon of honey.
2. *Breakfast:* Fresh fruit, a glass of milk sweetened with honey and some seeds or nuts.
3. *Lunch:* A bowl of freshly-prepared steamed vegetables, two or three whole wheat chappatis and a glass of butter milk.
4. *Mid-afternoon:* A glass of fresh fruit or vegetable juice.
5. *Dinner:* Raw vegetable sald and sprouts with lime juice dressing, followed by a hot course if, desired.

Home remedies: Raw potato juice, bitter gourd juice, fluid extract of celery seeds, lemon juice, white flour and products made from them, refined foods, fried foods, flesh foods, condiments, pickles, alcohol and smoking.

B - OTHER MEASURES

1. Application of heat and hot packs to the affected parts.
2. Hot tub bath and cabinet steam bath.
3. A hot-Epsom salts bath at night twice a week for three months.
4. Daily dry friction.
5. Fresh air, deep breathing, light outdoor exercises and yogasanas.
6. Avoid dampness and cold.

CHAPTER 56

Sexual Disorders

Sex plays an important role in shaping human lives. It is now realised that the sex impulse is present in various forms from the earliest months until the end of life. Being a basic instinct like hunger, its satisfaction is essential for sustained harmony and well-being.

The sexual act not only quietens the excitement which is a natural occurence during maturity, but also refreshes the body and mind. It also contributes to mental development. In fact, it exercises a powerful influence upon every organ and cell and every physical and chemical process, including the nervous system.

Sexual activity, however, demands complete concentration and relaxation. It cannot be performed in haste and tension. The modern men who are usually tense and highly occupied are unable to follow these norms. The consumption of alcohol also leads to inadequate sexual functioning. Many persons, therefore, suffer from sexual disorders.

Impotence

Impotence is the most common of all the sexual disorders in the male. It can be defined as failure to obtain an erection or maintain it for a reasonable length of time without attaining orgasm. The main causes of impotence are fatigue, devitalised condition of the system in general, abuse or misuse of the sexual organism over a long period, glandular deficiencies, infectious diseases including veneral diseases and psychological factors.

About 90 per cent cases of impotency are caused by psychological factors. Inadequate performance results from loss of confidence and other preoccupations of the mind. Many people carry their office problems to bed.

They are constantly under stress and stress is the deadly enemy of potency. It stimulates the sympathetic nerve which inhibits erection. These persons are haunted by the fear of the loss of manhood, particularly when a temporary loss of desire or an occasional failure of potency occurs. This may ultimately result in impotence which has a devastating effect on their personal lives.

Impotence may quite often result from one's feelings of guilt about masturbation, pre-marital sex or about having contracted venereal diseases previously. In fact, any act which arouses feelings of insecurity can precipitate impotency.

Premature ejaculation

Premature ejaculation is another extremely common sexual disorder prevalent among the males. In this condition, the man gets an orgasm even before penetration or soon thereafter without allowing his partner to reach a climax. This leaves both partners dissatisfied. If this inability continues in more than half the number of times a person has sex, he can be classified as "disturbed". This usually results from high level of sexual excitement accompanied by mental tension and anxiety. Apprehension of either the partner or the sexual act can aggravate or precipitate this problem.

Venereal Diseases

There has been an alarming increase in venereal or sexually transmitted diseases (V.D. or S.T.D.) due to promiscuity and free sex. These diseases are caused by bacteria and germs and can become very serious if not treated properly and early. The most common diseases in this category are syphilis and gonorrhoea.

Syphilis is probably one of the oldest diseases of the human race. Sexual contact is the commonest way in which this disease is spread through a community. But many of those who contract the disease are innocent. Little children are sometimes born with this disease. It may also be transmitted from one person to another by kissing or handling infected clothing or other articles.

Syphilis usually begins as a small ulcerating type of lesion which may occur anywhere in the body, the most common sites being the penis, the vulva or in the vagina. The violent or rough sex indulgence often results in abrasions and thus the virus comes in direct contact with blood.

Gonorrhoea is usually transmitted by sexual contact. An acute inflammation of the male urethra or the vagina of the female due to infection through pus by the gonorrhoea germs is known as gonorrhoea. The person having a high degree of toxaemia and a low vitality may develop this condition with the slightest secretion. A clean blood stream and a high vitality on the other hand may protect one from this disease.

This wise plan, however, is to avoid all chances of infection. The common chance is the sexual act in which one of the partners has this disease. Sometimes it may be contracted through other sources or it may be hereditary.

Gonorrhoea is a more difficult disease than syphilis to identify. About two-thirds of women with this disease have no symptoms at all or at most very trivial ones which may be passed off as an apparently harmless vaginal discharge. The usual symptom in the male is a discharge from the tip of the penis.

If the disease is neglected or improperly treated, it may spoil the entire blood stream which may produce gonorrhoeal rheumatism and will also affect the eyes. Proper treatment is, therefore, highly important soon after occurrence of the infection.

Dietetic Treatment

Taking of drugs or so called "remedies" in case of impotence and premature ejaculation is not only useless but dangerous. Diet is an important factor in these conditions. To begin with, the patient should adopt an exclusive fresh fruit diet from five to seven days. In this regimen, he can have three meals a day of fresh juicy fruits such as grapes, oranges, apples, pears, peaches, pineapples and melons. The bowels should be cleansed daily during this period with a warm water enema.

After the all-fruit diet, the patient may gradually embark upon a balanced diet of the three basic food groups, namely seeds, nuts and grains, vegetables and fruits with generous amounts of special rejuvenative foods such as whey, soured milks, particularly made from goat's milk, millet, garlic, honey, cold-pressed vegetable oils and yeast. The patient should avoid smoking, alcohol, tea, coffee and all processed, canned, refined and denatured foods, especially white sugar and white flour and products made therefrom.

Research has shown that malnutrition contributes to impotency. It has been established that protein, essential fatty acids, vitamin E and several of the B vitamins are essential for the production of sex hormones. A lack of protein can result in loss of sex interest and a decrease in sperm count. Lack of vitamin E can lead to degeneration of testicles and decrease in both the sex hormones and the pituitary hormone gonadotropin, which stimulate the sex glands.

Leland Kordel, one of the best known nutritionists, reports that hundreds of cases of impotency have responded to diets rich in protein, vitamin A, vitamin B-complex and Vitamin D. According to him, protein keeps the thyroid well-nourished and there is a close link between the thyroid and sex glands; vitamin A keeps the mucous membrane in good condition and thus helps the functioning of the testicles; vitamin B1 helps the pituitary gland to keep mating desire normal; choline helps the liver to manufacture hormones. Vitamin D found in codliver oil and other fatty foods help virility.

Vigorous massage all over the body is highly beneficial in the treatment as it will revive the muscular vigour which is essential for nervous energy. The nerves of the genital organs are controlled by the pelvic region. Hence, a cold hip bath for 10 minutes in the morning or evening will be very effective. Every effort should be made to build up the general health-level to the highest degree and fresh air and outdoor exercise are essentials to the success of the treatment.

The scheme of treatment outlined above will go a long way in restoring sexual function, but of course the results achieved will depend upon the age and condition of the sufferer. Where the troubles are of psychological origin, treatment should be just the same, but in these cases advice from a qualified psychotherapist would be highly desirable. The patient also requires a little gentle handling by a willing partner.

The venereal diseases like syphilis and gonorrhoea are quite amenable to successful treatment by proper dietary and other natural methods, leaving no ill-effects to mar the future life and happiness of their victims. The suppressive drugs employed by the modern medical system in their treatment simply halts the active manifestation of the diseases in the victim's system for the time being. The disease-poisons and the metallic drugs used are still left in the patient's system and these have a most destructive effect upon the tissues and structures of the body, especially upon the nervous tissues.

The only safe way of treating venereal diseases is fasting. All cases of syphilis and gonorrhoea can be cured through fasting. This will not only prevent dreaded after-effects, but will also greatly enhance the whole general health-level of the patient by thorough cleansing of his system. The juice of an orange, in a glass of warm water, may be taken during this period. If orange juice disagrees, vegetable juices may be taken. Each day while fasting, it should be ensured that the bowels are cleansed of the effete and poisonous matter thrown off by the self-cleansing process now set up by the body. This can be achieved through a warm water enema. The fast may be continued from seven to fourteen days.

After the fast, the patient, may adopt an exclusive fruit diet for further five days. He should, thereafter, gradually embark upon a balanced diet of three basic food groups as outlined in the treatment for impotence, avoiding all the foods mentioned therein.

Major A. Austin, a doctor in the Royal Army Medical Corps in Great Britain in his book, 'Direct Paths to Health' mentions the case of a syphilis patient aged 27 years who was cured only by dietetic treatment. Dr. Austin narrates the case as under:

"Mr. A., aged twenty-seven, came to me suffering from tertiary syphilis. The classic drugs had been used, including mercury and '606' (known now under various names, such as salvarsan, neo-salvarsan, arsenobenzol, all being similar and based on arsenic), but it had not stopped the ravages of the disease. His face and body were covered with rupial eruptions — ulcers covered with a scab — and the odour from his body was most unpleasant.

"I prescribed a fourteen days' fast with a saline purge daily, plenty of water and as much strained orange juice diluted with water as he liked to drink during the day. At the end of the fourteen days he was allowed two meals a day, one of them consisting of nothing but properly cooked vegetables and some butter, and the other of milk and fresh fruit.

"In six weeks from the date of commencing the treatment all the eruptions had disappeared, as well as the foul odour of the body, and he was feeling remarkably well and has remained so ever since."

Vegetable juices are highly beneficial in the treatment of venereal diseases. Juices which are particularly helpful include those of carrot, cucumber, beet and spinach. The patient may make liberal use of carrot juice either in combination with spinach juice or cucumber and beet.

In case of syphilis, a 'T' pack should be employed for an hour for the local treatment of the initial sore and it should be repeated twice daily. All clothes, sheets and towels, used by the patient should be handled carefully to avoid new sores and to prevent infection to others. It is better to boil all such articles. In case of eruption on the different parts of the body, a wet sheet pack for an hour is beneficial. It will help brign out all the poisonous substances of the skin by producing more eruptions which will gradually dry up.

Application of pelvic packs occasionally for an hour is one of the most effective methods of treatment in case fo gonorrhoea. As irritation in the prostate gland and urethra is present in this disease,hot hip bath for eight minutes has a beneficial effect as it tends to relieve irritation.

An occassional steam bath for eight minutes is of outstanding value in both syphilis and gonorrhoea. It will help remove the poisonous substances from the body and enable the kidney to perform its work effectively. An overall massage has also beneficial effect upon the entire body.

TREATMENT CHART FOR SEXUAL DISORDERS

A - DIET

I. An all-fruit diet for 5 days, with three meals a day at five-hourly intervals. The bowels should be cleansed daily during this period with a warm-water enema.

II. Thereafter, gradually adopt a well-balanced diet on the following lines:-
1. *Upon arising:* 25 black raisins soaked overnight in water alongwith water in which they are soaked as well as water kept overnight in a copper vessel.
2. *Breakfast:* Fresh fruit and a glass of milk, sweetened with honey and some nuts, especially almonds.
3. *Lunch:* A bowl of freshly-prepared steamed vegetables, two or three whole wheat chappatis with butter and a glass of buttermilk.
4. *Mid-afternoon:* A glass of carrot juice or sugar cane juice.
5. *Dinner:* A large bowl of fresh green vegetable salad with lemon juice dressing, mung bean sprouts and

cottage cheese.
6. *Bedtime:* A glass of milk sweetened with honey and few dates.

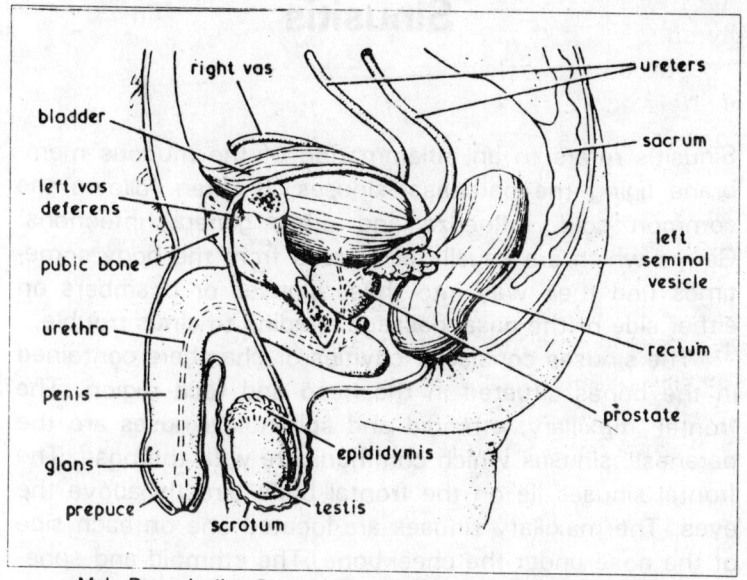

Male Reproductive Organs. The Genito-Urinary Tract in the Male

AVOID: Smoking, coffee, tea, alcohol and all processed, canned and refined foods, especially white sugar and white flour products.

Note: Make liberal use of garlic, onion, carrot, yeast, lady's finger, curd, millet, lecithin and food rich in vitamin E, A and C.

B - OTHER MEASURES

1. Physical activity in fresh air, sufficient exercise and yogasanas such as bhujanasana, shallabhasana, pavanmuktasana, and shavasana.
2. Vigorous massage all over the body, twice a week.
3. Cold hip baths for 10 minutes daily.

CHAPTER 57

Sinusitis

Sinusitis refers to an inflammation of the mucous membrane lining the paranasal sinuses. It often follows the common cold, influenza and other general infections. Germs which are usually eliminated from the body sometimes find their way into these sinuses or chambers on either side of the nasal passage, leading to sinus trouble.

The sinuses consist of cavities or chambers contained in the bones situated in the head and face region. The frontal, maxillary, ethmoid and sphenoid sinuses are the paranasal sinuses which communicate with the nose. The frontal sinuses lie on the frontal bone directly above the eyes. The maxillary sinuses are located one on each side of the nose under the cheekbone. The ethmoid and sphenoid sinuses are situated behind the nose or either side of it. These air sinuses lighten the weight of the skull and give resonance to the voice.

Symptoms

The symptoms of sinusitis are excessive or constant sneezing, a running nose, blockage of one or both nostrils, headaches and pressure around the head, eyes and face. Sinus headaches are usually felt in the forehead and in the face just below the eyes. The patient may suffer from a low grade fever, lack of appetite, loss of sense of appetite and toothache. He feels miserable because of difficulty in breathing. The voice is also affected because of the blocked nose.

Causes

Sinusitis results from the congestion of the sinus passages due to catarrh. It is caused by oversecretion of mucus in the membranes lining the nose, throat and head. This oversecretion is due to irritation caused by toxins in the blood.

A faulty diet is, thus, the real cause of sinus trouble. When a person consumes certain types of food or drinks regularly, these, in due course, have a conditioning effect on the entire system. As a result, some persons become more sensitive to certain allergens, whose reaction utlimately turns into sinusitis.

The modern medical system regards sinus trouble as the result of allergy. After identifying the allergen, it prescribes medicines and injections to build up resistance in patients. This is a lengthy treatment which may provide momentary relief but does not provide a lasting cure. Patients are advised to avoid the use of or contact with well-known allergens such as certain spices, flowers, perfumes, smoke, certain plants, animals and so on. Often, it is very difficult to determine what the individual is allergic to.

Dietetic Cure

Correcting the faulty diet is of utmost importance in the treatment of sinusitis. Patients should take a balanced diet. Most persons with sinus trouble also suffer from acidity. Their diet should, therefore, veer to the alkaline side. The intake of salt should be reduced to the minimum as salt leads to accumulation of water in the tissues and expels calcium from the body.

In the acute stage of the disease, when fever is present, the patient should abstain from all solid foods and only drink fresh fruit and vegetable juices diluted with water in the proportion of 50:50. After the fever subsides, he may adopt a low-calorie raw fruit and vegetable diet with plenty of raw juices.

After the acute symptoms are over, the patient may gradually embark upon a well-balanced diet of three basic food groups, namely seeds, nuts and grains; vegetables and fruits. In persistent chronic conditions, repeated short juice fasts may be undertaken for a week or so at intervals of two months.

Those suffering from sinusitis should completely avoid fried and starchy foods, white sugar, white flour, rice, macaroni products, pies, cakes and candies. They should also avoid strong spices, meat and meat products. Butter and ghee should be used sparingly. Honey should be used for sweetening. All cooked foods should be freshly prepared for each meal. Vegetables should be taken in liberal quantities. All kinds of fruits can be taken with the exception of those belonging to citrus group such as lemon, lime, orange and grapefruit. Milk should be taken in liberal quantities as it contains calcium which has a marked effect in overcoming inflammation of the tissues.

A diet rich in vitamin A is the best insurance against cold and sinus trouble. Vitamin A is the "membrane conditioner" and it helps build healthy mucus membranes in the head and throat. Some of the valuable sources of this vitamin are whole milk, curds, egg yolk, pumpkin, carrot, leafy vegetables, tomato, mango and papaya.

The carrot juice used separately or in combination with juices of beet and cucumber or with spinach juice is highly beneficial in the treatment of sinus trouble. Three ounces each of beet and cucumber juice or six ounces of spinach juice should be mixed with 10 ounces of carrot juices in these combinations.

At times, cold application over the sinus will give great relief; at other times alternate hot and cold application will prove beneficial. Plenty of sleep, adequate rest and fresh air are essential in the treatment of sinusitis.

TREATMENT CHART FOR CHRONIC SINUSITIS

A - DIET

I. Fast on fruit or vegetable juices for three days. Cleanse the bowels daily by warm water enema during this period.

II. An all-fruit diet, should be taken for further three days. During this period, take three meals a day of fresh juicy fruits such as oranges, papaya, pineapples, mangoes, pears and grapes at five-hourly intervals.

III. Thereafter, the following diet should be adopted:-
1. *Upon arising:* A glass of lukewarm water with half a freshly-squeezed lime and a teaspoon of honey.

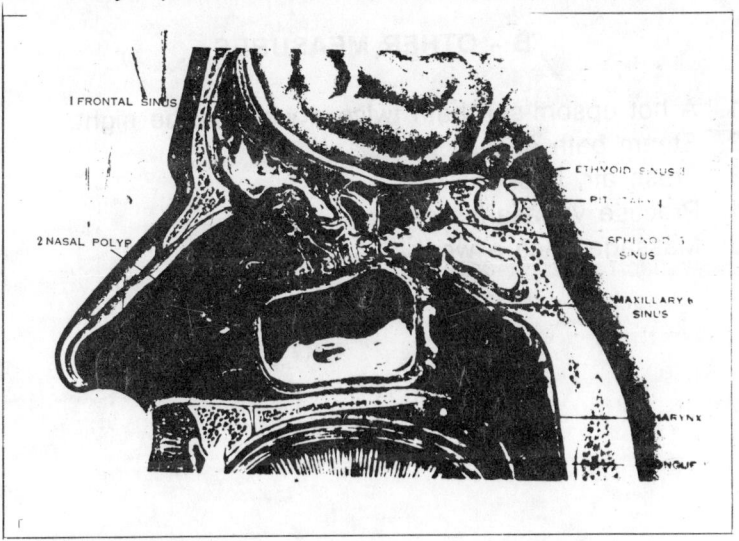

Cross section showing the nose and sinuses inflamed owing to a severe allergy. A thick grey discharge in all of the sinuses indicates an abnormal condition known as chronic sinusitis.

2. *Breakfast:* Fresh fruits and a cup of fresh milk, sweetened with honey:
3. *Lunch:* A bowl of steamed vegetables, whole wheat dry chappatis and a glass of buttermilk.

4. *Mid-afternoon:* A glass of fresh fruit or vegetable juice.
5. *Dinner:* A bowl of fresh green vegetable salad, sprouted seeds and fresh home-made cottage cheese or a glass of buttermilk.

Note: Repeat short fast on juices for three days, followed by an all-fruit diet for three days further, at an interval of one month till condition improves.

AVOID: Meats, sugar, tea, coffee, condiemnts, pickles, refined foods, fried, heavy or greasy foods, and products made from sugar and white flour.

Specially Beneficial: Garlic, onion, large doses of vitamin A, and C, carrot juice in combination with beet juice and pineapple juice.

B - OTHER MEASURES

1. A hot epsom-salt bath twice a week in the night.
2. Steam bath once a week.
3. Fresh air, brisk walks.
4. Practise yogasanas daily.
5. Massage once a week.

CHAPTER 58

Stomatitis

Stomatitis refers to inflammation of the mucous membrane lining the mouth. It is a painful condition resulting from infection. Ulcers may form on the gums and the mouth, particularly between the teeth. These ulcers contain numerous germs. Simple ulcers in the mouth, however, come and go spontaneously. The diesease is quite common both in adults and children.

Symptoms

A person suffering from stomatitis finds it very difficult to take his meals because of pain. At times, he has to go with small quantity of liquid food which he gulps down with difficulty. He also feels pain and difficulty in talking. Other symptoms of stomatitis are excessive salivation, coated tongue, bright red mouth, irritability, vomiting after taking meals, reduced appetite and bad breath. The patient may also suffer from mild fever and constipation.

Causes

Stomatitis may arise from a variety of causes. The most important causes which lead to this condition are defective functioning of the stomach and indigestion. Poor oral hygiene and nutritional deficiencies are other main causes of stomatitis. The disease may also result from infection with Candida albicans (thrush) and infection with Vincent's Spirochaete (Vincent's angina). It may also be found in blood disease such as leukaemia.

Dieatary Treatment

As stomatitis generally results from toxic condition of

the system, the treatment for this disease has to be constitutional. It should aim of improving the digestive system. Temporary measures will only supress the disease. To begin with, the patient should be placed on orange juice and water for three to five days. The procedure is to take the juice of an orange, diluted with water on 50:50 basis, every two hours during the day. If orange juice does not agree, carrot juice diluted with water, may be taken. The bowels should be cleansed daily with a warm-water enema during this period. If this is not possible in case of child-patient, a glycerine suppository may be applied.

After the juice diet, the patient should adopt an exclusive diet of fresh fruits for further three to five days. In this regimen, he should take three meals a day of fresh juicy fruits such as apple, grapes, grapefruit, orange, pear, pineapple, peach and papaya. Thereafter, the patient may gradually embark upon a well-balanced diet consisting of seeds, nuts and grains, vegetables and fruits. The emphasis should be on fresh fruits, whole grain cereals, raw or lightly-cooked vegetables and sprouted seeds like alfalfa and mung beans.

The patient should avoid meats, tea, coffee, sugar, white flour and all products made from them. He should also avoid condiments, pickles, refined and processed foods, soft drinks candies and ice cream.

Certain home remedies have been found beneficial in the treatment of stomatitis. The most important of these is the use of lemon (bara nimbu). Taking a tablespoon of lemon juice daily before meals will correct the functioning of the stomach and help cure the condition. The patient should also gargle several times daily with lemon juice mixed in water. This gargle can be prepared by mixing 20 ml. of lemon juice in 100 ml. of hot water.

Another simple but effective home remedy for stomatitis is the frequent use of a mouth-wash containing a teaspoon each of salt and baking soda in a glass of warm water. This should be used every two to three hours to keep the mouth as clean as possible.

The use of alum (phitkari) is also valuable in stomatitis.

The patient should gargle with alum diluted in hot water. Concentrated solution of alum may also be applied with the help of a swab on the ulceration spot.

Other Measures

Proper oral hygiene is of utmost importance in the treatment of stomatitis. The patient should carefully brush his teeth and gums to remove any foul material. He should also take multi-vitamin tablets, especially those high in vitamin C and B complex. This will aid in recovery. Other helpful methods include fomentations every three hours over the mouth, cheeks and jaws and hot foot bath twice daily. In case of hot foot bath, the patient should keep his legs in a tub or bucket filled with hot water at a temperature of 40° to 45°C. Before taking this bath, a glass of cold water shold be taken and the body should be covered with a blanket so as to ensure that no heat or vapour escapes from the foot bath. The duration of the bath is generally from 5 to 20 minutes. The patient should take a cold shower bath immediately after the bath.

TREATMENT CHART FOR STOMATITIS

A - DIET

I. Raw juice diet for three days. Take a glass of fruit or vegetable juice every two hours, diluted with water, from 8 a.m. to 8 p.m. and cleanse the bowels with warm-water enema during this period.

II. All-fruit diet for three further days. Take fresh juicy fruits at five-hourly intervals during this period.

III. Thereafter, the following diet may be adopted:-

1. *Upon arising:* A glass of lukewarm water with half a freshly-squeezed lime and a teaspoon of honey.

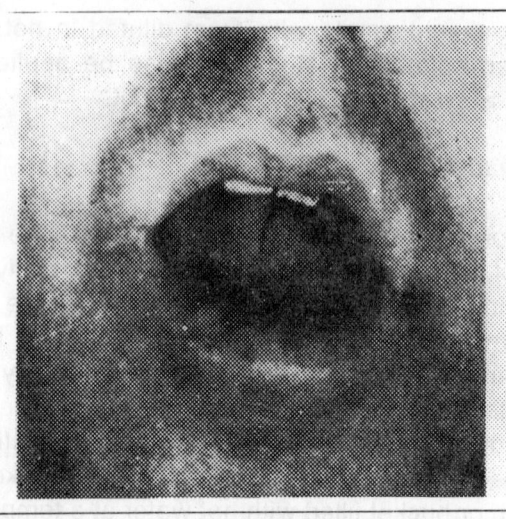

The Mouth and Tongue

2. *Breakfast:* Fresh fruit, a glass of milk and a handful of raw nuts.
3. *Lunch:* A bowl of freshly-prepared steamed vegetables, two or three whole wheat chappatis and a glass of buttermilk.
4. *Mid-afternoon:* A glass of vegetable or fruit juice or sugarcane juice.
5. *Dinner:* A large bowl of fresh green vegetable salad and mung bean sprouts.

AVOID: Meats, sugar, white flour, tea, coffee, condiments, pickles, refined and processed foods, fried foods and products made from sugar and white flour.

B - OTHER MEASURES

1. Maintain proper oral hygiene by careful brushing or teeth and gums.
2. Take multivitamin tablets, specially those high in vitamin C and B complex.
3. Fomentations every three hours over mouth, cheeks and jaws.
4. Hot foot bath twice daily.

CHAPTER 59

Stress

The term stress has been borrowed by biology from engineering, where it implies an ability to withstand a defined amount of strain. Dr. Hans Selye, a great medical genius and noted world authority on stress has described stress as "a state manifested by a specific syndrome which consists of all the non-specifically induced changes within a biological system".

The term implies any condition that harms the body or damages or causes the death of a few or many cells. The body immediately tries to repair the damaged cells but it can do so only if the diet is adequate, providing a generous supply of all the essential nutrients. If, however, rebuilding of cells is not able to keep pace with their destruction, the condition will result in disease. The most common diseases associated with stress are heart disease, diabetes, headache and peptic ulcer. Other diseases resulting from stress are ulcerative colitis, chronic dyspepsia, asthma, psoriasis and sexual disorders.

Reactions to stress are manifold. No one situation is stressful to all the people all the time. Some of the factors that can produce stress are children or the lack of them, the boss or the subordinate, the traffic, the telephone or the lack of it, overwork or not enough work to do, too much money or too little of it, making decisions, dull routine jobs, lack of authority and apprehensions about the future.

Symptoms

The body and the mind react to any stress factor. A large number of physical changes take place at the time of stress-induced arousal. The brain and nervous system becomes intensely active, the pupils of the eye dilate, digestion slows down, muscles become tense, the heart starts pumping blood harder and faster, blood pressure increases, breathing becomes faster, hormones such as adrenaline are released into the system along with glucose from the liver and sweating starts. All these changes take place in a split second under the direction of the nervous system. If the stress factors are immediately removed all the changes are reversed.

Stress in its earlier and reversible stage leads to poor sleep, bad temper, continual grumbling, longer hours of work with less achievement, domestic conflict with wife and children, repeated minor sickness, absenteeism and prolonged absence for each spell of sickness, accident proneness, feeling of frustration and persecution by colleagues and complaints of lack of cooperation and increase in alcoholic intake.

It is essential that these symptoms are recognised early by the patients or their well-wishers and remedial measures taken to overcome them. If, however, stress is continuous or repeated frequently, a variety of symptoms appear such as dizziness, stiff muscles, headache, vision problems, breathing difficulties, asthma, allergies, palpitation, digestive disorders, blood sugar irregularities, backache, skin disorders, bowel disorders and sexual difficulties.

Causes

Stress may be caused by a variety of factors both outside the body and within. External factors include loud noises, blinding lights, extreme heat or cold, X-rays and other forms of radiation, drugs, chemical, bacterial and various toxic substances, pain and inadequate nutrition. The factors from within the body include hate, envy, fear or jealousy.

Dietary Treatment

In dealing with stress, the life style of the patient needs a complete overhaul. He should be placed on an optimum diet and be encouraged to take regular exercise and adequate rest. If this is done, many diseases caused by stress can be eliminated.

Diet plays an important role in the prevention and healing of stress-induced diseases. Certain foods associated with stress and anxiety should be scrupulously avoided. These foods are caffeine in coffee and many soft drinks, which causes nervousness, irritability and palpitation; salt which has been associated with heart disease; cigarettes which cause tension, irritability and sleeplessness and which have been linked with cancer and alcohol which depletes vitamins of the B group considered essential for reducing stress.

Certain nutrients are beneficial in relieving stress. These are vitamins A and B, minerals such as calcium, potassium and magnesium which reduce the feeling of irritability and anxiety. Vitamin A is found in green and yellow vegetables. Some of the valuable sources of vitamin B are cashews, green leafy vegetables, yeast, sprouts and bananas.

An element of vitamin B-complex, pantothenic acid is especially important in preventing stress. It has a strong effect on the adrenal glands and the immune system and adequate amounts of this vitamin along with vitamin A can help prevent many of the changes caused by the stress.

Potassium deficiencies are associated with breathlessness, fatigue, insomnia and low blood sugar. Potassium is essential for healthy heart muscles. Nuts and whole grains are good sources of potassium. Calcium is a natural sedative. Deficiencies can cause fatigue, nervousness and tension. Dairy products, eggs, almonds and soyabeans are rich sources of calcium. Magnesium is known as nature's tranquiliser and is associated with the prevention of heart attacks. Deficiencies may lead to excitability, irritability, apprehension and emotional disorders. Magnesium is also necessary for absorption of calcium and potassium and is found in many fruits, vegetables, seeds, dates and prunes.

There are many foods which help in meeting the demands of stress and should be taken regularly by the patients. These include yogurt, blackstrap molasses, seeds and sprouts. Yogurt is rich in vitamin A, D and B-complex. It relieves migraine, insomnia and cramps associated with menstruation. Blackstrap molasses, a byproduct of the sugar refining process, is rich in iron and B vitamins. It guards against anaemia and is good for heart diseases. Seeds such as alfalfa, sunflower and pumpkins and sprouts are rich in calcium and quite effective as diterrents of listlessness and anxiety. Steam cooked vegetables are best, as boiling causes many vitamins and minerals to be dispelled into the water.

Regular physical exercise plays an important role in the fight against stress. Exercise not only keeps gthe body physically and mentally fit, it also provides recreation and mental relaxation. Recreation and rest are also important. The patient should get a definite time for recreational activities. He should take a holiday at regular intervals. And above all, he should simplify his style of living to eliminate unnecessary stresses.

TREATMENT CHART FOR STRESS

A - DIET

Take optimum diet, consisting of seeds, nuts and grains, vegetables and fruits supplemented by milk, high quality unrefined vegetable oils and honey, on the following lines:-

1. *Upon arising:* A glass of lukewarm water with half a freshly-squeezed lime and a teaspoon of honey.
2. *Breakfast:* Fresh fruit, few seeds or nuts, especially almonds, and a glass of milk, sweetened with honey.
3. *Lunch:* A bowl of freshly-prepared steamed vegetabls,

two or three whole wheat chappatis and a glass of buttermilk.

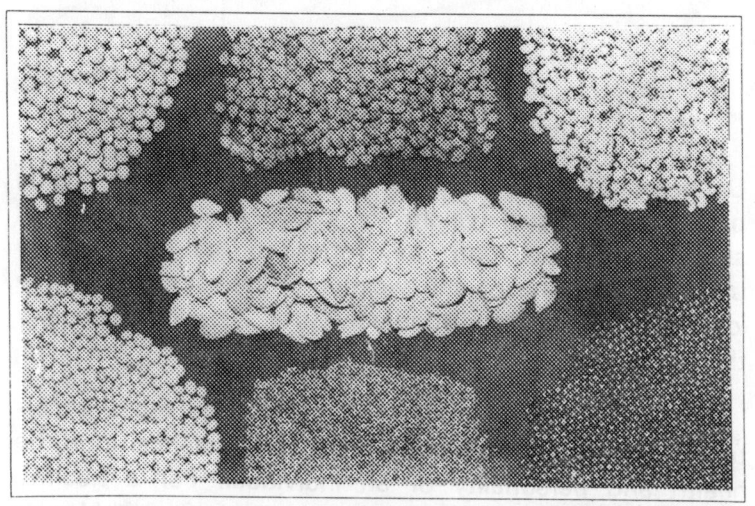

Seeds are among the most potent foods which help meet the demands of stress.

4. *Mid-afternoon:* A glass of fresh fruit or vegetable juice.
5. *Dinner:* A bowl of raw vegetable salad and sprouts, such as alfalfa and mung beans, with lime juice and vegetable oil dressing, followed by a hot course, if desired.
6. *Bedtime Snack:* A glass of milk or one apple.

Important: Take frequent small meals rather than three large ones.

AVOID: Tea, coffee, soft drinks, salt, white flour, white sugar, all products made from sugar and white flour, refined foods, flesh foods, tobacco, alcohol and smoking.

Especially Beneficial: Yogurt, blackstrap molases, seeds and sprouts, steam cooked vegetables, vitamins A and B, calcium, potassium and magnesium.

B - OTHER MEASURES

1. Regular physical exercise and yogasanas.
2. Recreation, adequate rest and proper sleep.

CHAPTER 60

Thinness

Underweight, like overweight, is a relative term, being based on the ideal weight for a given height, build and sex. A person can be regarded as moderately underweight if he or she weighs 10 per cent below the ideal body weight and markedly so if 20 per cent below the ideal.

Appropriate body weight is among the most important physical attributes and has a deep influence upon the health and personality of an individual. For a healthy body, weight slightly above the average is favourable upto the age of 30 years, as it serves as a good defence measure against certain diseases, especially tuberculosis, which are widely prevalent among the adolescent and the young. Between 30 and 40 years of age, weight should be maintained at the average level as during this period, many future diseases have their beginning. After the age of 40, it will be advisable to keep the weight slightly below the average, so as to lighten the burden on the heart, kidneys and other vital organs.

There are two types of thin people. One type is wiry and energetic, who eat heartily but never put on weight. Presumably, they burn up energy due to constant activity. Such persons need not worry as chances are that they do not have any disease as such. The other type of thin persons lack energy and drive, are unable to take normal meals and find that rich food usually makes them sick. Their body lacks fat cells thus providing no storage place for added fat and the calories they consume are probably wasted.

Symptoms

Underweight due to an inadequate calorie intake is a serious condition, especially in the young. They often feel easily fatigued, have poor physical stamina and lowered resistance to infection. Diseases like tuberculosis, respiratory disorders, pneumonia, circulatory diseases like heart disorders, cerebral haemorrhage, nepthritis, typhoid fever and cancer are quite common among them. The occurrence of the complications of pregnancy in young women may result from malnutrition due to an inadequate energy intake.

Causes

Thinness may be due to inadequate nutrition or excessive bodily activity or both. Emotional factors or bad habits such as skipped meals, small meals, habitual fasting and inadequate exercise are some of the other causes of thinness. Other factors include inadequate digestion and absorption of food due to a wrong dietary pattern for a particular metabolism; metabolic disturbances such as an overactive thyroid and hereditary tendencies. Disorders such as chronic dyspepsia, chronic diarrhoea, presence of parasites like tapeworm in the alimentary canal, liver disorders, diabetes mellitus, insomnia, constipation and sexual disorders can also lead to thinness.

It has been observed that most underweight persons are not healthy. They are usually tense and lack appetite. Eating large quantities of food will not help them to gain weight until and unless their health improves. They can gain weight only when these abnormalities are overcome. Building up their health is, therefore, of utmost importance.

Dietary Cure

Diet plays an important role in building up health for gaining weight. Nutrients which help keep the nerves relaxed are of utmost importance as nervousness causes all the muscles to become tense and the energy which goes into the tensing wastefully uses up a great deal of food.

Although all vitamins and minerals are required for relaxation, the most important ones are vitamin D and B6, calcium and magnesium. The richest sources of vitamin D are milk, cod-liver oil and sunshine. Calcium is also supplied by milk and yogurt. Magnesium can be obtained from green leafy vegetables such as spinach, parsley, turnip, radish and beet tops. These vegetables should preferably be taken in salad form or should be lightly cooked.

Lack of appetite can result from an inadequate supply of vitamin B, which leads to low production of hydrochloric acid by the stomach. Hydrochloric acid is essential for the digestion of food and absorption of vitamins and minerals into the blood. It is, therefore, necessary that the daily diet should be rich in vitamin B for normal appetite, proper digestion and absorption of foods and regular elimination. Foods rich in vitamin B are all whole grain cereals, blackstrap molasses, nuts, soyabean, eggs and butter. Vegetables oil is of special value to those wishing to gain weight as it is rich in vitamin E and essential fatty acids.

The underweight person should never make the mistake of over-stuffing himself. Weight can be gained without eating more than is desired, as the appetite, digestion and absorption can be improved and nerves relaxed by taking foods rich in vitamins A, B, D, calcium and magnesium.

Underweight persons should eat frequent small meals as they tend to feel full quickly. Meals may be divided into six small ones instead of three big ones. These may consist of three smaller meals and three substantial snacks between them. The weight-building quality of a food is measured by the number of calories it contains. To gain weight, the diet should include more calories than are used in daily activities so as to allow the excess to be stored as body fat. The allowances of 500 calories in excess of the daily average needs is estimated to provide for a weight gain of one pound weekly.

All refined foods such as products containing white flour and sugar should be avoided, as they destroy health. Excessive intake of refined carbohydrates and fats may help the individual to put on weight but this will be detrimental to general health. The diet should be tilted towards alkaline-forming foods such as fruits and vegetables. Alkaline food should comprise 80 per cent of the diet. The other 20 per cent should consist of acid-forming foods such as cereals and lentils. Beverages containing caffeine like soft drinks, coffee and tea should be curtailed. Smoking should be given up. Water should not be taken with meals but half an hour before or one hour after meals.

The following is the suggested menu for gaining weight:

Upon arising: A glass of orange, grapes or tomato juice.
Breakfast: One egg in any form except fried, whole meal bread and butter or porridge, a glass of milk with a tablespoon of honey.
Mid-morning: Fruit or carrot juice or butter-milk.
Lunch: Lightly cooked or steamed vegetable, baked potatoes, chappatis of whole wheat flour and butter, a glass of butter-milk with black molasses.
Mid-afternoon: Milk with ripe banana or dates.
Dinner: Raw vegetable salad with lemon and olive oil dressing or hot vegetable soup, cottage cheese, lightly cooked or steamed vegetables and whole wheat chappatis.
Before retiring: One apple, raw or baked.

A balaned diet together with adequate exercise, rest, emotional balance and the absence of acute disease will enable the underweight person to build a healthy body and put on weight.

Milk Cure

An exclusive milk diet for rapid gain of weight has been advocated by some nature cure practioners. In the beginning of this mode of treatment, the patient should fast for three days on warm water and lime juice so as to cleanse the system. Thereafter he should have a glass of milk every two hours from 8 am to 8 pm the first day, a glass every hour and a half the next day, and a glass every hour the third day. Then the quantity of milk should be gradually increased so as to take a glass every half an hour from 8 am to 8 pm, if such a qantity can be tolerated fairly comfortably. The milk should be fresh and unboiled, but may be slightly warmed, if desired. It should be sipped very slowly through a straw. The milk should be unpasteurised, if possible.

TREATMENT CHART FOR THINNESS

A - DIET

I. An all-fruit diet for three to five days. Take three meals a day of fresh juicy fruits at five-hourly intervals.

II. Thereafter, adopt a well-balanced diet on the following lines:-

1. *Upon arising:* 25 black raisins soaked overnight in water alongwith the water in which they are soaked and water kept overnight in a copper vessel.
2. *Breakfast:* Fresh fruit, a glass of milk, sweetened with honey and few nuts, especially almonds.
3. *Lunch:* Freshly prepared steamed vegetables, whole wheat chappatis with butter or brown rice and a glass of buttermilk.
4. *Mid-afternoon:* A glass of fruit juice or sugarcane juice.
5. *Dinner:* A good sized raw vegetable salad and sprouts with vegetable oil and lime juice dressing, followed by a hot course if desired.
6. *Bedtime Snack:* A glass of milk with few dates.

THINNESS

Milk is effective in removing thinness.

Home remedies: Musk melon, mango-milk diet, figs, raisins, vitamins D and B6, calcium and magnesium.

AVOID: Tea, coffee, sugar, white flour and products made from them, refined foods, fried foods, flesh foods, alcohol and smoking.

B - OTHER MEASURES

1. Brisk walk for 45 minutes morning and evening.
2. Yogasanas such as uttanpadasana, pavanmuktasana, vajrasana, yogamudra and shavasana.

CHAPTER 61

Tonsillitis

Tonsillitis refers to acute inflammation of the tonsils. It is one of the most common ailments encountered at childhood and is indicative of a toxic condition of the system. Chronic tonsillitis is a term applied to cases in which there is enlargement of the tonsils accompanied by repeated attacks of infection.

The tonsils are two almond-shaped small glands situated one on each side of the throat. They can be seen just at the back of the mouth between two folds of membranes running up to the soft palate. They are tiny at birth but show a spurt of growth and activity during the early months of life. They can become very much larger if severly infected. They protect the throat against disease germs.

In early childhood, especially in the first months at school, children meet a vide variety of infections, most of which are transmitted through the nose and mouth. So, the tonsils are ideally situated to attack and destroy these germs before they can enter the respiratory tract to set up a serious infection such as bronchitis or pneumonia. In fulfilling this protective function, the tonsils become red and swollen.

Symptoms

The main symptoms of tonsillitis are sore throat, fever, headache, pain in various parts of the body, difficulty in swallowing, hoarseness of voice and general weakness. The tonsils are seen to be inflamed and red when the mouth is opened wide. In many cases, spots of pus exude from them. Externally, the tonsillar lymph glands, which lie just behind the angle of the jaw, are tender and enlarged. In several cases there may be pain in the ear.

The children suffering from this disease are often listless and pale. They may vomit frequently due to the irritation of large tonsils. In case of chronic tonsillitis, the children may lose weight. They may be irritable, lethargic and weak in studies.

Causes

Inflammation of the tonsils is usually due to infection by streptococcus pyogenes. This infection is feciltated by the toxic condition of the system generally, resulting from wrong feeding habits and unhyenic condition of living. It is brought to a head by a sudden lowering of vitality due to exposure and sudden chill. Overeating, consumption of refined foods like sugar, white flour and products made from them, fried foods, condiments, excessive tea and coffee all contribute to this disease. Othe predisposing factors are cold, dyspepsia, loss of sleep and constipation.

Dietary Treatment

The treatment of tonsillitis by means of painting and spraying is both harmful and supressive. It does not help to rid the system of toxins, which are at the root of the trouble. In fact, it forces these toxins back into the system, which may cause more serious trouble later on. The removal of tonsils by surgery, in case of chronic tonsillities, may appear as a simple measure. But it is responsible for serious ill-health in later life, as the system of the child concerned will be working at a permanently impaired level of efficiency.

The correct way to treat the disease is to cleanse the system of toxic waste through proper dietary and other natural methods. The patient should be kept isolated in bed. The bedroom should be well-ventilated. He should not be given solid foods and should be encouraged to take sufficient fluids and juices. Orange an lemon juices, diluted with water and mixed with honey, will be especially beneficial. If he shows reluctance to take juices, he may be given juicy fruits such as apples, grapes, grape-fruit, oranges, pears, pineapple, peaches and melon. In no circumstances, he should be given foods which produce or increase acidity. He should be given warm water enema to cleanse the bowels for the first few days of the treatment.

After the acute symptoms of tonsillitis are over, the patient may gradually embark upon a well-balanced diet, according to his age. The emphasis should be on fresh fruits, raw vegetables whole grain cereals and milk.

Certain home remedies have been found beneficial in the treatment of inflammed tonsils. One of the most effective of these remedies is the use of lime. Half a fresh lime squeezed in a glass of warm water, mixed with two teaspoons of honey and little salt, should be sipped slowly in such cases.

The use of milk has been found valuable in this diease. A glass of pure boiled milk, mixed with a pinch of turmeric powder and pepper powder, should be taken every night for 3 nights. It will provide great relief.

Raw vegetable juices are also beneficial in the treatment of tonsillitis. The juices of carrot, beet and cucumber, taken individually or in combination, are especially valuable. Formula proportions found helpful, when used in combination, are carrot 150 ml. beet 50 ml. and cucumber 50 ml. to prepares 250 ml of combined juice.

Other Measures

A heating compress should be applied to the throat. It is a very valuable measure to relieve sore throat and reduce swelling and inflammation. The procedue is to take a piece of cloth and fold it about three inches wide and 12 to 15 inches long. This cloth should be dipped in cold water and wrung out as dry as possible. It may be wrapped round the patient's neck and covered with three or four folds of flannel or woollen material about four inches wide. The compress should be fastened in place with safety-pins and allowed to remain there the whole night. The patient will feel warm within a short time and this will have a soothing effect on the throat. This compress should be changed every eight hours.

The throat may be gargled with hot water mixed with a little salt and lime juice several times daily. This will help draw out fluids from the inflamed throat, thereby relieving discomfort. A gargle made from the fenugreek (methi) seeds is effective in severe cases. Hot packs may be applied to the neck. A warm-water bath will also be helpful. Massage of the throat is also very valuable in tonsillitis. Fresh air, deep breathing and other exercises should all form part of the daily health regimen of the patient.

Tonsillitis can be successfully treated by the natural methods outlined above. Surgery for the removal of the tonsils will be necessay only in very rare cases, when tonsils are seriously diseased, rugged and contain hopelessly incurable pus pockets.

TREATMENT CHART FOR TONSILLITIS

A - DIET

I. Raw juice diet for 3 to 5 days. Take a glass of fresh orange or lemon juice, diluted with water on 50:50 basis, every two hours from 8 a.m. to 8 p.m. and use lukewarm water enema daily during this period.

II. An all-fruit diet for further 3 to 5 days, with three meals a day of fresh juicy fruits such as apple, pear, peach, papaya, grapes, orange and pineapple.

III. Thereafter, gradually adopt a well-balanced diet on the following lines:-

1. *Upon arising:* A glass of lukewarm water with half a freshly-squeezed lime and a teaspoon of honey.
2. *Breakfast:* Fresh fruit and a glass of milk, sweetened with honey.

3. *Lunch:* A bowl of freshly-prepared steamed vegetable such as carrot, cabbage, cauliflower, squash and beans, two or three whole wheat chapatis and a glass of butter milk.

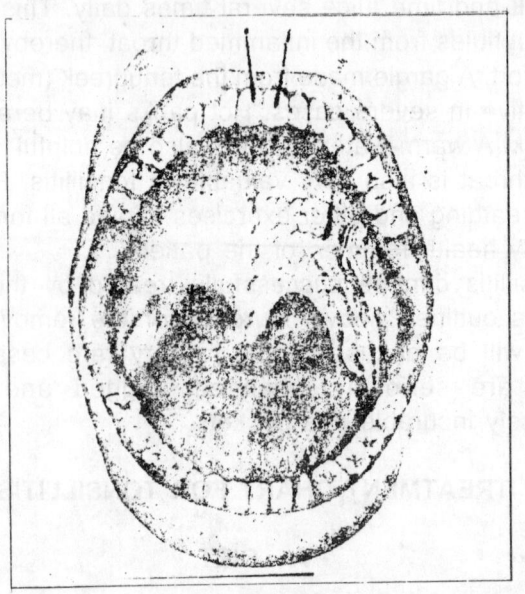

Many respiratory diseases begin with sore throat caused by streptococcus germs. It is the work of the tonsils and adenoids to destroy these germs, but sometimes they multiply so rapidly that they cannot be overcome by those organs.

4. *Mid-afternoon:* A glass of vegetable or fruit juice.

5. *Dinner:* A large bowl of salad of fresh green vegetable such as lettuce, carrot, cabbage, cucumber, tomatoes, radish, red beets and onion and sprouts such as alfalfa and mung beans with lemon juice dressing.

6. *Bedtime Snack:* A glass of milk.

AVOID: Tea, coffee, sugar, white flour, all products made with sugar and white flour, all refined foods, fried foods, and flesh foods as well as condiments and pickles.

B - OTHER MEASURES

1. Apply heating compress to the throat.
2. Gargle the throat with hot water, mixed with a little salt and lime juice, several times daily.
3. Massage the throat.
4. Take warm-water bath.
5. Fresh air, deep breathing and other exercises.

Tooth-Decay

Tooth-deay or dental caries is the main cause for loss of teeth. It is characterised by bacteria-induced progressive destruction of the mineral and organic components of the enamel and dentine, the two outer layers of the tooth. It is considered to be one of the most common diseases of modern age caused, in large measure, by eating denatured foods of today, which are too soft and too sweet.

Good teeth are an important part of one's health and appearance. They play a very important role in the digestion. One can look at one's best with a good smile, which emanates from good teeth.

Symptoms

In the beginning, the tooth may be merely sensitivity to hot and cold substances in the mouth and to pressure from biting. Later, an abcess forms at the base of the tooth and the pain becomes severe. If the tooth is not properly treated, it will eventually have to be extracted.

Causes

Tooth-decay results from faulty diet. The most common cause of this disease is the consumption of soft drinks, cakes, pasteries, refined carbohydrates an sugar in all forms. Lack of balance between carbohydrates and proteins and insufficient intake of vitamins and minerals also contribute to this disease.

Food particles lodged in the mouth provide a suitable place for the grwoth of bacteria. These, in turn, produce a local acid reaction which then attcks the surface of the tooth. Minute cracks or defects in the enamel, or hard outer covering of the tooth may also lead to this process. Once the enamel has been eroded away, the body of the tooth is more easily damaged.

Dietary Treatment

Diet plays a vital role in dental health. The condition of the teeth, after they are formed, depends upon the foods one eats from day to day. Tooth decay, the destruction of the bone around the teeth, and infections of the gums can be prevented with an appropriate diet. In fact, with the proper diet, the teeth and jaw-bones can be made harder and healthier as the years go by.

All sweets and refined foods and all products made with white flour and white sugar should be avoided as fibreless refined foods allow particles to accumulate on the teeth. It is important to ensure that the diet includes plenty of raw vegetables and whole meal bread. Whole foods are ideal. They are good for the teeth. The gums need friction to keep them firm and whole foods also help remove plaque. They are therefore called 'detergent foods' by some dentists. Millet and sesame (til) seeds are especially beneficial. Sesame seeds are extremely rich in calcium.

The use of onion is considered beneficial in the prevention of tooth-decay. Latest researches by Russian doctors have confirmed the bactericidal properties of onion. The Russian doctor, B.P. Tohkin, who has contributed to this research, has expressed the opinion that chewing raw onions for three minutes is sufficient to kill and the germs in the mouth. Tooth-ache is often allayed by placing a small piece of onion on th bad tooth or gum.

Tooth-decay can be pevented by regular consumption of apples, as they possess a mouth cleansing property. Dr. T.T. Hanks in his books 'Dental Survey' says, 'Apples have a mouth-cleansing property that no other fruit possesses, and taken after meal, they have the same effect as a tooth brush in cleansing the teeth with the added advantage that the acid content, aside from its nutritive value, is of assistance in promoting the flow of saliva in the mouth, which is also beneficial to the teeth'. The acids of the apple also exerts an antiseptic influence upon the germs present in the mouth and teeth when it is thoroughly chewed. Apples are thus regarded as natural preservers of teeth and should be taken during tooth troubles.

Lemon and lime also promote healthy teeth and gums, due to their high vitamin C content. They strengthen the gums and teeth and are very effective in preventing and curing acute inflammations of the gum margins. They should therefore form a part of our daily diet.

In preventing tooth-decay, what one eats is no doubt important, but equally important is when one eats. Frequent small snacks are very harmful to teeth, as they produce an acid medium in which the bacteria thrive. The number of times one eats sugar is one of the most important factor in determining the rate of decay. For this reason, it is better to eat sweets at the end of a meal rather than between meals.

Other Measures

Tooth-decay can be treated by removing decayed regions of the tooth and filling the cavities. If the cavities have reached to pulp, it may become necessary to extract the affected tooth.

Proper cleaning is the most important step towards healthy and sparkling teeth. Ideally, teeth should be cleaned after every meal, but one thorough cleansing each day will be far better than any number of hurried brushings. A quick brushing is a waste of time. The teeth may appear clean, but they will still be coated with a layer of plaque, a sticky, transparent substance. It is invisible, but it can be felt as a fuzzy coating on teeth. It is this substance which leads to decay.

There are many theories on how best to clean the teeth. The consensus of dental opinion, however, seems to back using a circular motion with the brush. This will fecilitate clean up of all dental surfaces. One should not be afraid to touch the gums with the brush, as this gentle stimulation improves the blood circulation in the gums.

Toothpaste is not in fact essential for the removal of plaque, although most people use it. It does help to keep the mouth fresh. The flouride, which is now being added to an increasing number of pastes, also helps to strengthen the outer enamel and this renders it less susceptible to decay.

TREATMENT CHART FOR TOOTH DECAY

A - DIET

Take a well-balanced optimum diet, with emphasis on whole grains and raw vegetables, on the following lines:-

1. *Upon arising:* A glass of lukewarm water with half a freshly-squeezed lime and a teaspoon of honey.
2. *Breakfast:* Fresh fruit, a glass of milk, sweetened with honey and some seeds or nuts.
3. *Lunch:* Freshly-prepared steamed or lightly-cooked vegetables, whole wheat chappatis and a glass of butter milk.
4. *Mid-afternoon:* A glass of fresh fruit or vegetable juice.
5. *Dinner:* A bowl of raw vegetable salad and sprouts, such as alfalfa and mung beans, with lime juice and vegetable oil dressing, followed by a hot-course, if desired.

AVOID: Sweets, refined foods, all products made from white flour and sugar, tea, coffee, flesh foods, condiments, pickles and frequent snacks.

Especially Beneficial: Whole foods, especially millet and sesame seeds, raw onion, apple, lemon and lime.

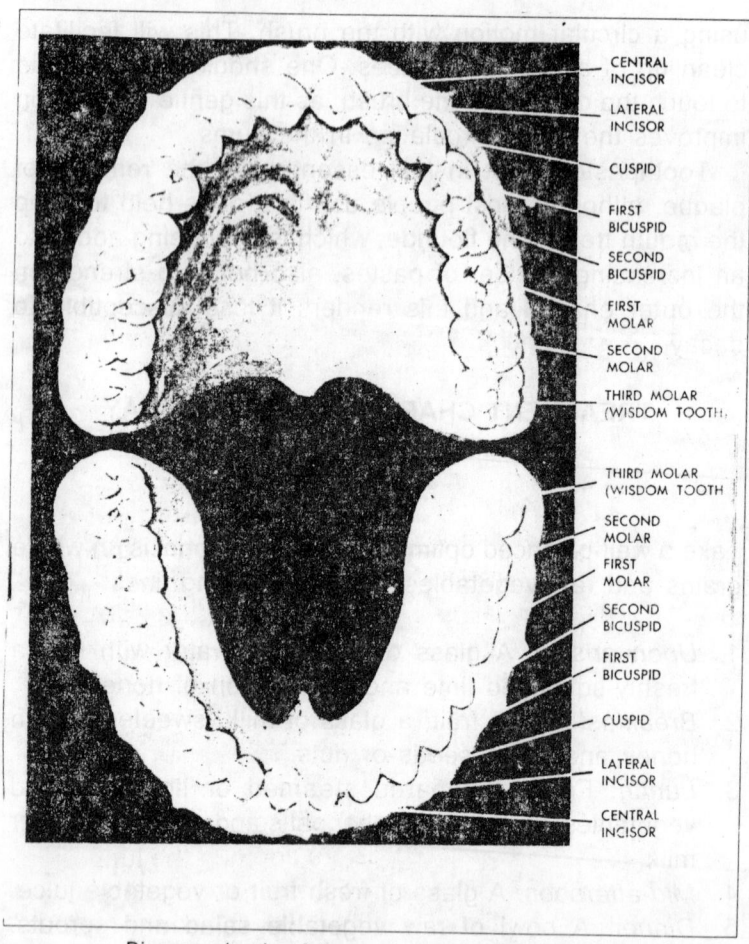

Diagram showing full set of upper and lower teeth

B - OTHER MEASURES

1. Proper cleaning of teeth, using circular motion of brush.
2. Removal of decayed regions of the tooth and filling the cavities.

CHAPTER 63

Tuberculosis

Tuberculosis is one of the most dreaded diseases. It is a major health problem in India and often rated the number one killer. It affects eight to nine million people at any one time and over five lakh people die of this disease every year in this country. This disease is also called consumption as it consumes the body and reduces the patient to a skeleton.

Tuberculosis has a very ancient origin. Traces of the existence of this disease have been found in Egyptian mummies as early as 5,000 B.C. It is described as *Rajrog* or the king of diseases in the Vedas. The noted ancient physicians, Charaka and Sushruta thought that it was difficult to cure. Aristotle expressed pity for the unfortunate "consumptives".

Tuberculosis is caused by a tiny germ called *tubercle bacillus* which is so small that it can be detected only by a microscope. The germ enters the body through the nose, mouth and the windpipe and settles down in the lungs. It multiplies by millions and produces small raised spots called tubercles. Sometimes this germ is called Kock's bacillus and the disease, Kock's disease after the name of Prof. Kock (1843-1910) who discovered this germ in March 1882.

Tuberculosis is not hereditary but an infectious or communicable disease. Those suffering from the disease for a considerable time eject living germs while coughing or spitting and when these enter the nose or mouth of healthy persons, they contract the disease. The spread of the disease is helped considerably by overcrowded and dirty conditions. Mouth-breathing and kissing as well as contaminated food and water are also responsible for spreading this disease. Tuberculosis does not spread merely by touching the persons suffering from it.

Symptoms

Tuberculosis is of four types, namely of lungs, intestines, bones and glands. Pulmonary tuberculosis or tuberculosis of the lungs is by far the most common type of tuberculosis. It commences normally with a dry cough. The patient loses strength, colour and weight and is unable to carry on his normal work. Other symptoms are a rise in temperature especially in the evening, hoarseness, difficulty in breathing, pain in the shoulders, indigestion, chest pain, and blood in the sputum.

Causes

Lowered resistence or devitalisation of the system is the chief cause of this disease. Most people have the germs present at all times, but they do not develop the disease unless their bodies are in a weakened condition. This condition is brought about mainly by mineral starvation of the tissues of the body due to an inadequate diet and the chief mineral concerned is calcium. In many ways, therefore, tuberculosis is the disease of calcium-deficiency. There can be no breakdown of the tissue and no tubercular growth when there is an adequate supply of organic calcium in the said tissue. Thus, an adequate supply of organic calcium in the system together with other organic mineral matter is a sure preventive of the development of tuberculosis.

Lowered resistance also results from a variety of other factors such as suppression of diseases by drugs and medication, use of stale, devitaminised and acid-forming foods; eating wrong combination of foods, such as taking fruits with starchy foods at one meal, causing fermentation in the stomach; wasting of energy through excessive loss of semen and living in ill-ventilated houses. Other causes include exposure to cold, loss of sleep, impure air, sedentary life, overwork, contaminated milk, use of tobacco in any form, liquor of all kinds, tea, coffee and all harmful drinks. These factors prepare the ground for the growth of germs of various kinds, including the tubercle bacillus. These germs, which may be present in the body, are quite harmless for those who are full of vitality and natural resistance.

Dietary Cure

Tuberculosis is no longer considered incurable if it is tackled in the early stages. An all round scheme of dietetic and vitality-building programme along natural lines is the only method to overcome the disease. As a first step, the patient should be put on an exclusive fresh fruit diet for three or four days. He should have three meals a day of fresh, juicy fruits, such as apples, grapes, pears, peaches, oranges, pineapples, melons or any other juicy fruit in season. For drinks, unsweetened lemon water or plain water either hot or cold may be taken. If losing much weight on the all-fruit diet, those who are already underweight may add a glass of milk to each fruit meal.

After the all-fruit diet, the patient should adopt a fruit and milk diet. For this diet, the meals are exactly the same as the all-fruit diet, but with milk added to each fruit meal. The patient may begin with two pints of milk the first day and increase by half a pint daily upto four or five pints. The milk should be fresh and unboiled, but may be slightly warmed, if desired. It should be sipped very slowly. The fruit and milk diet should be continued for four to six weeks. Thereafter, the following diet may be adopted.

Breakfast: Fresh fruits as obtainable and milk. Prunes or other dried fruit may also be taken, if desired.

Lunch: Steamed vegetables as available, one or two whole wheat chappatis and a glass of butter-milk.

Dinner: A bowl of raw salad of suitable vegetables with whole wheat bread and butter. Stewed fruit or cooked apple may be taken for dessert.

At bedtime: A glass of milk.

The chief therapeutic agent needed for the treatment of tuberculosis is calcium. Milk, being the richest food source for the supply of organic calcium to the body, should be taken liberally. In the diet outlined above at least two pints of milk should be taken daily. Further periods on the exclusive fruit diet followed by fruit and milk diet should be adopted at intervals of two or three months depending on the progress. During the first few days of the treatment, the bowels should be cleansed daily with a warm water enema and afterwards as necessary.

The patient should avoid all devitalised foods such as white bread, white sugar, refined cereals, puddings and pies, tinned, canned and preserved foods. He should also avoid strong tea, coffee, condiments, pickles and sauces.

The patient should take complete rest — of both mind and body. Any type of stress will prevent healing. Fresh air is always important in curing the disease and the patient should spend most of the time in the open air and should sleep in a well-ventilated room. Sunshine is also essential as the tubercle bacilli are rapidly killed by exposure to sunrays. Other beneficial steps towards curing the disease are avoidance of strain, slow massage, deep breathing and light occupation to ensure mental diversion.

TREATMENT CHART FOR TUBERCULOSIS

A - DIET

I. An all-fruit diet for three days. Take three meals a day of fresh juicy fruits at five-hourly intervals.

II. A fruit and milk diet for further 10 days, adding a cup of milk to each fruit meal.

III. Thereafter, adopt a well-balanced diet, on the following lines:-

1. *Upon arising:* A glass of lukewarm water mixed with half a freshly-squeezed lime and a teaspoon of honey.
2. *Breakfast:* Fresh fruit, a glass of milk, sweetened with honey, and few nuts, especially almonds.

3. *Lunch:* A bowl of freshly-prepared steamed vegetables, whole wheat chappatis with butter and a glass of butter milk.
4. *Mid-afternoon:* A glass of fruit juice or sugarcane juice.
5. *Dinner:* Raw vegetable salad and sprouts with vegetable oil and lime juice dressing, followed by a hot course, if desired.
6. *Bedtime Snack:* A glass of milk with few dates.

Home Remedies: Milk diet, custard apple (sitaphal), Indian gooseberry (amla), pineapple, banana, orange juice, drumstick (sanjana) leaves, bottle gourd (lauki) and mint.

AVOID: Tea, coffee, sugar, white flour and products made from them, refined foods, fried foods, flesh foods, alcohol and smoking.

B - OTHER MEASURES

1. Wet chest pack for one hour every morning on an empty stomach.
2. Neutral immersion bath for one hour at bedtime.
3. Fresh air, breathing and other light exercises and yogasanas.
4. Adequate rest and proper sleep.
5. Avoid all worries and mental tensions.

CHAPTER 64

Varicose Veins

Varicose veins are a condition in which the veins become enlarged, dilated or thickened. They have diminished elasticity and there are variations in the thickness of the vein wall. A varicosed portion of a vein may affect the whole length or be localised to portions only.

Veins are thin-walled vessels through which the impure blood is carried back to the heart. They usually have valves which regulate the flow of blood towards the heart. Varicose veins can occur in any part of the body but generally appear on the legs. The veins of the legs are the largest in the body and they carry the blood from the lower extremities upwards towards the heart. The direction of circulation in these vessels is largely determined by gravity. Though there are no mechanical obstacles to blood-flow, it is usually the incompetence of the valves which leads to an increase in pressure in the veins.

Varicose veins have an unsightly appearance and can be dangerous. A blood clot within a large, greatly dilated vein may break away and move towards the heart and lungs, causing serious complications. Varicose veins are about thrice as common an occurrence in women as in men. This disease is rare in underdeveloped rural societies.

Symptoms

The first sign of varicose veins is a swelling along the course of the veins. This may be followed by muscular cramps and a feeling of a weight and weariness in the affected leg, particularly at night, due to blood congestion. In some cases, the normal flow of blood towards the heart may be reversed when the patient is in an upright position. This results in veinous blood collecting in the lower part of the legs and the skin becomes purplish and pigmented, leading to what is known as varicose eczema or varicose ulcers. Both conditions cause severe pain.

Causes

There is evidence to show that those whose work involves much standing such as dentists, barbers and shop assistants are more subjected to this disease than those engaged in other occupations. While standing erect, the venous blood from the feet has to return to the heart against the force of gravity. Other bad habits which can lead to the formation of varicose veins are crossing the legs, wearing tight clothing and too much sitting.

A varicose condition of the veins also results from sluggish circulation due to various factors such as constipation, dietetic errors, lack of exercise and smoking. Pregnancy may cause varicose veins due to increased pressure in the pelvis and abdomen, which slows down the flow of blood from the lower extremities to the heart. Women usually suffer from this condition in the early years of child-bearing. Obesity can also cause varicose veins.

Dietetic Cure

The modern medical treatment of either a surgical operation or injections do not hold out hopes of a cure, as they do not even treat the basic cause. By surgically removing one affected vein, other veins may get affected.

For proper treatment in a natural way, the patient should, in the beginning, be put on a juice fast for four or five days or on an all-fruit diet for seven to ten days. A warm water enema should be administered daily during this period to cleanse the bowels and measures should be taken to avoid constipation.

After the juice fast or the all-fruit diet, the patient should adopt a restricted diet plan. In this regimen, oranges or orange and lemon juices may be taken for breakfast. The midday meal may consist of raw salad of any of the vegetables in season with olive oil and lemon juice dressing. Steamed vegetables such as spinach, cabbage, carrots, turnips, cauliflower and raisins, figs or dates may be taken in the evening. No bread or potatoes or other starchy food should be included in this diet, as otherwise the whole effect of the diet will be lost.

After the restricted diet, the patient may gradually embark upon a well-balanced diet of three basic food groups, namely seeds, nuts and grains, vegetables and fruits. About 75 per cent of the diet should consist of raw vegetables and fruits. All condiments, alcoholic drinks, coffee, strong tea, white flour products, white sugar and white sugar products should be strictly avoided. A short fast or the all-fruit diet for two or three days may be undertaken every month, depending on the progress being made.

The alternate hot and cold hip bath will be very valuable and should be taken daily. The affected parts should be sprayed with cold water or cold packs should be applied to them. A mud pack may be applied at night and allowed to remain until morning. A hot Epsom salt bath is also very valuable and should be taken twice a week.

The patient should undertake outdoor exercises like walking, swimming, cycling, take sun baths and do deep breathing exercises.

TREATMENT CHART FOR VARICOSE VEINS

A - DIET

I. Raw juice for 3 to 5 days. During this period, the bowels should be cleansed daily with warm water enema.

II. An all fruit diet for further 3 to 5 days.

III. Thereafter, adopt a well-balanced diet on the following lines:-

1 *Upon arising:* A glass of carrot and spinach juice.

VARICOSE VEINS

2. *Breakfast:* Fresh fruits and a glass of milk sweetened with honey.
3. *Lunch:* Freshly-prepared steamed vegetables, whole wheat chappatis and a glass of buttermilk.

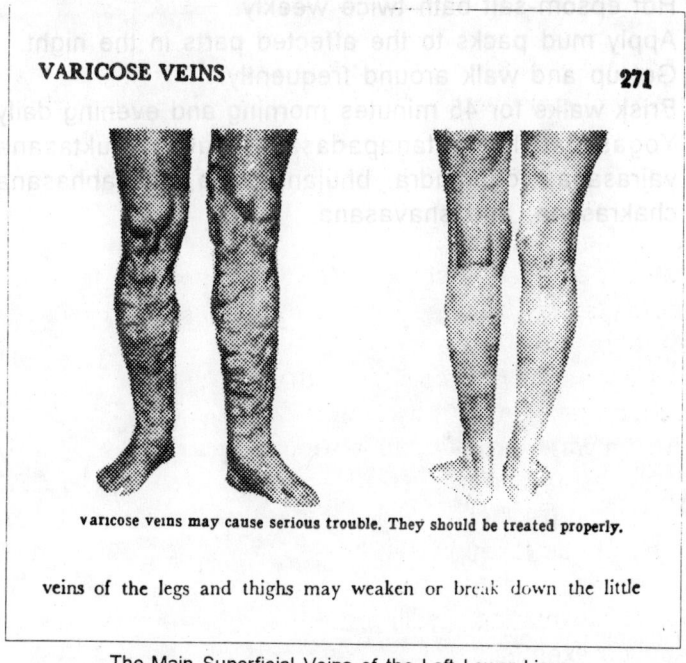

VARICOSE VEINS 271

varicose veins may cause serious trouble. They should be treated properly.

veins of the legs and thighs may weaken or break down the little

The Main Superficial Veins of the Left Lower Lime

4. *Mid-afternoon:* A glass of vegetable or fruit juice.
5. *Dinner:* Fresh green vegetable salad, and sprouts with lemon juice dressing, followed by a hot course, if desired.
6. *Bedtime Snack:* A glass of milk or one apple.

Note: Repeat a short juice fast or an all-fruit diet for two or three days every month.

AVOID: Tea, coffee, sugar, white flour, all products made with sugar and white flour, fried foods, flesh foods, condiments, pickles, alcohol and tobacoo.

B - OTHER MEASURES

1. Drink at least six to eight glasses of water daily.
2. Cold hip bath for 10 minutes daily.
3. Hot epsom-salt bath twice weekly.
4. Apply mud packs to the affected parts in the night.
5. Get up and walk around frequently.
6. Brisk walks for 45 minutes morning and evening daily.
7. Yogasanas like uttanapadasana, pavan muktasana, vajrasana, yogamudra, bhujangasana, shallabhasana, chakrasana, and shavasana.

CHAPTER 65

Women's Ailments

Menstrual Disorders

The maternal instincts of a woman arise almost entirely from the female hormones within her body. These hormones are produced in a pair of almond-shaped organs, known as the ovaries. They are situated deep within the pelvis, one on each side of the uterus or womb.

The two major female hormones are estrogen and progesterone. These hormones give the woman strength and the stamina and are largely responsible for the peculiarly feminine shape of her body. The ovaries start producing large quantities of estrogen, the dominant female hormone when a girl reaches about 12 years of age. This enables her to grow rapidly and develop into a normal young woman. The commencement of menustruation at this time heralds the reproductive phase of her life, when she can have children. This phase may last for about 35 years.

The menstrual flow is connected with the female function of ovulation or the passing of the egg cell or ovum from the ovary to the womb ready for fertilisation. It is a provision of nature to cleanse the inner surface of the womb and enable reproduction to take place normally. The flow normally lasts for about four days and has a rhythm of some 28 days.

The main problems relating to menstrual flow are premenstrual tension, painful menstruation, stoppage of menstruation and excessive menstruation. These disorders are quite common, but they are not normal. Healthy women, living according to natural laws and eating a diet of natural food do not suffer from the monthly ordeal. Most menstrual disorders are caused by nutritional deficiencies which lead to deficiency and improper metabolism of the female sex hormones. These disorders are discussed briefly in the following lines:

Pre-menstrual tension and menstrual cramps

Just before menstruation, some women become nervous and irritable. They suffer from depression, headaches, fulness in the breasts, insomnia and swelling in the lower extremities. Studies have shown that starting from 10 days prior to menstruation, when the ovaries are the least active, the blood calcium drops steadily and progressively. As the decreased blood calcium induces stress, the production of cortisone and aldosterone are stimulated and salt and water are retained in the body. This results in the symptoms of the pre-menstrual tension.

The blood calcium drops still further on the first day of menstruation, causing muscular cramps in the uterus and sometimes elsewhere in the body. Convulsions may occur if the blood calcium drops dangerously low. Both pre-menstrual tension and menstrual cramps can be prevented if adequate calcium is obtained and efficiently absorbed. Since more calcium is retained when magnesium and vitamin D are adequate, it is essential to take sufficient amounts of vitamin D, calcium and magnesium daily prior to and during menstruation in case of pre-menstrual tension.

Dysmenorrhoea

Painful menstruation or dysmenorrhoea, as it is called in medical parlance, is a very common occurrence these days. This disorder is traceable to a debilitated and toxic condition of the sytem in general and of the sex organs in particular due to wrong feeding, wrong style of living and nervous exhaustion. The pain may be felt either two or three days before or immediately before or during the flow.

Pain starting two or three days before the flow usually shows that the ovaries are not functioning properly. This is a glandular malfunction and a carefully planned natural diet will usually put matters right. For local treatment, hot hip baths on alternate nights for a week before the period is due will be highly beneficial. Between periods, the cold hip baths will increase the tone of the ovaries.

Pain immediately before the flow commences is indicative of uterine flexion, which means that the position of the womb is abnormal. A professional examination should be arranged to ascertain the position of the womb and corrective exercises undertaken under professional advice. Uterine flexion often occurs in women who are so thin that they have lost internal fat and the ligament, on which the womb is suspended. General treatment along the dietetic lines is essential along with corrective exercises.

When the pain occurs during menstruation, it usually means that the womb itself is inflamed. This condition can be relieved by proper attention to diet and hot hip baths just before the period is due and cold hip baths between the periods. The hot hip bath is generally taken for eight to ten minutes at a water temperature of 100°F which can be gradually increase to 120°F. The cold hip bath should be taken for 10 to 15 minutes at a water temperature of 50° to 65°F.

Menorrhagia or excessive menstruation:

Profuse menstrual flow is common in certain women and usually denotes a blood deficiency, especially blood calcium. A variety of causes may be responsible for this trouble, but a toxic condition of the system is at the root of the matter. It is essential to keep the patient absolutely quiet and confined to bed. The bottom of the bed should be raised four to five inches. In case of excessive bleeding, a gauze may be inserted in the vagina as a temporary measure.

For the first few days the diet should consist only of milk and raw vegetables. No stimulants should be taken as they tend to increase the flow. When the bleeding has stopped, great care should be taken to avoid over-exercising or straining the body in any manner. A full natural diet should then be adopted using fresh raw vegetable salads twice daily. As a long term measure, what is needed is a scheme of treatment which will thoroughly cleanse the system of toxic material.

Dietary Treatment

The various disorders relating to menstrual flow are indicative of the low level of a woman's health and a toxic condition of her sex organism, which has been brought about by the wrong living habits, especially wrong food habits. These disorders are made more deep seated and chronic by the modern medical efforts to deal with them through the suppressive agency of surgery and drugs. The disorders being systemic in origin, can be tackled only by treating the system as a whole so as to remove the toxicity from the body and build up the general health-level of the sufferer.

To undertake such a scheme of all-round health-building treatment, the sufferer from menstrual disorders should begin with an all-fruit diet for about five days. In this regimen, the patient should have three meals a day of fresh, juicy fruits, such as apples, pears, grapes, grapefruits, oranges, pineapples, peaches and melons. No other foodstuff should be taken, otherwise the value of the whole treatment will be lost. However, if there is much weight loss on the all-fruit diet, those already underweight may add a glass of milk to each fruit meal. During this period the bowels should be cleansed daily with a warm water enema.

After the all-fruit diet, the sufferer should adopt a well-balanced diet consisting of three basic food groups, namely, seeds, nuts and grains, vegetables and fruits as outlined in Chapter 1 on Diet in Health and Disease.

Further short periods on the all-fruit diet for two or three consecutive days can be undertaken at monthly intervals, according to the needs of the case. The morning dry friction and cold hip baths should form a regular feature of the treatment. All cold baths should, however, be suspended during the menstrual period.

The diet factor is of the utmost importance. Fruits and salads, nature's body-cleansing and health-restoring foods, must form the bulk of the future diet along with whole grains, nuts and seeds, especially in sprouted form. The diet should contain an adequate, but not excessive, amount of high quality protein, preferably from raw, unpasteurised milk, sour milk and home-made cottage cheese. The emphasis should also be on iron-rich foods such as apricots, milk, eggs and nuts. Raw juices such as spinach juice, red beet juice and grape juice are also beneficial in the treatment of menstrual disorders. Vitamin B12 has been found helpful in restoring normal menstrual cycle and the patient should take upto 50 mg. of this vitamin daily.

The patient should take frequent small meals instead of few large ones to prevent low blood sugar, which is common during menstruation. The foods which should be avoided in future are white flour products, sugar, confectionery, rich cakes, pastries, sweets, refined cereals, flesh foods, rich, heavy or greasy foods, tinned or preserved foods, strong tea, coffee, pickles, condiments and sauces. Smoking, if habitual, should be given up completely as it aggravates menstrual disorders.

The utmost care of the body, combined with scrupulous cleanliness, is essential to the success of the treatment. Fresh air, outdoor exercise and deep breathing are also important and should be practised daily.

Menopausal Disorders

A significant event occurs around the mid or late forties in women. It is called a change of life or menopause, to give it a proper medical term and is a perfectly normal event. It signifies the end of the female reproductive period of life, which commenced during a woman's early teens. In physical terms, it refers to the cessations of the monthly periods.

There are several misconceptions about menopause. Many women at this time feel that they are growing old and that they are well past their full physical vigour. Other woman feel that the menopause brings a cessation of sexual pleasure. These apprehensions are far from the truth. Menopause may be considered an end to woman's fertility, but certainly not to her virility. It does not decrease a woman's physical capacity and sexual vigour or enjoyment.

Symptoms

During the menopause, the entire chain of endocrine glands is disturbed, particularly the gonads, the thyroid and the pituitary glands. In a really healthy woman, the menopausal change takes place without any unpleasant symptoms. In such a woman, the only sign of the change of life is the cessation of the menstrual flow. There are, however, many women who do not enjoy good health due to dietetic errors and a faulty style of living. In these cases, the menopausal change often leads to all kinds of distressing physical, emotional and nervous systems and manifestations.

Hot flushes, night sweats, nervous tension, menstrual disturbances, insomnia, a diminished interest in sex, irritability and depression are the typical symptoms of menopause. Other symptoms are a feeling of fatigue, palpitations, dizziness, headaches and numbness. Not every woman, will get these severe reactions. The severity or otherwise of the symptoms depends on a variety of factors such as general health, previous surgery and radiation. The problems of menopause are usually over when menstruation stops.

Causes

The annoying symptoms associated with menopause arise from the fact that the ovaries are no longer producing their normal amount of estrogen, the dominant female hormone. Anything which interferes with the normal functioning of the ovaries may also bring about these symptoms. The same strange feelings may occur if the ovaries are removed by surgery because of a disease. This can also result from heavy X-ray therapy or the use of radiation.

A lack of normal hormone balance may also result in a severe backache. This is caused by the thinning of the bones because of the low level of estrogen in the blood stream. Unless properly treated, this may eventually lead to a collapse of one or more of the vertebrae.

Treatment

Although menopause cannot be avoided, it can be postponed for as long as 10 to 15 years and it can be made a smooth affair when it arrives, with a proper nutritional programme, special supplements and the right mental attitude.

When a woman is affected by the menopausal change to any marked extent, it is a sure sign that her body is in a toxic condition and in need of a thorough cleansing. For this purpose, she should undergo a course of natural health-building treatment.

Diet is of utmost importance in such a scheme of treatment. In fact, the problems of menopause are often much more severe than those of puberty, largely because the diet has been deficient for years prior to its onset in many nutrients such as protein, calcium, magnesium, vitamins D, E and pantothenic acid.

The diet should be made up of three basic food groups, namely, seeds, nuts and grains, vegetables and fruits. The emphasis should be on vitamin E-rich, raw and sprouted seeds and nuts, unpasteurised, high quality milk and home-made cottage cheese and an abundance of raw, organically — grown fruits and vegetables. Plenty of freshly made juices of fruits and vegetables in season should also be included in the diet.

All processed, refined and denatured foods, such as white sugar, white flour and all articles made with them, should be completely eliminated. Special supplements such as vitamin C, B6 and panthothenic acid should be taken. They have a specific property of stimulating the body's own production of estrogen or enhancing the effect of existing estrogen.

During menopause, the lack of ovarian hormones can result in a severe calcium deficiency. For this reason, a larger than usual intake of calcium may help a lot. Vitamins D and F are also essential for assimilation of calcium. Any woman having difficulty at this time should supplement her daily diet with 1,000 IUs of natural vitamin D, 500 milligrams of magnesium and obtain daily two grams of calcium which can be supplied by one quart of milk.

During menopause, the need for vitamin E soars 10 to 50 times over that previously required. Hot flushes and night sweats often disappear when 50 to 100 IUs of vitamin E are taken daily. The symptoms recur quickly if this vitamin is discontinued.

Of late, it has become popular to take estrogen to prevent or postpone the menopausal symptoms. Although hormone therapy is apparently successful and will, in many cases, help the patient to feel and act younger, it cannot be recommended in all cases because of its carcinogenic (cancerous) effect. If, however, estrogen therapy is undertaken, it should never be administered at the same time as vitamin E therapy. Ingestion of estrogen and vitamin E should be separated by several hours.

Plenty of outdoor exercise, such as walking, jogging, swimming, horse-riding or cycling, is imperative to postpone menopause. Other helpful measure in this direction are avoiding mental and emotional stresses and worries, especially the worry about getting old, sufficient sleep and relaxation and following all the rules of good health. The healthier a woman is, the fewer menopausal symptoms she will experience.

Menopause can be made a pleasant affair by building one's physical health and adopting an optimistic attitude. From puberty to menopause, a woman has been somewhat of a slave to her female glands. She was inconvenienced by her periods. She bore children, enduring the pain and discomfort of pregnancy. Menopause relieves her of this bondage to her feminity. It is only now that she will begin to experience some of the most carefree days of her life. A whole new life is given to her, if she is wise enough to prepare for it and accept it as such.

Leucorrhoea

Leucorrhoea, commonly known as whites, refers to a whitish discharge from the female genitals. It is an abnormal condition of the reproductive organs of women. If not treated properly in the initial stages, it may become chronic.

Recent investigations have shown that secretions from the uterus and the upper part of the vagina flow down and are reabsorbed in the lower part of the vagina. This is the normal constant flow within the female organs. The whitish discharge is, however, caused by the presence of infection in any of these tissues and a variety of other factors. The condition may continue for weeks or months at a time.

Symptoms

In addition to the whitish discharge from the vagina, the patient feels weak and tired. She also suffers from pain in the lumbar region and the calves and a dragging sensation in the abdomen. Other symptoms are constipation, frequent head-aches and intense itching. In the chronic form, the patient feels irritable and develops black patches under the eyes.

Causes

Leucorrhoea does not develop suddenly in an acute form. It denotes a devitalised and toxic condition of the system generally. The condition also involves one or many parts of the reproductive organs. Whenever the body is loaded with toxins due to wrong food habits and the eliminative organs such as skin, bowels, lungs and kidneys are unable to eliminate them, woman's produces profuse discharge or elimination through the mucous membrane of the uterus and vagina in the form of leucorrhoea. In the case of advanced, chronic inflammatory conditions of these organs, it leads to discharge with pus, offensive in odour and colour varying from cream to yellow or light green.

In young girls, leucorrhoea may occur during the few years before and after the start of the menstrual flow. It may be due to an irritation of the genital organs caused by various factors such as dirt, soiled undergarments, intestinal worms and excessive mental stimulation of sex or masturbation. Some excess secretion is normal when the girl reaches puberty, due to the overactivity of her sex glands and organs. This usually disappears within a short time.

In young women, leucorrhoea may occur during intermenstrual periods, due to a thickening of the mucous membrane in the reproductive organs. Such discharge is associated with painful menstruation and other menstrual disorders.

In mature women, a profuse yellowish discharge, associated with burning on urination, may be caused by gonorrhoea. This is a serious infection which should be treated promptly. During the child-bearing years, from adolescence to mid-forties, the infection may sometimes follow the birth of a child due to damage of the cervix during delivery. This is increased by prolonged ill-health, anxiety, neurosis, sedentary occupation and standing for long period. If not treated properly, this infection may continue for months or even years and may spread to other areas of the genital tract.

Leucorrhoea may also result from a chill. A chill causes inflammation of the womb and vaginal membranes. Other common causes are the displacement of the womb and unhygienic conditions which attract the bacteria to the genital organs.

Dietetic Cure

A total health-building scheme is essential for the removal of the systemic toxicity which is primarily responsible for the disease. Such a scheme should consist of correct feeding habits, proper sleep, exercise, fresh air and sunshine.

To begin with, the patient should fast for three or four days with lemon water or fruit juices for the elimination of the morbid matter from the body. During this period, the bowels should be cleansed daily with a warm water enema. In case of habitual constipation, steps should be taken for its eradication.

After a short fast, the patient may adopt an all-fruit diet for about a week. In this regimen, she should have three meals a day of fresh juicy fruits such as apples, pears, grapes, grapefruits, oranges, pineapples and peaches. If the patient is suffering from anaemia, or is very much underweight, the diet may consist of fruits and milk. The patient may then gradually embark upon a well-balanced diet on the following lines:

Upon arising: A glass of lemon or orange juice in lukewarm water.

Breakfast: Fresh acid-bearing fruits such as apples, oranges, pears, all berries or fruit juice and milk.

Lunch: Steamed vegetables, whole wheat chapattis and butter-milk.

Dinner: Vegetable soup, a large salad of all available vegetables in season and dates, figs and raisins.

Fresh fruits or fruit juices only should be taken between meals. All forms of white flour, white sugar, fried and greasy foods, condiments, preserves, tea and coffee should be avoided.

Treatment through water is extremely beneficial in curing leucorrhoea. A cold hip bath twice a day for 10 minutes will help relieve congestion in the pelvic region and facilitate quick elimination of morbid matter. A warm vaginal douche at 30° to 40°C is beneficial for general cleaning and elimination of the putrid discharge. The procedure is to fill the douche can with three pints of warm water and hang it at a level of three feet above the body. The patient should lie with the hips slightly raised above the body and special nozzle applied for this purpose should be oiled and inserted slowly into the vagina. The flow can be regulated by the small valve at the nozzle. In severe cases of leucorrhoea, the douche should be taken daily.

The patient should completely relax and should avoid mental tension and worry. Abdominal exercise and walking are also helpful.

Sterility

Sterility in case of the female refers to the incapacity to conceive and give birth to a living baby. It ranks high as a reason for unhappy marriages. Sterility or failure to reproduce must be distinguished from fridigity which denotes failure to perform the sex act or to perform it imperfectly.

It may be relevant to first examine the mechanism of conception. The sperms of the male are injected into the vagina during sexual intercourse. At the very same time an alkaline fluid is secreted from the vaginal walls. The mobile sperms are able to move up the womb and through the fallopian tubes to fertilise the ova or the female egg only when this fluid is present.

Two factors are important in ensuring a normal secretion of this fluid. Firstly, there should be an adequate nerve supply to the vaginal ducts. This is the reason why a very nervous woman fails to conceive. The nervous system in such cases must be strengthened by rest, relaxation and proper diet. The second important factor is to ensure that the fluid flowing from the vaginal walls is alkaline. If this is not so, the sperms are destroyed by the acidic fluid, usually present in the vaginal canal and womb. To ensure the necessary alkalinity of the fluid, it is essential to take a predominantly alkaline diet, with a liberal intake of raw vegetables and fruits, and eliminate acid-forming foods.

Causes

Sterility among the female may be due to physical defects, physical debility and functional faults. Physical defects or structural abnormalities of the genital and reproductive organs may be congenital or accidental. These structural abnormalities may result from a malformation or the sagging of the womb, collapse of the fallopian tubes and rigidity of the hymen.

Sterility due to physical debility may result from poor health as a consequence of certain acute or chronic diseases. The diseases may affect not only the physical body but also the genital organs. Complaints like gonorrhoea, syphilis and inflammation of the fallopian tubes also come under this category. Chronic anaemia, constipation and leucorrhoea may aggravate these conditions.

Sterility may also be caused by a loss of essential glands or organs of reproduction or a decrease in their functions. These conditions may be brought about by a variety of factors such as surgical injuries, tumour, excessive radiation and lack of normal menstrual cycle. Obesity or emaciation due either to dietetic errors or faulty metabolism are yet other factors which may contribute to female sterility.

Psychological factors like emotional stress, tension, mental depression, anxiety and fear may also result in psychosomatic sterility. This condition is generally temporary and can be corrected by psychotherapy.

Dietary treatment

Structural defects can be ascertained by thorough physical examination and radiology and can be set right by surgery. Physical debility and the functional faults of organic nature can be cured by simple and effective methods of natural treatment. These methods include hygienic living, optimum nutrition and following all the laws of nature.

Fasting is the best remedy for the treatment of disorders resulting from the toxins in the system. A short fast of two or three days may be undertaken at regular intervals by the women who are unable to bear children. The bowels should be cleansed by a warm water enema during the period of fasting and afterwards when necessary. They will have beneficial effect not only on the digestive system but also on the surrounding organs of urinary and genital system.

Diet is the most important factor in the treatment of sterility. It should consist of the three basic health — building food groups namely, seeds, nuts and grains, vegetables and fruits. These foods should be supplemented with milk, vegetable oils and honey. The best way to take milk is in its soured form, that is, curd and cottage cheese. Each food group should roughly form the bulk of one of the three meals. About 70 to 80 per cent of the diet should consist of foods in their natural uncooked state, because cooking destroys much of the nutritional value of most foods. Sprouting is an excellent way of consuming seeds, beans and grains in their raw form as in the process of sprouting the nutritional value is multiplied, new vitamins are created and the quality of protein is improved.

The daily menu of a health-building and revitalising diet may be on the lines prescribed in Chapter 1 on Diet in Health and Disease. Excessive fat, spicy foods, strong tea, coffee, white sugar, white flour, refined cereals, flesh foods, greasy or fried foods should all be avoided.

Smoking and drinking, where habitual, must be completely given up.

Other helpful measures in overcoming female sterility are mud packs and cold water treatments like hip bath and wet girdle pack. These treatments will greatly improve internal circulation in the genital organs and will relieve them of all kinds of inflammation and other abnormalities. Mud packs may be applied to the abdomen and the sexual organs. For hip baths, a common tub may be used. The tub may be filled with sufficient water to cover the hips, when a person sits inside it. The cold hip bath should be taken for 10 minutes at a water temperature of $50°$ to $65°F$. For the wet girdle pack, a thin underwear wrung in cold water should be worn. Above this wet underwear, a thick dry cotton or woolen underwear should be worn. All cold treatments should be suspended during menstruation.

Certain yogasanas which help tone up the gonads should also be practised regularly for overcoming female sterility. These asanas are sarvangasana, matsyasana, ardhamatsyendrasana, paschimottanasana and shallabhasana.

All these measure along with clean habits, proper rest and relaxation will go a long way in overcoming female sterility.

TREATMENT CHART FOR MENSTRUAL DISORDERS

A - DIET

I. An all-fruit diet for 3 to 5 days, with three meals a day. If already underweight, add a glass of milk to each fruit meal.

II. After the all-fruit diet, adopt the following diet:-
1. *Upon arising:* A glass of lukewarm water mixed with the freshly-squeezed juice of half a lime and a teaspoon of honey.
2. *Breakfast:* Fresh fruits and a glass of milk.
3. *Lunch:* A bowl of freshly-prepared steamed vegetables,

whole wheat chappatis and a glass of butter milk.

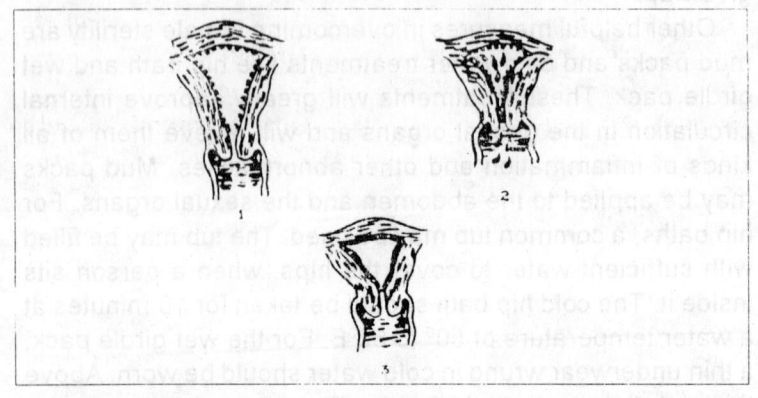

Menstruation: 1. womb before; 2. during; 3. after menstrauation.

4. *Mid-afternoon:* A glass of fruit juice or vegetable juice.
5. *Dinner:* A bowl of fresh green vegetable salad and mung bean sprout with lime juice dressing.

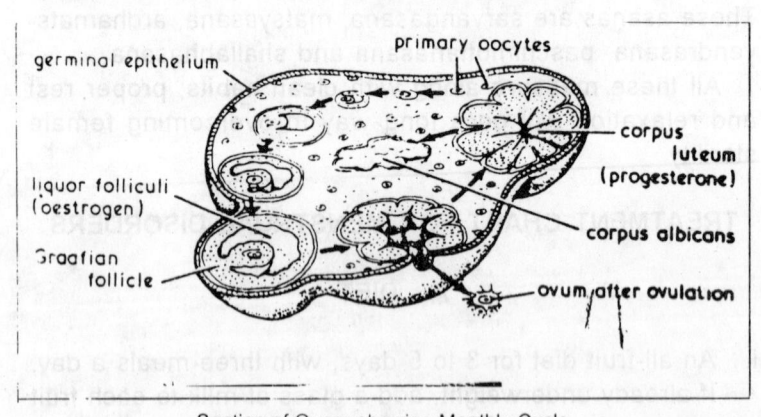

Section of Ovary showing Monthly Cycle

6. *Bedtime Snack:* A glass of fresh milk or an apple.

Note: Spend short periods on all-fruit diet for two or three days at monthly intervals.

2. Take six small meals instead of three large ones.

AVOID: Meats, sugar, white flour, tea, coffee, condiments, pickles, fried foods, soft drinks, candies, and products made from sugar and white flour.

B - OTHER MEASURES

1. Cold hip bath for 10 minutes daily. Suspend all cold baths during the menstrual period.
2. Fresh air and moderate exercise.

DR. BAKHRU'S OTHER BESTSELLERS WITH JAICO

A Complete Handbook of Nature Cure
(Revised & Enlarged Edition)

This revised and enlarged handbook is a most comprehensive family guide to health the natural way. Author makes a compelling case, for treating diseases through natural methods which rely on natural foods, natural elements, yoga and observance of other laws of nature. This well illustrated book is no doubt beneficial for those who desire good health through the use of natural remedies. The book also contains numerous food charts to enable the readers to plan their daily diet for good health.

In view of its valuable contents, this book has been awarded first prize under the category Primer on Naturopathy For Healthy Living by the jury of judges. This prize was given at "Book Prize Award Scheme" for the year 1997-1998 instituted by the National Institute of Naturopathy, an autonomous body under Government of India, Ministry of Health and Family Welfare.

Diet Cure for Common Ailments

This book covers the whole gamut of ailments which can be cured merely by proper food habits and regulation of one's life, without recourse to medicinal treatment. The book is based on the theories and fundamentals of Nature Cure that go to preserve health and vitality and regain these when lost. It is a useful guide to those who wish to treat themselves through this system at home.

A Handbook of Natural Beauty
This book is every woman's guide to Looking Good, Feeling Good and Staying Fit. It enlightens readers on:
— Which foods make you fairer
— Why water will do more for you than any skin cream
— A delicious way to prevent tooth decay
— How to prevent your hair from falling and greying and a natural hair dye
— Exercises for a healthier, lovelier you and ..... a lot more.

Nature Cure For Children
This book gives all essential tips you require to put your "little one" at ease. It is an alternative way out to treat your child and keep the doctor at bay. It helps you discover:
— What to do when worms infest your child's tummy
— What to do when lice swarm all over your child's head
— How to give a hot water enema
— How to apply mud packs
— How to give a massage and ..... a lot more.

Naturopathy For Longevity
The book deals with diseases commonly prevalent in the elderly and prescribes time-tested nature cure methods for their treatment. It contains invaluable nature cure methods which if practised sincerely can work miracles for problems related with ageing viz. poor health, loss of functions, slower mental faculties and development of other frightening diseases.

Indian Spices And Condiments As Natural Healers
Spices and condiments are one of the most important forms of natural foods. Besides culinary uses, they have been used in indigenous system of medicine as natural healers since ancient times. They thus form part of our heritage healing. This book describes in great detail the medicinal virtues of different specific spices and condiments, and their usefulness in the treatment of various common ailments. This information can serve as a guide to the readers to solve their common health problems through the use of specific spices and condiments, besides adopting a well-balanced natural diet.